THE STORIES OF L

CW00417310

Also by Kim Ballard:

The Frameworks of English (3rd edition, 2013)

THE STORIES OF LINGUISTICS

AN INTRODUCTION TO LANGUAGE STUDY PAST AND PRESENT

KIM BALLARD

© Kim Ballard 2016

All rights reserved. No reproduction, copy or transmission of this publication may be made without written permission.

No portion of this publication may be reproduced, copied or transmitted save with written permission or in accordance with the provisions of the Copyright, Designs and Patents Act 1988, or under the terms of any licence permitting limited copying issued by the Copyright Licensing Agency, Saffron House, 6–10 Kirby Street, London EC1N 8TS.

Any person who does any unauthorised act in relation to this publication may be liable to criminal prosecution and civil claims for damages.

The author has asserted her right to be identified as the author of this work in accordance with the Copyright, Designs and Patents Act 1988.

First published 2016 by
PALGRAVE

Palgrave in the UK is an imprint of Macmillan Publishers Limited, registered in England, company number 785998, of 4 Crinan Street, London, N1 9XW.

Palgrave Macmillan in the US is a division of St Martin's Press LLC, 175 Fifth Avenue, New York, NY 10010.

Palgrave is a global imprint of the above companies and is represented throughout the world.

Palgrave® and Macmillan® are registered trademarks in the United States, the United Kingdom, Europe and other countries.

ISBN 978–1–137–00067–5 paperback

This book is printed on paper suitable for recycling and made from fully managed and sustained forest sources. Logging, pulping and manufacturing processes are expected to conform to the environmental regulations of the country of origin.

A catalogue record for this book is available from the British Library.

A catalog record for this book is available from the Library of Congress.

Printed in China

Contents

List of figures and illustrations

Acknowledgements

The author would like to thank the following people:

Dr Doug Arnold, Peter Cheshire, Julia Cooper and Jane Dawson for their assistance on various points of detail

Professor Andrew Linn for his invaluable feedback and suggestions

Professor Peter Rhodes for his help with Plato's *Cratylus*

Maureen Ballard for providing some nice examples of speech errors

Imogen Simmonds for her illustrations of the sheep and the human brain

Professor Deb Roy of MIT for permission to reproduce the image from the Human Speechome Project (Figure 9.1).

Special thanks are also due to Paul Stevens at Palgrave for his excellent editorial advice and his unfailing enthusiasm for this book, and to Cathy Scott and Amy Wheeler at Palgrave for all their painstaking help with the various stages of production.

Sources

Figure 4.1 is from Wikimedia Commons, provided by: strangemaps.wordpress.com.

Figure 5.1 is from Wikimedia Commons, provided by a private contributor.

Figures 8.1 and 8.3 are from Wikimedia Commons, both provided by Wellcome Images (a website operated by Wellcome Trust, a global charitable foundation based in the United Kingdom).

Finding your way around this book

The majority of textbooks on the history of linguistics take a broadly chronological approach, but this one is slightly different because the chapters are organised thematically in order to highlight the specific aspects of language that have been of interest to scholars over the centuries. Although the chapters are arranged in a loosely connected sequence, you may prefer to read them in a different order depending on your interests.

At the end of each chapter there are suggestions for further reading and research, ranging from challenging academic titles to books aimed at a more general readership and written with a lighter touch. The majority are on language and linguistics, but occasionally titles from other disciplines have been included. Some useful websites are also listed. For readers who wish to find out more about the history of linguistics as a field of study, some information about relevant societies and journals is provided at the back.

In the body of the text, you will find that the references that accompany quotations sometimes contain two dates, for example (Jones, 1786/1799, p. 26). In these instances, the first date refers to the original year of publication or composition, and the second to any later edition or translation used for the quotation. Full details of references can be found at the back, where many of the titles are accompanied by URLs to help you find the texts online, especially if they are older works that are difficult to access in hard copy. The titles of foreign works are given first in English, except in any instances of Latin texts whose titles are not normally translated.

During the course of this book, you will encounter many of the thinkers and researchers who have played a part in the stories of linguistics. They are all listed in alphabetical order at the back, along with their life dates, nationalities, and a brief note giving the reason for their inclusion. In addition, at the beginning of Chapters 2–10, you will find a list of the key people introduced in that particular chapter, grouped according to their field of study or the period in which they lived.

Although this book covers a wide range of approaches to language and aims to do so in a way that is easily accessible to the reader whatever their academic background, inevitably there are sections and chapters (particularly Chapters 6 and 7) where a working knowledge of language structures will be needed. An overview of these linguistic frameworks is provided in the final section of Chapter 1. In the body of the book, linguistic terms are emboldened when first introduced. Their definitions can be found in the glossary at the back, as can a list of the phonetic symbols that are used occasionally.

Timeline of some key events in the history of linguistics

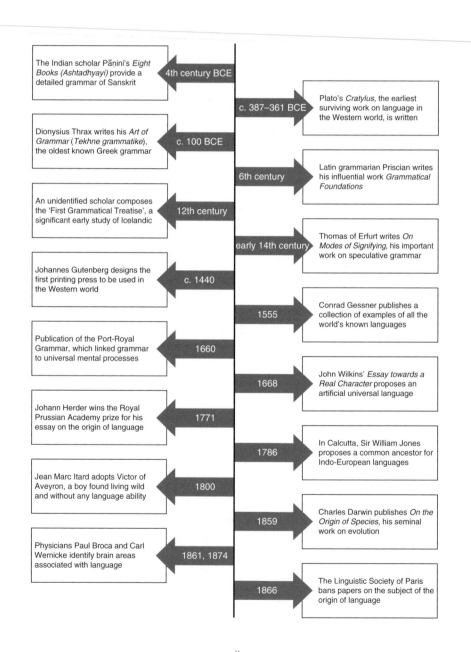

The Indian scholar Pāṇini's *Eight Books (Ashtadhyayi)* provide a detailed grammar of Sanskrit — 4th century BCE

c. 387–361 BCE — Plato's *Cratylus*, the earliest surviving work on language in the Western world, is written

Dionysius Thrax writes his *Art of Grammar (Tekhne grammatike)*, the oldest known Greek grammar — c. 100 BCE

6th century — Latin grammarian Priscian writes his influential work *Grammatical Foundations*

An unidentified scholar composes the 'First Grammatical Treatise', a significant early study of Icelandic — 12th century

early 14th century — Thomas of Erfurt writes *On Modes of Signifying*, his important work on speculative grammar

Johannes Gutenberg designs the first printing press to be used in the Western world — c. 1440

1555 — Conrad Gessner publishes a collection of examples of all the world's known languages

Publication of the Port-Royal Grammar, which linked grammar to universal mental processes — 1660

1668 — John Wilkins' *Essay towards a Real Character* proposes an artificial universal language

Johann Herder wins the Royal Prussian Academy prize for his essay on the origin of language — 1771

1786 — In Calcutta, Sir William Jones proposes a common ancestor for Indo-European languages

Jean Marc Itard adopts Victor of Aveyron, a boy found living wild and without any language ability — 1800

1859 — Charles Darwin publishes *On the Origin of Species*, his seminal work on evolution

Physicians Paul Broca and Carl Wernicke identify brain areas associated with language — 1861, 1874

1866 — The Linguistic Society of Paris bans papers on the subject of the origin of language

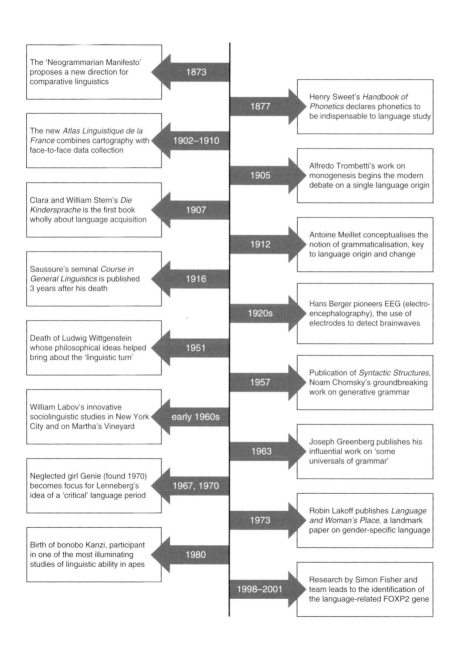

The 'Neogrammarian Manifesto' proposes a new direction for comparative linguistics — 1873

1877 — Henry Sweet's *Handbook of Phonetics* declares phonetics to be indispensable to language study

The new *Atlas Linguistique de la France* combines cartography with face-to-face data collection — 1902–1910

1905 — Alfredo Trombetti's work on monogenesis begins the modern debate on a single language origin

Clara and William Stern's *Die Kindersprache* is the first book wholly about language acquisition — 1907

1912 — Antoine Meillet conceptualises the notion of grammaticalisation, key to language origin and change

Saussure's seminal *Course in General Linguistics* is published 3 years after his death — 1916

1920s — Hans Berger pioneers EEG (electro-encephalography), the use of electrodes to detect brainwaves

Death of Ludwig Wittgenstein whose philosophical ideas helped bring about the 'linguistic turn' — 1951

1957 — Publication of *Syntactic Structures*, Noam Chomsky's groundbreaking work on generative grammar

William Labov's innovative sociolinguistic studies in New York City and on Martha's Vineyard — early 1960s

1963 — Joseph Greenberg publishes his influential work on 'some universals of grammar'

Neglected girl Genie (found 1970) becomes focus for Lenneberg's idea of a 'critical' language period — 1967, 1970

1973 — Robin Lakoff publishes *Language and Woman's Place*, a landmark paper on gender-specific language

Birth of bonobo Kanzi, participant in one of the most illuminating studies of linguistic ability in apes — 1980

1998–2001 — Research by Simon Fisher and team leads to the identification of the language-related FOXP2 gene

1 Introduction

Defining linguistics as a discipline

Linguistics is often referred to as a 'new' discipline but the formal study of language has actually been taking place for well over two thousand years, a fact which sometimes comes as a surprise to new students of the subject. Certainly, it was the twentieth century which saw the growth of university linguistics departments across Europe, the USA and many other parts of the world. The first department of linguistics to be founded in Britain, for example, was at London University's School of Oriental and African Studies (SOAS) in 1932. This expansion in the last hundred years or so has helped to generate the breathtaking amount of language research that is taking place today. However, the study of language has a long and intriguing tradition, and many aspects of linguistic study in the present day owe a considerable amount – directly or indirectly – to the inquiries of the more distant past.

Linguistics is the formal and systematic study of human language. Some prefer a definition of linguistics as the *scientific* study of language. If 'scientific' is meant in relation to the study of the natural world, then linguistics may certainly be viewed as a science, treating as it does what is now believed to be a genetically driven function of the human species. Equally, if 'scientific' refers to methodology, then it is still applicable because linguists frequently adopt methods of analysis in which exactness and a logical approach are crucial. Significant areas of linguistic inquiry have become increasingly empirical. In other words, conclusions about language are based on evidence and close, systematic observation.

On the other hand, the term 'scientific' is less appropriate if it overlooks the common ground which linguistics shares with humanities subjects, where there is room for multiple interpretations, and where conjecture, intuition and argument often provide the insights that move the discipline forward. Over two thousand years ago, the speculations of philosophers such as Plato and Aristotle laid down foundations that provided a starting point for the theoretical debate about the nature of language. More recently, the speculations of Noam Chomsky, one of the great linguists of the twentieth century, about the internal structure of language have given the discipline its strongest impetus yet. Whether linguistics is viewed as a science or as a humanities subject is immaterial to its recognition as a serious academic and intellectual pursuit. The fact that this question is raised at all is a reflection of the wide variety of activities and approaches that linguists undertake in their work. Essentially, linguistics is the study of human language in all its forms and uses. However, in true scientific spirit, linguists are concerned not simply to identify and describe the characterising features of language but also to formulate rules (in the sense of predictable patterns) and theories which explain linguistic phenomena.

Probably because communication is so important to us, all language users seem to exhibit some degree of interest in language itself. This often gives rise to perceptive and illuminating linguistic observations, but equally there are many popularly held views about language which are either mistaken or at odds with the positions linguists adopt. One commonly held opinion among non-specialists, for instance, is that some languages are superior to others. This is reflected in the impression that a language is attractive (Italian is often given as an example) or unattractive to the ear. An associated view is that some languages 'have no grammar' or that one language is logical (usually Latin), by comparison with which another is illogical (probably English). Speakers may also have views about usage, believing, for example, that a double negative (*I ain't got none*) is not permissible or is incorrect because 'two negatives make a positive'. Linguists and other scholars of language have also held beliefs about language (including the views just discussed) that we now know to be misguided or mistaken. It is easy to mock the errors of the past but far better to consider them in the context of the time when they were conceived. Often these misconceptions have been the catalysts for new and more accurate insights, just as the belief of the Greek astronomer Ptolemy that the sun orbited the earth was questioned and then disproved by Copernicus and Galileo. As far as attitudes to language use are concerned, linguists nowadays take a dispassionate, detached view of language, as befits a scientific approach to the subject. This non-prescriptive position is one of the central operating principles of modern linguistics.

Linguists at work

For two and a half millennia, all kinds of scholars have been studying language. As just mentioned, some of the earliest Western scholars to theorise about it were philosophers, and over the centuries they have continued to make significant contributions to our understanding. Thinkers and researchers from many other fields have also helped to shape the stories of linguistics, and in the course of this book we will be meeting – as well as the philosophers – various scientists, physicians, psychologists, anthropologists and more.

In the eighteenth and particularly the nineteenth century, as the study of language first became a discipline in its own right, most of the scholars involved in language study were philologists. ('Philology' comes from the Greek, and means, among other things, 'love of language'.) Their primary aims were to compare languages in order to identify any relationships between them, and to explore the historical dimensions of these language families. Nowadays, linguists are a very diverse bunch, some of whom would label themselves purely as linguists, while others prefer a term which indicates the specific area they work in, hence theoretical linguist, sociolinguist, psycholinguist and so on. It will come as little surprise that the vast majority of linguists, whatever their particular interests, have been male. This is largely a reflection of the socio-historical contexts in which earlier scholars lived and worked. Thankfully, female linguists feature more prominently in the research of recent decades.

In the modern age, the work of linguists – disparate though it is – has sometimes been broadly divided into two categories: 'desk' (or, more disparagingly, 'armchair') linguistics and 'field' linguistics, setting up a contrast between those linguists who typically work introspectively, drawing on their intuitions about their own native language for their data, and those who are out and about collecting and examining data from large numbers of speakers. The former typically concentrate on 'internal' aspects of language, the latter on 'external' ones. The division of linguistic research into these two general areas is, of course, oversimplifying the work that linguists do, work they can be found doing in a wide variety of locations.

The work of theoretical ('desk') linguists is often regarded as central to the discipline because it has resulted in a considerable number of theories about how language is structured, how 'correct' sentences are generated and how meaning is conveyed. Their focus is on the phenomenon of language itself, often as a seemingly abstract, idealised entity. They can generate their own data as they know what constitutes acceptable or ill-formed sentences and how their chosen examples can be interpreted. Even when comparing languages, the linguists who take a more theoretical approach will rely for information about languages they do not speak themselves on fellow linguists working within a similar framework.

Field linguists, by contrast, largely concentrate their attention on the way speakers use language in everyday life – particularly in terms of how this is related to personal and social aspects such as age, gender, occupation and class – and how language is affected by developments in society as a whole. For them, the collection of data involves meeting people, conducting interviews and making recordings in all kinds of situations and locations, from the workplace, to the railway station, to coffee shops and bars. Their interest in variation typically centres on accents and dialects, but there is also much interest in spoken interaction and how it operates in various contexts, and in relation to the participants. Linguistic change is of central importance to field linguists: their search to discover how and why change occurs – for instance, by examining the differences in accents between several generations in the same geographical region – is underpinned by the principle that fluidity is the constant condition of living languages.

Currently there is considerable concern about the number of languages in the world that are disappearing. Very occasionally, a language will be wiped out in an instant. This happened when the 2007 tsunami in the Far East destroyed tiny communities of people who spoke languages not spoken or known in the rest of the world. More often, there is a steady reduction in the number of speakers of a language, which can in turn lead to its decline or 'death'. This is usually the result of the encroaching dominance of a more widely used language. Across the planet, groups of field linguists are working hard to record and describe these critically endangered – usually indigenous – languages before it is too late. Every lost language represents some degree of personal and cultural loss, and the (sometimes extreme) human suffering involved should never be forgotten or overlooked. But a lost language is also a lost piece of human knowledge and creativity, and field linguists do invaluable work in their efforts to preserve threatened languages if at all possible.

Linguists then are to be found in locations as diverse as the secluded corner of a university library ideal for the contemplation of some grammatical conundrum, or a remote stretch of the Upper Amazon among a tribe whose language and culture is under threat from external forces. They can lurk on street corners to pick up telling examples of spontaneous language in use, or surf the internet for varieties of discourse (found on websites and social media) that embody our cultural beliefs and values. But a significant number of linguists can also be found in laboratories using sophisticated technology and equipment for a variety of purposes, studying language in ways that were effectively impossible for researchers in the pre-electronic age. Some, working in conjunction with both the sick and the healthy, will be using scanning devices to learn about how the mind and the brain process language, and what happens when people suffer from language disorders resulting from an accident, a congenital condition or a degenerative disease. Others will be using computers to analyse vast linguistic corpora, or data collections, consisting of thousands of examples and amounting to millions of words, while their colleagues take advantage of the computer's processing power to model theories about the way human languages work. Linguists can be found among the newborn and the very young, scrutinising their development to understand the miracle of language acquisition, and even among the dead, examining the bones and DNA of prehistoric humans in an attempt to unravel the mystery of the origin of language.

The stories of linguistics

A century ago, two former colleagues of the Swiss linguist Ferdinand de Saussure (1857–1913) published a textbook based on the notes taken by students during his lectures at the University of Geneva. This *Course in General Linguistics* (*Cours de linguistique générale*) of 1916 is considered a landmark in the development of ideas about language and is often seen as the start of the modern age of language study. Current students and researchers in the field of linguistics therefore tend to position themselves – understandably – within the context of what has happened in the last 100 years, and particularly in the last 50 to 60 years, when much of linguistics has been influenced by the giant figure of Noam Chomsky (b. 1928). (We will be finding out more about both Chomsky and Saussure in later chapters.) However, linguistics as a discipline has its roots in the far more distant past, as far back as at least the fifth century BCE in Western civilisation (which this book will focus on), and even longer ago in India and ancient Mesopotamia. The linguist Pieter Seuren commented that 'modern linguistics has, regrettably, grown accustomed to living without its history' (Seuren, 1998, p. xi). Although much of the thinking of the past now seems naïve to the contemporary student, there is a great deal in the ideas and approaches of previous centuries which can illuminate the modern discipline.

By exploring the history of linguistics, we can identify the topics that have been of perpetual interest to various scholars and linguists, as well as those which have come to interest them more recently. We can understand how some of the conclusions linguists reached in the past were the product of the information and research methods available to them at the time. We can appreciate how ideas about language were bound up with ideas about the human condition and about society and culture. In addition to all this, an exploration of the past reveals the way in which language study has shaped itself into a discrete discipline, yet at the same time has developed many branches of research, with significant connections to a host of other disciplines. In other words, the history of linguistics is not one unified, self-contained account of the past but a collection of interwoven stories, each of them in some way distinct. Linguistics too has its epics, its mysteries and its tales of human interest. Of course there are some obvious difficulties in attempting to tell the many stories which make up the history of language study. Inevitably, it is necessary to be selective in an introductory textbook like this. But, more to the point, we can only reconstruct the history from the evidence that has survived the passage of time. There may well be ideas and observations that have been lost to us and which, if known, would change the way we view or interpret the past. By contrast, when we arrive at the present day, it is, in principle and thanks largely to modern technology, possible to present a more comprehensive account of current thinking, although the confines of an introductory work will again require selections to be made. Either way, then, it is inevitable that there will be gaps in the stories – but then all stories are, by nature, incomplete in one way or another.

In telling the stories of linguistics, this book will focus on the central questions that have been asked down the ages, and the way in which linguists have searched for answers to those questions. We will start by looking at the various ideas about what human language actually is, and how thinkers have treated the claim that language is unique to the human species. We will then move on to the question that we will almost certainly never know the complete answer to, the intriguing mystery of the origin and emergence of human language. From there we will shift to the diversity of human language, to see what thinkers have made of the differences and similarities between languages, and how they have investigated the variation that occurs among speakers of the same language. After that, we will move into more theoretical territory, looking at how, over the last two millennia or so, the structure of language has been described and explained. This will bring us on to the possibly even knottier question of how meaning is constructed and conveyed in human communication. Then we will consider questions that have become particularly salient in the last two centuries: how does the human brain process language, and how do we acquire it in the first place?

These are all questions which characterise and define the discipline of linguistics. Together, they unify the vast and eclectic body of scholarship and research undertaken over many centuries. Today, this work continues in its different guises all over the world. What is more, the body of knowledge accumulated by linguists has spawned an impressive range of applications in many areas of our lives, from education to healthcare, from government and politics to crime. Finally, then, based on an overview of the current fields and applications of linguistic research, we will try to anticipate what the future holds for the study of human language.

Piecing together the stories of linguistics

There are certainly several reasons why it is valuable to spend time exploring the history of linguistics. But the study of the history of any discipline always comes with some warnings about the challenges of delving into the past. One of these challenges, which we touched on in the previous section, is that of forming a full understanding of the ideas or periods under consideration. Historical evidence may be lacking or known to have gone missing: we know, for example, that an extensive work on Latin by Marcus Terentius Varro originally consisted of 25 books in total, but just 6 survive intact. We can do nothing to restore lost material like this, but we can improve our chances of forming an accurate picture of the past if we approach it in a detached way, setting aside any preconceptions about what we will find as well as any thoughts about what we would like to discover. It's a little like standing outside a house, imagining the lives of its inhabitants simply by looking through the windows. If we could go inside, we would doubtless realise that many of our assumptions were wrong.

Of course, the most important clues to understanding the history of linguistics are found in primary sources – philosophical works, essays, articles, monographs, grammars, dictionaries, language atlases, letters, diaries, data collections and so on – which reveal the linguistic activities and theories of scholars and researchers both past and present. (And, on that subject, it's worth bearing in mind that writers themselves sometimes revise their work, and significant changes can be made from one version to another. In Chapter 3, for instance, we will see the effect of Darwin's revisions of his 1871 work *The Descent of Man*.) Not so very long ago, it would have been almost impossible for most students to access many of these materials, but the digitalisation of them over the last few years means that a significant number can now be accessed without even having to leave your desk. (The 'References and sources' section at the back includes URLs to many of the works listed.) So hopefully you will feel inspired to take a look at some of these primary sources, and see for yourself what light they cast on the historical recesses of linguistics.

Something else to bear in mind when looking at historical sources is the language in which they were originally written. Many of the works considered in this book were written in English, but several other languages are represented, particularly Latin, French and German. If you are able to read any of these, all well and good, but we all have to rely on translations sometimes, and in those instances, it's important to be mindful of the fact that a translation may not capture all the subtleties of the original. Many works (especially those of the ancient Greek and Roman philosophers) have been translated several times, and translations are often worth comparing in order to see how they put different slants on the subject matter. Whether a translation exists or not, it's worth taking a look at the original work if you can, even if you don't know the language it's written in, as this can give you a better feel for it as an intellectual creation from a particular period in time, especially if you can examine it in its original form. For example, there is no English translation of the diaries kept by Clara and William Stern (and written in German) to record their children's language development (discussed in Chapter 9), but these are well worth perusing to gain an insight into the scope and methodology of their work.

As we will see, it is impossible to study the history of linguistics in isolation from other disciplines: many of the developments in the field owe a great deal to ideas and research undertaken within fields such as neuroscience, philosophy and anthropology. So studying the history of linguistics provides many opportunities for interesting diversions into all kinds of territory. Similarly, it is important to take account of the social and political contexts in which linguistic ideas were being hatched, as this can help us interpret the past appropriately, and in turn make us more aware of how our own age influences the way we think.

The way we view the past, the nature and availability of primary sources, the influence of other disciplines on the one we are exploring and the effect of the cultural climate on the thinkers we encounter – these are all matters of **historiography**, the way we go about studying something from a historical point of view. Researchers into the history of linguistics spend a lot of time thinking about how best to study, interpret and understand the past, and in the last 40 years or so they have been particularly concerned to write about and debate their methods. The result has been the formation of various societies and the birth of several publications all devoted to piecing together the history of linguistics. Hopefully, the stories constructed in this book will give you a taste to know much more about this fascinating historical endeavour.

Language frameworks

This section provides an overview of linguistic frameworks, and introduces the terminology associated with them. Readers who are already familiar with the basic frameworks for linguistic analysis are invited to skip this section. Any readers wanting to learn more might like to consult *The Frameworks of English* (Ballard, 2013), where much of the material is applicable to language in general.

Language is often talked about as existing on several interconnected levels, and this is a systematic way of presenting the basics of language structure you will need in this book. The following sentence, adapted from Shakespeare, provides a useful example for illustrating these different levels:

All the world's a stage, and all the men and women merely players.

We can begin with words – or **lexis** – as the building blocks of language. Words can be categorised in different ways, but most important is the **word class** to which a word belongs as this indicates the roles the word can play in sentences. These word classes include **noun**, **verb**, **adjective**, **adverb**, **pronoun**, **determiner**, **preposition** and **conjunction**, categories with which people are generally familiar. If we wish to break words down into component parts, we enter the world of word formation or **morphology**. We can see that most of the words in the example are in fact indivisible, although *merely* (an adverb) is derived from a combination of the adjective *mere* with the adverb ending *-ly*. We can then consider the **grammar** of the example. Grammar concerns the way in which the sentence is constructed and involves two factors: **syntax** – the order in which the words occur – and **inflections** – the special endings on words indicating features such as tense. (Inflections are also treated as another aspect of morphology.) Syntax involves language-specific constraints on where words can occur in sentences according to their word class. For example, the determiners in <u>all</u> <u>the</u> *world* can only occur in this order, and the substitution of the adjective *whole* for *all* would require some restructuring of the phrase: *the whole world*. As for inflections, one regular inflection can be seen in the example: this is the regular *-s* inflection which makes *players* plural. The nouns *men* and *women* are also plural, although they have irregular plural forms. Irregularity can also be seen in the verb form *is* (*all the world <u>is</u> a stage*), the third person present tense of the highly irregular verb *BE*. If we replaced *BE* with a regular verb, then the regular inflection (also *-s*) would appear: *the world resemble<u>s</u> a stage*. Inflections, then, provide the adjustments needed to certain words according to their functions within the context of the sentence. Moving beyond morphology, lexis and grammar, **discourse** concerns how sentences (which serve as the basic unit of syntactic structure) combine to build **text** – stretches of language such as those we create when we tell a story or have a conversation (or write a play!).

Language is essentially a spoken phenomenon, and the study of spoken language requires us to consider **phonetics** and **phonology**. Phonetics is the study of individual speech sounds or segments – how they are both produced and received. How these speech sounds make up a system of sounds in any particular language is the domain of phonology. In their idealised, abstract state, these sound segments are referred to as **phonemes**. Speech sounds are usually represented using phonetic symbols within slant brackets to distinguish them from alphabetical letters, since many of the phonetic symbols take the same form as letters. A phonemic representation of *all the world* spoken in a standard British English accent, for example, would look like this: /ɔːl ðə wɜːld/. (Only occasional use is made in this book of phonetic symbols, and their associated sounds are generally easy to deduce, but a list can be found at the end, just before the glossary.) Phonology also incorporates **prosodics**, the aspects of speech production such as volume, pitch and intonation. An actor performing the speech from which the example is taken would need to make some prosodic decisions. How much, for instance, should he emphasise the adverb *merely*? Where, and for how long should he pause, if he should pause at all?

The levels of language outlined above relate to the complex, multi-layered structure of language. Relevant to all these levels is **semantics**, the exploration of meaning. Meaning is, of course, an essential quality of a word (as dictionaries show us), but not fixedly so. This is demonstrated in the example, where the words in combination take on an extended metaphorical significance. The relationship between language components and meaning has produced much lively debate over the centuries, as we shall see in due course.

To summarise, language is constructed and functions on a range of levels:

morphology	the internal structure of words
lexis	the words themselves
grammar	the combination of words into sentences (grammar includes syntax and inflections)
discourse	the combination of sentences into texts
phonetics	the articulation and reception of speech sounds
phonology	the system of speech sounds and prosodic features
semantics	meaning

The structural levels (morphology to phonology) operate in different ways, but are interconnected. Linguists disagree about their precise relationship to each other, although phonology, grammar and semantics are often regarded as the central elements that make up a language system. Beyond this system is the need to consider language in use, and particularly how we activate and interpret meaning according to context – in other words, **pragmatics**. For some linguists, pragmatics falls within semantics, while others regard it as a separate layer in the study of linguistic structures.

Suggestions for further reading and research

On the study of language in general

Allan, Keith et al. (eds) (2010) *The English Language and Linguistics Companion* (Basingstoke: Palgrave Macmillan)

A very accessible introduction to the gamut of linguistic interests, with helpful advice on how to conduct your own research in the various fields.

Aronoff, Mark and Janie Rees-Miller (eds) *The Handbook of Linguistics* (Oxford: Blackwell)

A useful collection of articles from a wide range of linguists. It also contains a chapter by Lyle Campbell on 'The History of Linguistics'.

Bauer, Laurie (2012) *Beginning Linguistics* (Basingstoke: Palgrave Macmillan)

A student-friendly introduction to the core areas of linguistics, with examples drawn from a wide range of languages.

Yule, George (2014) *The Study of Language*, 5th edn (Cambridge: Cambridge University Press)

A perennially popular introduction to all the main concepts and areas of linguistics.

On the history of linguistics

Allan, Keith (2010) *The Western Classical Tradition in Linguistics*, 2nd edn (London: Equinox)

A detailed scholarly account, containing a wealth of examples and extracts. Ideal for readers who particularly enjoy linguistic theory.

Harris, Roy and Talbot J Taylor (eds) (1997) *Landmarks in Linguistic Thought Volume I: The Western Tradition from Socrates to Saussure* (London: Routledge)

Each chapter begins with an extract from a primary source, which is followed by a discussion of the text in relation to its cultural context. Volume II in the same series contains further extracts relating to the Western tradition, while Volume III covers the Arabic tradition.

Koerner, E F K (1976) 'The importance of linguistic historiography and the place of history in linguistic science', in *Foundations of Language*, vol. 14, no. 4, pp. 541–47

An interesting article outlining the value of the study of the history of linguistics. Available at www.jstor.org/stable/25170087 (accessed October 2015).

Law, Vivien (2003) *The History of Linguistics in Europe: From Plato to 1600* (Cambridge: Cambridge University Press)

This book is excellent in the way it provides so much useful historical background. Although it mainly covers the period to 1600, there is a chapter on the following four centuries.

Robins, Robert (1997) *A Short History of Linguistics*, 4th edn (London: Longman)

Published originally in 1967 and written by a former professor at SOAS, this was the first textbook in English on the history of linguistics. Organised chronologically, it reflects the author's strong interest in the classical world, and also includes coverage of linguistic thinking beyond the Western world.

Seuren, Pieter (1998) *Western Linguistics: An Historical Introduction* (Oxford: Blackwell)

A comprehensive survey of theoretical linguistics from Plato to the end of the twentieth century.

Thomas, Margaret (2011) *Fifty Key Thinkers on Language and Linguistics* (Abingdon: Routledge)

A very useful reference book for those wishing to find out more about the lives and work of influential thinkers from the fifth century to the present day.

Useful website

All About Linguistics (Sheffield University)
https://sites.google.com/a/sheffield.ac.uk/all-about-linguistics/branches/history-of-linguistics (accessed October 2015)

This excellent website has several pages devoted to the history of linguistics, including video talks by their Professor of the History of Linguistics, Andrew Linn.

2 The nature of language

Thinkers and researchers introduced in this chapter

From the ancient world of Greece and Rome:

Plato (428–348 BCE)	Greek philosopher
Aristotle (384–322 BCE)	Greek philosopher
Lucretius (c. 95–c. 55 BCE)	Roman philosopher

From the Age of Enlightenment:

René Descartes (1596–1650)	French philosopher
John Locke (1632–1704)	English philosopher
Gottfried Leibniz (1646–1716)	German philosopher
Offray de La Mettrie (1709–51)	French philosopher and physician
Jean-Jacques Rousseau (1712–78)	French philosopher

Ferdinand de Saussure, who appears frequently in this book, and some of his contemporaries:

Ferdinand de Saussure (1857–1913)	Swiss linguist
Otto Jespersen (1860–1943)	Danish linguist
Charles Bally (1865–1947)	French linguist
Albert Sechehaye (1870–1946)	Swiss linguist

Noam Chomsky, who is also very prominent in this book, and some of his fellow American researchers:

Winthrop Kellogg (1898–1972)	psychologist
Charles Hockett (1916–2000)	linguist and anthropologist
Noam Chomsky (b. 1928)	linguist
R Allen Gardner (b. 1930)	psychologist
Beatrix Gardner (1933–95)	psychologist
Sue Savage-Rumbaugh (b. 1946)	primatologist
Marc Hauser (b. 1959)	evolutionary biologist
Tecumseh Fitch (b. 1963)	evolutionary biologist

Also mentioned are the following animals whose lives have contributed to the study of human language:

chimpanzee Gua (1930–33)
chimpanzee Washoe (1965–2007)
chimpanzee Nim Chimpsky (1973–2000)
bonobo Kanzi (b. 1980)

The object of study

Ideas about the nature of language can be traced back well over 2,000 years in the Western world, but we will begin our exploration in 1913, with the death of the Swiss linguist, Ferdinand de Saussure, who has already been mentioned in Chapter 1. Since he is generally regarded as the founder of modern linguistics, it seems fitting to start this chapter with him. Saussure himself appears to have had no awareness of the considerable part he would play in shaping the emerging discipline. Following an already distinguished academic career, he had been appointed a professor at the University of Geneva in 1891 where, every other year between 1906 and 1911, he taught a course in **general linguistics**. When he died just two years later, the content of this course remained unpublished and may well have been destined to vanish forever had it not been for his two colleagues, Charles Bally and Albert Sechehaye. Recognising the importance of Saussure's 'seminal lectures', they approached his widow to request access to his papers and she kindly agreed to let them search through her late husband's study. To their dismay, however, Bally and Sechehaye opened the drawers of his desk to find nothing but some 'old jottings'. Undeterred, and with the help of eight of Saussure's former students, they managed to piece the course together from lecture notes containing what the students had 'heard from his own lips'. The collection was published in Paris in 1916 as Saussure's *Cours de linguistique générale* – the *Course in General Linguistics*.

Although there has been some controversy as to whether this re-creation is an entirely accurate representation of Saussure's theory of language, it is generally considered to reflect the most significant part. Saussure recognised that, because there are so many aspects to language, it could be hard for the linguist to know what to prioritise. 'Other sciences are provided with objects of study given in advance', he remarked, whereas 'no one object of linguistic study emerges of its own accord' (Saussure, 1916/1983, p. 8). We saw in the previous chapter that the extent and variety of the work that contemporary linguists do is itself a reflection of the many guises which language takes as well as of the different views held by linguists as to what language essentially is. Saussure did not propose that the external aspects of language – whether social, political or cultural – were unimportant, but for him the true focus of language study was the internal linguistic system residing in the minds of speakers. This should be the 'primary concern' of the linguist. It seems rather fitting that Saussure was delivering this message to his students around the same time as scientists across Europe were discovering more and more about the internal structure of the building block of matter – the atom – and his proposal may well have captured the scientific mood of the time. The internal nature of language became and has arguably remained the central concern at the heart of linguistic study – what is still termed general or, alternatively, **theoretical linguistics**.

Saussure's system of signs

Saussure, then, saw language primarily as a system. This view has been a powerful and influential one in the last hundred years, and remains so today. In one respect, it is true to say that language was seen as systematic long before the twentieth century. This is borne out by the wealth of reference books, particularly grammars, that had already been written to describe individual languages across the world. The compilation of a grammar, with its many tables or lists of **conjugations** (verb forms) and **declensions** (chiefly noun forms), as well as its various 'rules', seemed to encapsulate the language in question as something organised and, to a large extent, governed by regularity. For Saussure, what made any language system distinctive (and, by extension, language as a whole) was that it was self-contained, with the elements within the system being defined only in relation to each other.

Judging from the *Course in General Linguistics*, Saussure enjoyed selecting analogies for the benefit of his students, for whom many of his ideas were certainly new. His comparison of a language system to a game of chess is clearly one that struck a chord with his audience, since it was preserved in their notes. Here are his observations:

> In the case of chess, it is relatively easy to distinguish between what is external and what is internal. The fact that chess came from Persia to Europe is an external fact, whereas everything which concerns the system and its rules is internal. If pieces made of ivory are substituted for pieces of wood, the change makes no difference to the system. But if the number of pieces is diminished or increased, that is a change which profoundly affects the 'grammar' of the game. … Everything is internal which alters the system in any degree whatsoever. (ibid., p. 23)

This analogy illuminates Saussure's distinction between the internal and external elements of language. It also demonstrates his point about the interdependence of the units which constitute the language system. A game of chess could, in theory, be altered to contain a greater or lesser number of pieces (or a different distribution of the six types), but this would unavoidably affect the way in which the game is played out.

Some of Saussure's own examples can be used to illustrate how this idea of a system of interdependent elements applies to language. First, we can compare languages to see how systems may vary. For example, in English, 'sheep' refers to the living animal but we use 'mutton' when we refer to its meat. In French, however, '*mouton*' is used for both these concepts:

French		*mouton*	
English		*sheep*	*mutton*

In French, then, the internal system differs from English in using only one word to cover the same semantic territory as the two English words. Someone translating from French into English would need to consider which of the two English words would be appropriate. Words of very similar meanings – **synonyms** – taken from the same language can also be used to demonstrate how a language system is structured, such as these French examples:

redouter ('to dread')	*craindre* ('to fear')	*avoir peur* ('to be afraid')
craindre		*avoir peur*

Here, the loss of '*redouter*', for instance, would require a repositioning of its synonyms to fill the gap left by its disappearance. This shows how the values of these different elements are not absolute, but defined by the presence of other related elements within the same overall structure. This is the essence of **structuralism**, a theoretical approach which, as well as influencing work in other disciplines, was to have a strong influence on the study of language over the following decades, as we will see in Chapter 6.

Also integral to Saussure's view of language is a distinction he makes between the current and historical dimensions of language. For Saussure, it was inappropriate to mix the two together. You either had to study language change and development over time (a **diachronic** approach, which had been predominant in the century preceding the publication of the *Course*) or focus on the language at any one point in time (a **synchronic** approach). Again, the chess analogy is useful. Someone looking at a chessboard where a game has already been started cannot determine exactly what moves have already been made, or in what sequence. This is comparable to a language user who, unaware of previous states of the language he or she speaks, simply draws on the system as it is at the moment of speaking. This is why the synchronic view of language should, according to Saussure, take precedence over a diachronic approach 'since for the community of language users that is the one and only reality' (ibid., p. 89). Saussure actually thought that too much recent attention had been paid to the history of languages and looked forward to a return to 'the static viewpoint of traditional grammar, but in a new spirit and with different methods' (ibid., p. 82). His prediction was certainly destined to come true, as we will see shortly.

The language system, for Saussure, is a set of interrelated linguistic **signs**, each sign standing for something meaningful within the system. In fact, he saw human society as made up of many such systems including 'symbolic rites, forms of politeness, military signals' (ibid., p. 15). (The pieces in a game of chess could be included here too!) Language just happened to be the most important of these systems. Saussure suggested that there should be a science devoted to the study of signs: it would be called 'semiology', and the study of language would be one part of this discipline. That science does of course exist now under the name of **semiotics**, although linguistics tends to be viewed as a discipline in its own right.

The idea of the linguistic sign was not original to Saussure. It can be traced as far back as Aristotle, the Greek philosopher of the fourth century BCE, who summarises his view of signs (translated here as 'symbols') in the opening section of his treatise *On Interpretation*, stating that 'spoken words are the symbols of mental experience ...' (Aristotle c. 350–330 BCE/1928, 16ᵃ/Ch. 1). The seventeenth-century English philosopher, John Locke, echoes this view in his 1690 work *An Essay Concerning Human Understanding*, where he makes use of the notion of 'verbal signs'. He describes these articulated sounds in a human being as 'signs of internal conceptions' which act 'as marks for the ideas within his own mind, whereby they might be made known to others, and the thoughts of men's minds be conveyed from one to another' (Locke, 1690, III.i.2).

In Saussure's terms, every linguistic sign (and he distinguishes a sign from a word) is made up of two elements: the **signified** (*signifié* in French) – the mental concept in question – and the **signifier** (*signifiant*) – usually the sound image associated with the concept, although it could take some other form, such as a gesture. Here is an example from English:

linguistic sign	
mental concept	sound image
	"sheep"
= signified	= signifier

Again, Saussure's idea can be traced back to earlier times. The Stoic philosophers of ancient Greece (whose thinking dates from just a few years after the death of Aristotle) made a very similar connection between a signified concept and its signifier. Medieval thinkers also took up this idea: in the Latin terminology of the time, the signified idea was the *significatum* and its signifying element or name the *significans*. Together these formed a 'meaning' or *significatio*. Saussure, however, reworked the idea of the sign particularly by showing how it is defined in relation to other signs within the same language: in English, as we have seen, the sign 'sheep' is partly defined by not being 'mutton'. In turn, these interdependent elements make up a self-contained system: 'A linguistic system is a series of phonetic differences matched with a series of conceptual differences' (Saussure, 1916/1983, p. 118) is how Saussure summed it up. Or, to put it even more simply, 'a language is a system of signs expressing ideas' (ibid., p. 15).

The arbitrariness of signs

Another important point Saussure makes is that the linguistic sign is arbitrary. In other words, there is no particular reason why (in English) the mental concept 'sheep' should be signified by the sound sequence 'sh-ee-p'. It could just as easily be 'd-o-g'! The signifier is 'unmotivated': there is no natural connection between it and the concept it signifies. The sign then is a convention that has become established by mutual agreement among a community of speakers. This notion of **arbitrariness** is an important one in modern linguistics, but the earliest debate about whether signs (or names, in this instance) are conventional or natural can be found in *Cratylus*, a short work (written probably between 387 and 361 BCE) by the Greek philosopher Plato. Partly because the issue relating to arbitrariness was a very pressing one in the ancient world, and partly because *Cratylus* is the oldest surviving European work on language, it is worth devoting some space to it here.

Like many of Plato's writings, *Cratylus* takes the form of a conversation or dialogue. This one is between three acquaintances: Cratylus himself, his friend Hermogenes, and Socrates, another philosopher who was also Plato's teacher. The subtitle of the work is 'The Correctness of Names' and the debate explores the question of whether the original forms of names (here, mainly nouns, but also some verbs and adjectives) are predominantly conventional, arbitrary forms agreed on by their users (the view held by

Hermogenes), or whether they express the true nature of what they refer to, as Cratylus believes. To use two examples offered by Socrates, is the Greek word for 'day', *emera*, with its similarity to *imeros* ('desire'), intended to reveal the essence of 'day' as something which is longed for during the night? And can someone be correctly named *Theophilus*, meaning 'loved by God', if they are, by nature, irreligious? These are important questions because, as Socrates observes near the beginning of the debate, 'a name is a tool for giving instruction', allowing us to 'divide things according to their natures' (Plato, c. 387–361 BCE/1997, p. 107). The purpose of the dialogue, then, is to establish whether the original forms of names can indeed reveal truths about the world around us and whether names are therefore reliable tools for philosophical inquiry.

From a contemporary perspective, the debate in *Cratylus* can be perplexing, partly because it is hard to gauge the seriousness of Socrates' etymological explanations (**etymology** – the origins and history of words – was a popular topic of discussion in Plato's time and he may be gently satirising the etymologists) but also because the conventional nature of language seems fairly self-evident to the modern thinker. Of course, many words (other than onomatopoeic words which supposedly imitate the sounds they refer to) do have identifiable, 'motivated' origins. In contemporary English, for example, a *crossroads* is clearly a place where roads cross. Less obvious, but also explicable, is the origin of the noun *trivia*, which actually derives from the Latin for 'three ways' – *tres viae*. At the point where roads intersected, travellers who bumped into each other would probably stop and exchange some small talk – trivia. So the more recent history of these words is relatively transparent. But what about the earliest incarnations of the elements which make up these words? What forms did they take, and did they in some way encapsulate the essence of what they referred to? Cratylus is asking about the original forms of words. Surely these reflect some unchanging, universal truths? This was a powerful view of the time.

Hermogenes, however, was not alone in casting doubt on the naturalistic view of his friend Cratylus. The arbitrary nature of words was strongly supported by Aristotle, who was actually Plato's pupil. So for him, mental experiences and impressions are expressed through conventionally agreed forms. This was particularly important given that language was the medium for logical argument: words can only be useful here if they are independent of what they refer to. John Locke, who was mentioned above, was of a similar opinion that words are an agreed means by which humans can convey their thoughts to each other for the 'comfort and advantage of society'. For him, words 'came to be made use of by men as the signs of their ideas; not by any natural connexion that there is between particular articulate sounds and certain ideas, for then there would be but one language amongst all men; but by a voluntary imposition, whereby such a word is made arbitrarily the mark of such an idea' (Locke, 1690, III.ii.1).

To return to Saussure, his insistence on the sign as arbitrary clearly has a good pedigree, but it has additional importance as part of his theory of signs in general. The arbitrariness of signs was the first principle of his semiology as this unites all the systems of meaning used in human society. Language, the most complex and widespread of our sign systems, actually provides the fullest expression of how we establish and make use of signs by mutual agreement. Also, Saussure's view is the first to position linguistic signs within a closed system of interrelated signs. This takes us back once more to the game of chess. When Saussure comments on the irrelevance of the pieces being ivory or wood (or even taking the forms they do, for that matter), he is thinking of his view of the sign as arbitrary. No matter what material the chess piece is made of, what it represents on the board remains the same. Arbitrariness was to be picked up as a feature of language 50 years after Saussure in the work of Charles Hockett, but in a very different context. We will come to this shortly.

The Chomskyan revolution

Saussure's anticipation of a new era of theoretical language study based on a static (namely, synchronic) viewpoint was effectively realised within a decade or so of his death (as we shall see in Chapter 6), but his hopes were even more richly fulfilled in 1957 when the American linguist Noam Chomsky published his slim but revolutionary volume *Syntactic Structures*. As the title announces, syntax (which Saussure's *Course* deals with only briefly) takes centre stage in this work and was to remain the central focus of Chomsky's subsequent research. There is much to say about Chomsky's role in the stories of linguistics and he will be making further appearances in later chapters, particularly when we come to look at linguistic structure (in Chapter 6, where we will consider Chomsky's innovative theory of **generative grammar**) and at children's language acquisition (Chapter 9). If Saussure can be regarded as the founder of modern linguistics, many would regard Chomsky as its most influential figure.

Born in 1928, Chomsky's interest in language began early under the influence of his father, who was a proclaimed expert in Hebrew. After completing his PhD, which already marked a departure from the analytical approaches of linguists he had met and worked with, Chomsky took up a post at the Massachusetts Institute of Technology (MIT), with which he is still associated. As a thinker, he positions himself in a long tradition of rationalism, stretching back to the French philosopher René Descartes in the early seventeenth century and to his German counterpart Gottfried Leibniz in the late seventeenth century who both believed only humans were endowed with reason, a fact which was exhibited through their possession of language. This idea was justified by Descartes in 1637 when he wrote: 'It is a very remarkable thing that there are no men so dull and stupid, not even lunatics, that they cannot arrange various words and form a sentence to make their thoughts understood; but no other animal, however perfect or well bred, can do the like' (Descartes, 1637/1970, p. 42). To Descartes, this was evidence 'that brutes not only have a smaller degree of reason than man, but are wholly lacking in it' (ibid.). For Chomsky, our specific capacity for language – the means by which reason finds its expression – is itself innate, something which sets us even more firmly apart from other creatures.

As we will see in more detail in Chapters 6 and 9, Chomsky's unique claim was that this innate language capacity takes the form of a mental **universal grammar** (**UG**) which provides the knowledge a speaker needs, first to learn language (any language), and then to be able to produce and understand a limitless number of sentences from the limited resources (its rules and vocabulary) which make up that language. As in Saussure's chess game, where fixed rules and a set number of pieces nevertheless allow a countless number of ways in which the game can be played out, so in language. The grammatical principles determine how sentences are constructed (and restrict the production of ungrammatical constructions), but do not limit the number of different sentences that can be generated. The proposed existence of a universal grammar is a way of accounting for what Chomsky sees as a defining characteristic of human language – its extraordinary creativity, a sharp contrast to the limited range of communicative messages that can be conveyed by other species.

Chomsky, then, like Saussure, sees language as a system, although Chomsky's system is all about syntax rather than signs. Both linguists therefore place considerable emphasis on the internal rather than external aspects of language, employing contrastive labels in order to represent this:

	Saussure	early Chomsky	late Chomsky
internal aspect of language	*la langue*	competence	I-language
external aspect of language	*la parole*	performance	E-language

For Saussure, the system of linguistic signs – ***la langue*** – is internalised in the minds of its speakers, even though it has a social, interactive aspect – ***la parole***.

Chomsky's internal language system is innate, so **competence**, the speaker's knowledge of how to produce and understand sentences, is of considerable importance for what it reveals about the human mind. By contrast, **performance**, language as it is used in social interaction and which is often affected by a host of non-linguistic factors, is of little interest to Chomsky. His later terms **I-language** (internalised language) and **E-language** (externalised language) make this distinction even more explicit. It is his concern with formulating a model of the internal, mental nature of language which led him to propose that linguistics as a discipline is really a branch of cognitive psychology. He also emphasises the innate mental aspect on the basis that it encapsulates the uniformity which he believes underlies all human language as opposed to the diversity of the forms which it can take – something he sees largely as a distraction.

Chomsky has never shied away from controversy, and it is probably true to say that his ideas about the nature of language have had as many detractors as supporters. Although he continues to participate in linguistic debates (most recently, getting involved in questions relating to language evolution), much of his time in recent decades has been devoted to his work as a social and political commentator. Despite this, Chomsky remains the most influential living linguist, and his ideas the orientation points by which other linguists position themselves.

Human language, animal communication

Language – but not communication – is unique to human beings. For Saussure and Chomsky this meant that the linguist's priority should be the study of the internal structures of language. This would reveal not only the essential nature of language as a phenomenon, but also the condition of the human mind. The comparison of one language with another was a valuable pursuit for understanding language in general, but a comparison with anything other than human language less so. As we will see in Chapter 9, for example, Chomsky was highly critical of behavioural psychologists who thought they could learn about human language acquisition by studying the learning behaviour of other species. However, for many researchers, the study of animal communication has been regarded as a productive means to learn more about human language, and a comparative method has proved useful in helping to define human language and unravel the nature of its uniqueness. In this way, members of many other species have acted as unwitting participants in the stories of linguistics.

The tradition of studying animal communication in relation to human language is a long-standing one. Over 2,000 years ago, for example, the Roman philosopher Lucretius compared humans to animals in his work *On the Nature of Things* (*De rerum natura*) when he considered the range of sounds different species could produce. For Lucretius, the ability of humans to utter a range of distinctive meaningful sounds is comparable to the ability of animals and birds to do the same, and he gives several examples of this (Lucretius, c. 49 BCE/1951, pp. 203–4). Many centuries later, in 1748, largely as a response to the Enlightenment view that both language and reason were unique to humans, the French philosopher Julien Offray de La Mettrie in his *Man a Machine* (*L'Homme Machine*) proposed that an ape, 'whose external and internal organs so strikingly resemble man's' (La Mettrie, 1748/1912, p. 101), could be taught some form of speech. Animal dissections, particularly of great apes such as chimpanzees and orang-utans, helped to fuel the debate about their communicative abilities. Jean-Jacques Rousseau (another French philosopher) drew comparisons, but, like Descartes, was firmly of the opinion that, although animals were not without capabilities, 'conventional language is characteristic of man alone' (Rousseau, 1781/1966, p. 10). In the same essay (published three years after his death), he also writes:

> It appears … that the invention of the art of communicating our ideas depends less upon the organs we use in such communications than it does upon a power proper to man, according to which he uses his organs in this way, and which, if he lacked these, would lead him to use others to the same end … Animals have a more than adequate structure for such communication, but none of them has ever made use of it. This seems to me a quite characteristic difference. (ibid.)

In the modern age, DNA analysis has shown that we humans share 99.9% of our genetic code with each other, and just under 99% with our nearest living relatives, chimpanzees and bonobos. This seemingly reinforces the particular benefits of using them in language (and other associated) research. In the last 80 years or so there have been many research projects involving these animals (mostly in the USA), and many have become minor celebrities in the linguistic world. One of the earliest studies was in 1931, when Donald, the ten-month-old son of a psychologist, Winthrop Kellogg, was introduced to his new 'sister', a seven-month-old chimp named Gua! The boy and the chimp were raised together for just over a year, with the aim of discovering whether this environment would enable the young chimp to develop socialised human behaviour, including some ability to vocalise and comprehend language. Although Gua developed nothing in the way of human language sounds, when Donald started to imitate the chimp's calls, his father decided the experiment was perhaps not such a good idea after all.

Contrary to what Julien de La Mettrie believed, the great apes do not have the vocal apparatus to articulate the sounds of human speech. When the first attempts to teach chimps to speak failed miserably, researchers adopted signing as a preferable medium for learning. The most successful experiment of this kind was carried out by Allen and Beatrix Gardner in the 1960s with a chimpanzee named Washoe, who was nearly a year old when she was adopted by them and, like Gua, raised as a human child. In the five years she spent with the Gardners, she acquired well over a hundred signs, and showed some remarkable interactions with the people she encountered. The Gardners argued that Washoe developed the ability to use language creatively by combining signs into simple syntactic structures, but some commentators were sceptical about this claim. The question was never resolved. Washoe died in New York in 2007, aged 42.

In the following decade, a similar project was carried out under the guidance of Herbert Terrace, who had been one of the critics of the Gardners' findings. The chimp in question was named Nim Chimpsky – a nod of course to Noam Chomsky, whose views about the uniqueness of human language the project was designed to challenge. Although, like Washoe, Nim learned a range of signs, the ultimate conclusion of the researchers was that it was not possible for chimpanzees to learn human language as Chomsky defined it. The growing academic and ethical controversy surrounding projects like these was starting to cast doubt on the value of long-term experiments with chimpanzees. Attention instead was diverted to our other close relatives, the bonobos.

One such bonobo was Kanzi, who was born in captivity in Georgia, USA, in 1980 and studied by a team of primatologists led by Sue Savage-Rumbaugh. This time, sign language was replaced with lexigrams as the medium of communication. These were symbols (chosen in preference to actual pictures) representing toys, games, plants, animals and food – 'ball', 'chase', 'banana', for example – all arranged on a very large keyboard. What is extraordinary about Kanzi is that he picked up some of the meanings of the symbols without initially being taught them, but by being present as a young animal when his adoptive mother Matata was being trained in the lexigrams. Before long, his growing lexigram repertoire enabled Kanzi to communicate his needs and intentions in a variety of contexts, and he even showed he was capable of two-word combinations such as 'hide peanut', or 'peanut hide' – arguably but not indisputably the faintest beginnings of grammatical development. As is also the case with young children, Kanzi's comprehension skills were greater than his production skills. He could correctly follow closely related instructions such as 'put the ball on the rock' and 'put the rock on the ball', again suggesting some sensitivity to word order. However, Kanzi, who is 35 at the time of writing, has never exhibited more than the linguistic capabilities of a very young child.

Projects involving chimpanzees and bonobos are fascinating to read about but have proved highly controversial in terms of the treatment Gua and her successors received and also the methodology used by the researchers which, some detractors claim, casts doubt on the validity of their findings. What is indisputable is that the animals involved have shown some ability to learn to communicate in a new way, as determined by their human companions. Reflecting on the experiments, most linguists would now agree that language requires an ability not possessed by even our closest genetic cousins – not the ability to speak, but the ability to construct a fully developed mental grammar as they grow up. However, the responses of the chimps and bonobos have served not simply to confirm this central ingredient for human language, but also to throw light on what had to happen in the process of evolution for the human species to develop language in the first place. This takes us back to 1960 and a new approach to defining language.

The design-features of language

The September 1960 issue of the journal *Scientific American* included a paper by the linguist and anthropologist Charles Hockett entitled 'The Origin of Speech'. This particular edition contained various articles on the theme of human development, and Hockett's article proposed that clues to the origin of human language could be found through a comparison of its various characteristics with the features of more primitive animal communication systems. By isolating those features unique to human language, it would be possible to determine the stepping-off point of human language. In other words, what had to happen to animal communication to turn it into human language? We will be looking more closely at the origin of language in the next chapter, but here we will use Hockett's approach to further our exploration of the nature of human language, an approach which remains influential over half a century after the article's publication.

There is no doubt that other species possess some remarkable abilities for conveying messages to each other. Hockett gives consideration, for example, to bees and the extraordinary 'waggle dances' they are able to perform in order to alert fellow bees to the exact location of water or pollen sources. But a detailed comparison with human language reveals the ways in which our communication system has evolved to a greater level of complexity. In his paper, Hockett presents a set of 13 **design-features** (although he added three more later on) with the aim of identifying 'the basic features of design that can be present or absent in any communicative system, whether it be a communicative system of humans, of animals, or of machines' (Hockett, 1960/1982, p. 5). This classification was effective in being able to deal with the multifaceted nature of human language, at the same time as making viable comparisons with other creatures. Most significantly, all of his design-features occur in human language, but only a subset of the complete list applies to any other species.

Several of Hockett's design-features relate to the mechanism we use to transmit our messages to other members of our species. In many species, including humans, this is primarily by use of the **auditory-vocal channel**. In other words, the mouth is used to generate the signal and the ear to hear it. Another of the design-features is **semanticity**, the ability of a transmitted signal to convey meaning to other members of the species. Of course, both humans and animals use involuntary, non-linguistic cries in response to emotions such as fear and pain. But in terms of intentional signals, there is no doubt that animals can convey quite specific messages to each other. This is well documented through recent research. Meerkats in Southern Africa's Kalahari Desert, for example, have an alarm call which appears to alert the group to a possible predator on the move, while Campbell's monkeys in West Africa seem to have distinct calls for predators depending on whether they are on the ground or in the air. Like humans, they use the auditory-vocal channel to transmit their messages and they rely on direction and the relative proximity of their fellow creatures to be heard.

In addition to semanticity, many species – Hockett chooses gibbons as an example – exhibit the feature debated by ancient philosophers and emphasised by Saussure – arbitrariness. As it turns out, this is found quite commonly in the animal world: a monkey may produce a particular screech to indicate 'eagle as predator' but a different screech would serve just as well as long as the other monkeys knew what it meant. Arbitrariness is not then unique to human language – but is particularly salient to it. We can demonstrate this by comparing languages, as this can often highlight the arbitrary quality of words. For instance, the flying creature that would elicit 'bird' in English is '*oiseau*' in French, '*fugl*' in Danish and '*ptitsa*' in Russian. The arbitrariness of these signals of meaning is certainly thrown into sharp relief when languages are compared, but also when we consider that none of these words could have been predicted. They are, as we saw above, unmotivated.

What then are the design-features which distinguish human language? In Hockett's original article, three features emerge. The first of these is **displacement** – the ability to convey messages about things that are not physically present, that have already happened, or that will happen in the future. So humans can talk about complex subjects like politics and history and the future of the planet as well as give a simple danger warning, whereas meerkats and monkeys can only do the last of these things. (Although the bees' waggle dance is also said to exhibit displacement, this only has one specific 'topic' and purpose.) **Productivity** is another feature that sets us apart: our language is endlessly creative. In our 'open' language system, there is no limit to the number or type of messages we can convey whereas animal calls are a small 'closed' set, largely concerned with safety, food, reproduction and territory, and lacking the option for endlessly new combinations. Hockett described productivity as one of the 'most important features' – 'the capacity to say things that have never been said before and yet to be understood by other speakers of the language' (ibid., p. 6). Of course, as we saw earlier, Chomsky had a considerable amount to say about the significance of linguistic productivity, placing emphasis on the power of our mental grammar capacity to generate a limitless number of sentences, but Hockett has his own less sophisticated take on this: 'one can coin new utterances by putting together pieces familiar from old utterances, assembling them by patterns of arrangement also familiar in old utterances' (ibid.). As he wrote, the Chomskyan revolution was already gathering pace.

Lastly, Hockett identified the two-tiered system of human language which he termed **duality of patterning**. (It is also known as **double articulation**.) What this means is that we combine sounds which have no specific meaning (unlike animal alarm calls) into groups of sounds which do convey meaning. So the separate (meaningless) sounds of /d/ and /g/ combined with a third sound /ɒ/ give us 'dog' in one combination and 'god' in another – two distinct meaningful elements. With a set of about 45 meaningless sounds (in English) we are able to produce thousands of meaningful combinations (namely, words) and in turn combine them to convey an infinite number of messages, making human language highly productive, as we have already noted. Nothing like this – not even in the complexities of birdsong – exists elsewhere in the animal kingdom. Human language is often described as a symbolic system, since it is built on this principle.

Hockett's work provides an interesting way to classify human language in terms of animal communication in general. Later, Hockett added three more defining features of human language: prevarication, reflexiveness and learnability. Prevarication concerns the way we can use language to lie or deceive – something a dancing bee would never do. Reflexiveness is our ability to think about how we use language. We show this openly through **metalanguage**, making comments such as 'that's not what I meant' or 'what I'm trying to say is …' which reveal our ability to monitor the messages we are trying to convey. Learnability taps into the fact that human language relies on cultural transmission from one generation to another. Moreover, it takes many different forms (although some regional variation has been identified among different populations of other species, such as whales) and it is, in theory, possible for a human being already in possession of one language to learn any other language at any stage of their lives.

One of the strengths of Hockett's approach was to define the characteristics of human language at the same time as establishing what it had in common with animal communication from which it must, he argues, somehow have evolved. So where do Washoe, Kanzi and the other chimps and bonobos fit into his taxonomy? Clearly their natural communication systems lack certain design-features but to what extent were they able to acquire them? And in any case, would the acquisition of these features result in the possession of a language like ours? There has been considerable debate about whether the difference between human language and the communicative abilities of our nearest relatives is absolute, or a matter of degree. Undoubtedly, Washoe and Kanzi share some of our ability to acquire and use linguistic signs, but display only a very limited ability to connect them in a syntactic way. In any case, caution needs to be exercised with regard to Hockett's design-features. They may collectively identify the properties possessed by human language, but that does not mean it is true to say that, from an evolutionary point of view, the human species, once in possession of the capability for all these properties, would automatically produce language.

A more recent suggestion – proposed by the evolutionary biologists Tecumseh Fitch and Marc Hauser in an unexpected collaboration with Noam Chomsky – is that human language is dependent on one design-feature alone, and that is **recursion** (Hauser, Chomsky and Fitch, 2002). This is closely linked to productivity but places more emphasis on the syntactic processes which enable us to be so productive. Recursion operates by embedding one syntactic unit inside another. For example, the simple sentence *the earth is flat* can be embedded in *Terry believes [the earth is flat]* and this in turn can be embedded inside *Julia believes [Terry believes [the earth is flat]]*, and so on. It's hard to imagine a chimpanzee being able to achieve this level of complexity in its messages. The scientific paper by Chomsky, Fitch and Hauser caused something of a surprise when it was published, since up to this point Chomsky had largely dissociated himself from any discussion of language evolution. Interestingly, though, the paper seems to present a compromise between linguistics and biology, as it makes a distinction between language in a broad sense (where it shares features with other species) and language in a narrow sense, its 'internal computation system' (ibid., p. 1570) which deals with syntax or, effectively, recursion. As a design-feature, recursion has not been without its detractors, but as the one feature that seemingly makes human language into what it is (particularly perhaps to linguists who regard syntax as the core of linguistic study), the concept undoubtedly has a certain appeal.

The difficulty of defining language

Language seems to defy precise definition. As we have seen already in this chapter, ideas about the nature of language have been explored for more than two millennia and the thoughts of the earlier thinkers keep resurfacing in one form or another in the ideas of their successors. What makes human language unique has been a powerful question, and its potency can still be perceived in the work of many present-day researchers.

To study the ideas of Saussure and Chomsky, with their considerable emphasis on the internal aspects of language, the reader could be beguiled into thinking that systems of linguistic signs or grammatical rules lie at the heart of this human phenomenon. But many thinkers – and they too can be traced back through the centuries – have disputed this, arguing that it is perverse to study language without any consideration for the communicative function it fulfils. In other words, can you understand language without understanding how speakers use it? The Danish linguist Otto Jespersen emphasised this point in the preface to his 1922 work on language: 'Language is activity, purposeful activity, and we should never lose sight of the speaking individu-als and of their purpose in acting in this particular way' (Jespersen, 1922, p. 7). So the external aspects of language are equally important, and they too capture something of what language actually is. Even Saussure recognised the collective aspect of language, as knowledge shared by a community of speakers, describing language as 'a fund accumulated by the members of the community through the practice of speech, a grammatical system existing potentially in every brain, or more exactly in the brains of individuals; for the language is never complete in any single individual, but exists perfectly only in collectivity' (Saussure, 1916/1983, p. 13).

Our intuitions about language may well incline us to feel that it has some independent life or existence of its own, although common sense tells us that if human beings became extinct, then human language would of course die with us. Nevertheless, the notion that language is in some sense 'alive' is a powerful one. Our feeling that language 'exists' is perhaps reinforced by the evidence of specific languages having been embodied, so to speak, in dictionaries and grammar books, not to mention all the other written texts which are part of our linguistic and cultural heritage. For many people in the past – until just a few centuries ago, in fact – the reality of language was the result of it having been created. As we will see in the following chapter, Plato suggested that language had been devised by some semi-mythical leader, or name-maker. More significantly, the spread of Christianity promoted language as a divine creation, given by God to Adam, the first man. This belief was reinforced by some thinkers on the basis that language was far too complex to have been created by human beings – although others doubted this on the grounds that language was too irregular and even illogical for it to be the work of God. In the last 300 years or so, the 'divine creation' view of language has given way to the belief that language is part of the evolutionary development of our species. What is more, it is recognised that the emergence of language in humans was, in all likelihood, not a single, discontinuous event, but an extended process taking place over thousands and thousands of years. Language then can be viewed as a biological product, not just as a system or a social phenomenon.

The history of linguistics reveals how, over time, ideas about the nature of language have changed and developed, and some of course have been superseded. Yet the true nature of language remains elusive. Ultimately, it can only be fully understood by reference to all its features and functions, and to both its internal and external qualities, but it is left to the reader to determine which – if any – of these capture the essence of human language most powerfully. Our exploration of the nature of language is far from finished, and the rest of this book will reveal many more of its extraordinary facets.

Suggestions for further reading and research

On different ways of looking at language

Chapman, Siobhan and Christopher Routledge (eds) (2005) *Key Thinkers in Linguistics and the Philosophy of Language* (Edinburgh: Edinburgh University Press)

The ideas about language of 80 different thinkers are presented in this useful reference book, each thinker with their own separate entry.

Chapman, Siobhan (2006) *Thinking About Language* (Basingstoke: Palgrave Macmillan)

A very clear and readable exploration of the many different ideas linguists and philosophers have had about what language is.

Crystal, David (2010) *The Cambridge Encyclopedia of Language*, 3rd edn (Cambridge: Cambridge University Press)

A linguistic treasure trove, great for browsing but also a coherently organised survey of language in all its guises.

Everett, Daniel (2012) *Language: The Cultural Tool* (London: Profile Books)

Based on personal experience with different cultures, Everett's account focuses on human language not as an innate endowment but as a set of tools devised in response to cultural needs.

On structural aspects of language

Chandler, Daniel (2007) *Semiotics: The Basics*, 2nd edn (Abingdon: Routledge)

A clear introduction with plenty on language, but also demonstrating how Saussure's ideas apply to other areas of our lives, such as the media.

Chomsky, Noam (1986) *Knowledge of Language: Its Nature, Origin and Use* (New York: Praeger)

The work in which Chomsky introduced the concepts of I-language and E-language, although he focuses on the former as a means of understanding the human mind.

Corballis, Michael C (2014) *The Recursive Mind: The Origins of Human Language, Thought and Civilization* (Princeton, NJ: Princeton University Press)

Also relevant to Chapter 3, Corballis explores recursion as a distinguishing feature of both thought and language.

Pinker, Steven and Ray Jackendoff (2005) 'The faculty of language: what's special about it?', in *Cognition*, vol. 95, issue 2, pp. 201–36

A response to the proposal by Hauser, Chomsky and Fitch that human language is distinguished by being recursive. This article is also relevant to Chapter 3 on the origin of language.

On the communicative abilities of animals

Anderson, Stephen R (2004) *Doctor Dolittle's Delusion* (New Haven, CT: Yale University Press)

A fascinating exploration of what the author sees as the fundamental inability of animals to communicate in a way that is comparable to human language.

Savage-Rumbaugh, Sue and Roger Lewin (1996) *Kanzi: The Ape at the Brink of the Human Mind* (New York: John Wiley)

The intriguing story of Kanzi the bonobo leads on to an exploration into the human mind and the origin of language.

Terrace, Herbert (1987) *Nim: A Chimpanzee who Learned Sign Language* (New York: Columbia University Press)

A detailed account of Terrace's project, this is an updated edition with a new preface by the author.

3 The emergence of language

Thinkers and researchers introduced (or reintroduced) in this chapter

From the ancient world of Greece and Rome:

Herodotus (c. 484–c. 425 BCE)	Greek historian
Plato (428–348 BCE)	Greek philosopher
Epicurus (341–270 BCE)	Greek philosopher
Lucretius (c. 95–c. 55 BCE)	Roman philosopher

From the Age of Enlightenment:

John Locke (1632–1704)	English philosopher
Carl Linnaeus 1707–78	Swedish naturalist
Johann Peter Süssmilch (1707–67)	German scholar and theologian
Jean-Jacques Rousseau (1712–78)	French philosopher
Étienne Bonnot de Condillac (1715–80)	French philosopher
Johann Gottfried Herder (1744–1803)	German philosopher

Working in the nineteenth century:

Charles Darwin (1809–82)	British naturalist
August Schleicher (1821–68)	German philologist, supporter of Darwin
Friedrich Max Müller (1823–1900)	German philologist
Alfred Russel Wallace (1823–1913)	British naturalist and evolutionist
Ernst Haeckel (1834–1919)	German naturalist

Publishing works in the twentieth century:

Otto Jespersen (1860–1943)	Danish linguist
Antoine Meillet (1866–1936)	French linguist
Derek Bickerton (b. 1926)	British linguist
Noam Chomsky (b. 1928)	American linguist

Also in this chapter, we'll be discussing various extinct members of the human (or hominid) family tree, including some of our direct ancestors:

Homo habilis	who lived about 2.4–1.4 million years ago
Homo erectus	about 1.8 million to 200,000 years ago
Homo heidelbergensis	about 600,000–250,000 years ago

and our close relatives:

the Denisovans	about 500,000–40,000 years ago
Homo neanderthalensis	about 400,000–35,000 years ago

Two starting points: Berlin and Paris

Eighteenth-century Berlin is just one of the many places where we could begin the story of the quest to uncover the origin of human language. In 1769, the Royal Prussian Academy of Sciences announced (in French) the subject for its next annual essay-writing competition with this rather inviting question: 'Are human beings, left to their natural abilities, in a position to invent language, and by what means do they, by themselves, accomplish that invention?' In an age when scientific investigation into the natural world was gathering increased momentum, this was an opportunity to speculate and theorise on one of the hot topics of the day. The wording of the question would have been particularly significant to contemporary thinkers in that it asked them to step aside from the traditional belief that language was a God-given faculty, and explore how humans might have 'invented' language without divine assistance. There were 34 entries in the competition, which was won by Johann Gottfried Herder, a German philosopher, theologian and literary critic. Herder took up the challenge of the competition enthusiastically: 'since this great subject promises such rewarding insights ... who would not wish to try his hand at it?' he wrote (Herder, 1772/1966, p. 103). We will return to his prize-winning essay later.

The excitement caused by the Berlin Academy's competition is in stark contrast to an event which occurred in Paris less than a hundred years later. Although the question of the origin of language was still of considerable interest to contemporary scholars, a newly formed society for the study of language, the *Société de Linguistique de Paris,* incorporated into its founding statutes of 1866 a ban on the submission of papers on this very topic. The society's reason for this was simply the strongly held belief that it was a waste of time to speculate further on a question that could never be answered. Of course, the ban didn't stop the speculation, and it is ironic that it was issued at a time when beliefs and knowledge about the origin and development of the human race itself were changing radically, a change which would inevitably affect the study of spoken human communication and how it came into existence.

The society's founders would probably be pleasantly surprised to learn about the progress that has been made since 1866 in our understanding of how language began. Having said this, we still know very little. In fact, it is probably true to say that we know more about the beginning of our universe than we know about the origin of human language. Nevertheless, we now have some idea of when and where language emerged, together with an array of theories about how this might have happened which are certainly more grounded in knowledge and research than anything proposed previously. What is also significantly different now is that the subject that was once largely the territory of thinkers within a comparatively limited sphere has become a vast interdisciplinary enterprise, with researchers from many scientific fields contributing to the debate. In fact, the diversity of approaches to tackling one of the great unanswered questions in science is remarkable, notwithstanding the fact of so much activity still having yielded relatively few answers.

Questions we need to ask

There are many questions that need to be asked about how human language emerged. We can begin with the relatively simple questions: how old is human language, who were the first 'speakers' and where did they live? A more perplexing question is why did language develop in our species? What benefits could such a communication system bring to us? What cognitive abilities needed to have developed in the brain before language could begin, and what form did the earliest traces of human language take? How did words as we know them first appear, what might they have referred to and how were these meanings agreed on? What prompted or enabled the development of our highly productive double articulation system, whereby a small set of meaningless sounds combine to form these meaningful elements (in the way the same three sounds form either 'dog' or 'god')? How did the grammatical system develop, enabling us to produce an infinite number of complex messages through rule-governed word combinations? Which role, if either, was more important in the development of language: that of the producer or the receiver? Did human language develop out of a system of instinctive animal cries (like that of monkeys) or did it arise independently? Did language originate from one human group alone or from several geographically disparate groups? Was the emergence of language a relatively sudden or a gradual process? What were the environmental, social and cultural conditions that fostered language? What were the biological and anatomical ones?

The vast array of questions which now preoccupy linguists have not always been investigated in equal measure by those who have pondered the origins of language. There are a handful of reasons for this. The earliest thinkers had no evidence available to them about how the human race developed, and ideas about human evolution were only just emerging fully in the mid-nineteenth century, around the time the Linguistic Society of Paris imposed its ban. Before this, the majority of thinkers accepted the view that the human race was created by whichever god (or gods) they believed in, or at least that human existence had only undergone a brief developmental stage from primitive savages to civilised beings. Language, therefore, was either God-given as a kind of fully developed package or was 'invented' in some fairly spontaneous way by humans themselves, possibly due to the divine bestowal of a capacity to do so. Until the start of the scientific age in the seventeenth century, these notions went largely unchallenged. Scientific breakthroughs (such as the theory of evolution and the deeper understanding of genetics) have subsequently changed the way language is viewed and studied as part of the human condition. So too has the development of linguistics as a discipline in its own right in the last hundred years or so. These events have taken the question of the origin of language away from scholars such as theologians and philosophers and placed it firmly in the hands of scientists and, of course, linguists.

Three very early thinkers, and the story of Adam

In the Western world, the earliest ideas about the origin of language for which we have any evidence were those of ancient Greek and Roman philosophers concerned to understand the precise nature of the world around them. Their observations, therefore, need to be understood within this context. Unlike later writers, they were not necessarily studying language for its own sake, but as part of a wider endeavour, which is why any discussion of the origin of language is often embedded in a work on some other subject. These early texts, and indeed some much later ones, can seem rather alien to a modern reader, both in the way they are composed and also in the beliefs on which they are based. However, it is striking how previous debates about language also contain ideas which still bear a clear relationship with modern thinking.

In the previous chapter we discussed Plato's *Cratylus*, the oldest surviving work on language in the Western world. Although *Cratylus* is predominantly a discussion of 'the correctness of names', and whether they are natural or arbitrary, it also considers the means by which names were first given, thus revealing something of the contemporary beliefs about the origin of language. Socrates (who is effectively Plato's mouthpiece) tells Hermogenes:

> ... it isn't every man who can give names ... but only a name-maker, and he, it seems, is a rule-setter – the kind of craftsman most rarely found among human beings. (Plato, c. 387–361 BCE/1997, p. 107)

Socrates presents the 'rule-setter' (or 'legislator' as some translators term him) as a respected and authoritative forebear who, with some guidance from a 'dialectician' (or expert in logic), knew how to put 'the natural name of each thing' into sounds and syllables (ibid., p. 109). However, this was no easy matter, and the names would only be appropriate if this name-maker had understood the world correctly and therefore chosen the right name. Language, then – or at least this particular aspect of it – is presented by Plato as something 'given' piece by piece by one particularly capable person to his countrymen (and as a predominantly male activity), a process which would have occurred among all the peoples of the ancient world.

The Greek philosopher Epicurus, who was born in Athens just a few years after the death of Plato, offers a slightly different take on the origin of names from Plato's. In a letter to the historian Herodotus, summarising for him what Epicurus saw as the 'chief doctrines' for explaining the workings of the natural world, Epicurus also touches briefly on language:

> … the names of things were not originally created by convention. On the contrary, the various ethnic groups of mankind, on experiencing their own peculiar emotions and sensory impressions, uttered sounds conforming to these various emotions and impressions … later on, characteristic terms were assigned by common agreement in the various ethnic groups in order to make their intentions mutually more intelligible and to convey them concisely. Also, people who knew them brought in certain things never seen before and suggested certain words for them. Sometimes these persons were forced to invent natural sounds for the objects; at other times they chose the sounds by a rational process in conformance with ordinary conventions … (Epicurus, c. 305 BCE/2012, p. 108)

Not unlike Plato, Epicurus explores the question of whether names are natural in some way or conventional, suggesting that convention ('reason or analogy') stepped in when instinctive sounds were lacking. The adoption of names, however, seems to be a more collective process. Even when names for 'things never seen before' were introduced, this was down to 'people who knew them' as opposed to one single name-maker. Epicurus gives a sense of language somehow developing along with human culture as a collaborative human activity, an approach that has far more resonance with a modern reader.

About 250 years later, the Roman philosopher Lucretius expounded the many ideas of Epicurus about matter and the universe in a work already mentioned briefly in the previous chapter, *On the Nature of Things* (*De rerum natura*). This takes the form of a poem of over 7,000 lines, the poetic style and the length of the work befitting both the subject matter and the grand educational purpose of the piece. It is divided into six books, with a short passage in Book 5 devoted to language. Lucretius tackles head-on the notion found in *Cratylus* that names were given by one person to the rest of the community: 'To suppose that someone on some particular occasion allotted names to objects, and that by this means men learnt their first words, is stark madness' (Lucretius, c. 49 BCE/1951, p. 203). Lucretius has several reasons for rejecting the idea of the legislator or name-maker. Why would only one person have the power to do this and not others at the same time? In any case, how could a name-maker acquire the knowledge of words in the first place? And how could the name-maker force others to use his words, or even understand them? Lucretius has his own ideas about how humans developed language. First, he proposes that uncivilised humans, who possessed no language, used cries and gestures to ensure that the stronger men protected the women and children, thus implying that the earliest human communication developed for a very particular purpose. Following this, 'it was nature that drove men to utter [the various sounds of spoken language], and practical convenience that gave a form to the names of objects' (ibid., p. 202). Like Epicurus, Lucretius presents the emergence of language among humans as a collective process, resulting from a natural urge to communicate using vocal signals.

Although early philosophers, then, had considered what kind of creation language actually was, the coming of Christianity constrained thinking in the Western world about the origin of language for many centuries. Here is the biblical account from the book of Genesis (the 1611 English version) of the creation of animals and birds, which followed the creation of Adam, the first man:

> And out of the ground the Lord God formed every beast of the field, and every fowl of the air; and brought them unto Adam to see what he would call them: and whatsoever Adam called every living creature, that was the name thereof. (Genesis 2.19)

Although there is considerable scholarly debate about when Genesis was composed (originally in Hebrew), it is likely to have been written earlier than Plato's *Cratylus*. The shared preoccupation with the giving of names seems to reveal some regional cross-fertilisation of ideas about the origin of language. The implication of the biblical passage is that Adam was created equipped with language, hence his ability to name the new creatures. It is probably unsurprising that, in accepting a divine view of creation for many centuries, the majority of Western Christian thinkers, like their Islamic counterparts, also accepted the human language capacity as part of that creation.

The coming of the scientific age

By the seventeenth century, and in the wake of the Renaissance, there had been a marked shift away from simple acceptance of nature as a divine creation requiring no explanation towards a greater curiosity about the world and the interrelationship of the living things within it. Natural philosophers (as scientists were then called) were hard at work in a frenzy of scientific inquiry. They looked into space and studied planetary motion; they dissected corpses and learnt about human anatomy. William Harvey showed for the first time how the blood circulated around the body, while Isaac Newton published his findings on light, motion and gravity. The world was explored with microscopes and telescopes, and measured with barometers and even mechanical calculators, the first of which was invented by Blaise Pascal in 1642.

With regard to language, travel and exploration had made scholars rethink ideas about the number of languages in the world and their relationship to one another. Dissections of animals resulted in some interesting ideas about their language potential and whether, like humans, animals had the ability to reason. As far as the origin of language was concerned, however, this new scientific age yielded no substantial evidence to advance the search, although scientific ideas about the human mind and the development of the human race began to permeate some of the speculation. In fact, by the eighteenth century, in what is now known as the Age of Enlightenment, speculating about the origin of language had become a very popular pursuit among philosophers and intellectuals.

Initially, all this scientific and intellectual activity was largely carried out within the framework of belief in the all-powerful divinity who created Adam and endued him with language. For example, in his influential *Essay Concerning Human Understanding* published in 1690, the English philosopher John Locke begins the section on language with the statement:

> God, having designed man for a sociable creature, made him not only with an inclination … to have fellowship with those of his own kind, but furnished him also with language … (Locke, 1690, III.i.l)

By the eighteenth century, however, philosophers were starting to reconsider this position, with the majority adopting the view that, while God was the creator of all living things, language itself was an entirely human creation.

Two French philosophers

One of the key thinkers of this time was Étienne Bonnot de Condillac, who trained in Paris as a priest, and later became the Abbott of Mureau, about 300 km east of Paris. He outlined his ideas in his 1746 *Essay on the Origin of Human Knowledge*, a section of which is devoted to the origin of language.

As a priest and abbot, Condillac could hardly question the concepts of divine creation or the divine gift of language; as a philosopher he seems to have been keen to take part in the debate about how language developed in humans. So he adopts a tactical position which enables him to satisfy the requirements of both roles. He begins by asserting his theological belief that it was through divine assistance that Adam and Eve were able to communicate their thoughts to each other. However, in order to free himself from the constraints of this theological tenet, he imagines a scenario in which two very young children, a boy and a girl, lost and left to wander alone after the flood described in the book of Genesis, might develop language as they grew up.

Condillac's work illustrates one of the central preoccupations of his time, which was the likely role of cries and gestures as precursors to a fully developed language among humans. He describes how the children would at first have expressed themselves with 'the cries of the passions and the different motions of the body' (Condillac, 1746/2001, p. 115), and would gradually have come to recognise each other's meanings from the context in which the cries and gestures appeared. From these mutually understood signals, language gradually developed: 'when they had acquired the habit of connecting some ideas to arbitrary signs, the natural cries served as a model for them to make a new language' (ibid., p. 116). Condillac even goes on to suggest how the production of sounds and names may have developed:

> They articulated new sounds, and by repeating them many times to the accompaniment of some gesture that indicated the objects to which they wished to draw attention, they became accustomed to giving names to things. Still, the first progress of this language was very slow. The organ of speech was so inflexible that it could articulate only very simple sounds with any ease. (ibid.)

Later, the birth of a child to the couple would have helped this new language to develop since the child, whose tongue was 'very flexible', had a greater capacity to form new sounds. Although the scenario described by Condillac seems rather quaint to a modern reader, his discussion of the recognition of shared meaning and of how the range of speech sounds may have emerged has a faintly plausible ring to it.

Condillac's friend and fellow philosopher, Jean-Jacques Rousseau, also entered the language-origin debate in the mid-eighteenth century. His 1755 *Discourse on the Origins and Foundations of Inequality among Men* contains a detailed section on the origin of language, despite his initial comments about the difficulties of formulating a convincing hypothesis. This work was followed some years later by his *Essay on the Origin of Languages* (published posthumously in 1781), although this focuses more on how human language came to be so diverse, something we will be considering in the following chapter. In the 1755 *Discourse*, Rousseau too explores the possible role of gestures and cries in the development of language. He proposes a primitive, or savage, stage of human development when instinctive cries were uttered in situations of danger or suffering. Gradually human thought developed and communication methods expanded. Gestures were used to denote any-thing visible and sounds to mimic what was audible, such as the call of a bird or animal. 'Inarticulate cries, many gestures and some imitative noises must have been for long the universal human language', writes Rousseau (1755/1984, pp. 111–12). However, gestures, he points out, were of no value in the dark or when the gesturers were not face-to-face, and so words developed in their place.

Elsewhere, Rousseau considers the nature of these early words, suggest-ing that they 'each … had the meaning of a whole proposition' (ibid., p. 94). In contrast to Epicurus and Lucretius, Rousseau includes some sug-gestions as to how the development of the 'sublime art' of language might have progressed in terms of specific linguistic elements. He argues, for example, that the earliest words were nouns for observable objects (such as a tree) and that adjectives would have been slow to develop because of their more abstract nature. In his later work, however, he seems to take a slightly different position by proposing that gestures were sufficient to fulfil physical needs such as hunger and thirst, but feelings of love, hatred, pity and anger were what prompted the first words. 'It seems then that need dictated the first gestures, while the passions stimulated the first words', he says in his *Essay on the Origin of Languages* (Rousseau, 1781/1966, p. 11). Either way, Rousseau is at pains to emphasise the difficulty of this process and the importance of collaboration among those early speakers, who must have achieved this outcome 'by a common consent' (Rousseau, 1755/1984, p. 94).

This idea of collaboration, which is also implicit in Condillac's tale of the lost children, touched on a contemporary debate relating to the human con-dition itself: if humans were essentially sociable creatures then language may have developed to facilitate sociability. On the other hand, if early humans preferred solitude (as Rousseau believed), then the development of language must have been a response to difficult conditions that forced them to start cooperating with each other in order to survive. In the *Discourse*, Rousseau invites 'anyone who will undertake it' to discuss 'the following difficult problem: which was the more necessary, a society already established for the invention of language, or language already invented for the establishment of society?' (ibid., pp. 96–7).

Gottfried Herder's prize-winning essay

This brings us back to Johann Gottfried Herder, the prize-winning essayist mentioned at the start of this chapter. He won his prize from the Academy of Sciences in Berlin in 1771. Just five years earlier, the German pastor and theologian, Johann Peter Süssmilch, had published a paper on the origin of language maintaining, like Condillac, that language was the gift of God. Unlike Condillac, however, who seemed more interested in speculating on how humans would have invented language if left to their own devices, Süssmilch bases his argument on the premise that language is far too complex to have been created by humans, and sets out to prove that the first language did not come from human beings, 'but from the creator alone', as he puts it in his lengthy title (Süssmilch, 1766). Herder's essay was partly a response to this paper as for him language was undoubtedly a human creation, but it was also a response to the other philosophers of his own age and earlier who had debated the origin of language. To read Herder's essay, with his many references to these thinkers and their ideas, is to understand how lively the debate was in the eighteenth century.

Herder harshly attacks Condillac's tale of the lost children, calling it 'a hollow explanation' of language origin (Herder, 1772/1966, p. 101). He also criticises Rousseau for not drawing a clear boundary between human language and the animal cries which express instinctive emotional reactions to particular situations: 'sounds of emotion will never turn into a human language', he contests (ibid.). For Herder, it is 'precisely through language' that human beings 'distinguish themselves from all animals' (ibid., p. 103). He contrasts the 'narrow sphere' of other living creatures with the very diverse sphere which humans inhabit. A spider, for example, whose principal function is to weave its web, has no need of language to fulfil what is an instinctive action. No animal, says Herder, has 'so much as the faintest beginning of a truly human language' (ibid., p. 99). Humans, on the other hand, have a far broader perspective and, hand-in-hand with this, a disposition towards reflection and reason. In fact, reason and language are inextricably linked so that 'not even the first and most primitive application of reason was possible without language' (ibid., p. 120).

To illustrate his ideas, Herder offers the example of a lion or wolf encountering a lamb. Their instincts compel them to attack it. A human being has no such instinct towards the lamb and instead tries to observe and understand what makes it distinctive. When the lamb bleats, that enables the human to distinguish it from other creatures and therefore that bleat becomes a distinguishing sign – 'and what is that other than a word?' Herder asks (ibid., p. 117). For him, such an act of reason is also a linguistic moment. 'The first vocabulary was thus collected from the sounds of the world', Herder goes on to say (ibid., p. 132). Again there are echoes of Plato's *Cratylus* when Herder proposes that every living creature 'delivers … its distinguishing word' (ibid., p. 130) and he even interprets the biblical story of Adam ('whatsoever the man called every living creature, that was the name thereof') as a statement that 'man invented language for himself – from the tones of living nature' (ibid., p. 131). Perhaps surprisingly, he rejects the role of 'arbitrary convention' and agreement among speakers in the development of language, so strong is his belief that language is part of what makes us human: 'to me it is incomprehensible how a human soul could be what it is and not, by that fact alone – without the help of a mouth and without the presence of a society – be led to invent language' (ibid., p. 119). Quite how humans came to share their newfound linguistic abilities is a question he chooses not to pursue.

With Herder, we have covered a span of more than two thousand years. Certain themes recur: the emphasis on names (although both Rousseau and Herder consider other word functions), the natural versus conventional quality of the names, the role of cries and gestures, and the purposes for which language developed. Language has been presented as a gift to humanity, as a product of social collaboration and as an inevitable result of the human capacity for reason. Some of these ideas are still of relevance to linguists; some have been left to posterity. The idea which has been most readily abandoned is of course the belief that language was bestowed by a divine or authoritative being. (Having said this, there are some scientists working today who believe, like Süssmilch, that the complexity of language is not something which humans could naturally have developed but is the result of what they call 'intelligent design'. This is not, however, the view of the vast majority of linguists.) As we will see next, long-held beliefs about the natural world and the status of humankind within it were about to be shattered.

Darwin's giant leap forward

A development which was to have significant implications for the study of the origin of language came in 1859 with the publication of Charles Darwin's *On the Origin of Species by Means of Natural Selection*, to give it its full title. It was a book that marked a watershed in scientific thinking. Darwin and some of his contemporaries had, for some time, questioned the belief that the living creatures of the natural world had been created exactly as they now appeared. Based on biblical stories and genealogies, their predecessors had believed that creation was a relatively recent event and that humans had only existed for about 6,000 years. By Darwin's time, fossil-hunting had become a very popular pursuit, and evidence from growing fossil collections had thrown doubt on this: the earth was clearly much older. (Over 300 million years old was Darwin's estimate.) There was also greater appreciation of the similarities between different species. Over a hundred years before Darwin, Carl Linnaeus, a Swedish naturalist, had classified living creatures into family groups in his *Systema naturae* (first published in 1735). As new ideas about the relationships of living things to each other gathered momentum in the mid-1800s, Darwin went much further, proposing that not only were there distinct similarities between certain groups of living species but that those species had evolved over a long period of time from common ancestors, their survival being the result of their ability to adapt to whatever environmental conditions they found themselves in.

Darwin himself seems to have had some inkling of the 'considerable revolution' his theory would bring about when, in the conclusion of his book, he wrote:

> In the distant future I see open fields for far more important researches. Psychology will be based on a new foundation, that of the necessary requirement of each mental power and capacity by gradation. Light will be thrown on the origin of man and his history. (Darwin, 1859, p. 488)

The publication of *On the Origin of Species* certainly caused considerable excitement among many naturalists and scientists, although Darwin's ideas were shocking to those who maintained a traditional view of creation, and many found his suggestion that humans and apes were very close relatives unpalatable. As far as language was concerned, scholars who practised what was becoming known as 'linguistic science' or the 'science of language' were quite possibly already thinking along evolutionary lines and were quick to identify the implications Darwin's theory had for the origin of language in the human species. If humans evolved from animals, then the human mind must have evolved from an animal mind. In principle, then, other animals could develop language too. Not everyone agreed. One of the chief dissenters was the German scholar Friedrich Max Müller, who became a professor at the University of Oxford. In the early summer of 1861, he delivered his first series of *Lectures on the Science of Language* at the Royal Institution in London, the last of which was devoted to the theoretical question of the origin of language. In his introductory lecture he stated:

> We cannot tell as yet what language is … If it be a production of nature, it is her last and crowning production which she reserved for man alone. If it be a work of human art, it would seem to lift the human artist almost to the level

of a divine creator. If it be the gift of God, it is God's greatest gift … (Müller, 1861/2013, p. 3)

For Müller, as for Herder, language remained the feature which would always distinguish humans from all other living creatures, a view he promoted in many public lectures.

On the Origin of Species contains relatively little discussion about human evolution and language. Conscious of this gap and the opinions of scholars like Müller, Darwin addressed the question of language in his next major work, *The Descent of Man, and Selection in Relation to Sex* (published in 1871) and again the following year in *The Expression of Emotions in Man and Animals*. In *The Descent of Man*, Darwin shows that he has read the remarks of both his critics and his supporters, and he is at pains to counter Müller's argument that the faculty of language proves human beings to be unique. For Darwin, the mental powers of humans are more advanced than, not distinct from, those of other animals, and this includes their ability to reason. Breaking language down into its various components, Darwin proposes that animals too can understand the meanings of sounds and connect them with ideas, and that they have some ability to articulate sounds themselves. Humans differ only by degree, having what he originally termed a 'large power of connecting definite sounds with definite ideas' (Darwin, 1871, p. 54), but described with far greater force in the revised second edition, where he talks of an 'almost infinitely larger power of associating together the most diversified sounds and ideas' (Darwin, 1874, pp. 85–6). Darwin goes on to propose that language may have begun with singing, especially during courtship rituals – an idea that had also been proposed by Rousseau a century earlier. He believes singing may have helped early humans discover their voices and it is 'probable that the imitation of musical cries by articulate sounds may have given rise to words expressive of various complex emotions' (ibid., p. 86), although he also recognises that 'the imitation and modification of various natural sounds, the voices of other animals, and man's own instinctive cries, aided by signs and gestures' were central factors (ibid., p. 87). What is particularly striking, though, is Darwin's discussion of the human brain and its function in the development of language, proposing that the mental capacity in some human ancestor needed to have become more highly developed before language could begin (precisely why or how it was impossible to say), and that once started, the growing power of speech would have reacted on the mind itself and encouraged 'long trains of thought' to develop (ibid., p. 88). In this way, Darwin establishes what he describes as the 'intimate connection between the brain … and the faculty of speech' (ibid.), a topic we will return to in Chapter 8.

The middle decades of the nineteenth century were certainly abundant with new or reworked theories about the origin of language. Max Müller himself had collected some of the theories together, several of which had been given slightly contemptuous nicknames, such as the bow-wow theory and the pooh-pooh theory. It is perhaps no wonder that papers on the origin of language were banned by the Linguistic Society of Paris in 1866, even though the debate was thriving. The line of inquiry relating to the role of gestures remained productive, leading to the idea of so-called 'mouth-gestures' in the development of language. This idea was taken up by another naturalist, Alfred Russel Wallace, who developed his own theory of mouth-gestures. His paper, 'The Expressiveness of Speech', was published in the *Fortnightly Review* in 1895 as 'a contribution to the fascinating subject of the origin of language' (Wallace, 1895, p. 543). He describes how 'primitive man' would have had to 'struggle hard to make himself understood, and would, therefore, make use of every possible indication of meaning afforded by the positions and motions of mouth, lips, or breath' (ibid., p. 530). Although many of them seem fanciful, Wallace offers a range of examples to demonstrate how this 'primitive word-formation' may have worked, for example by showing how the mouth closes at the end of 'come' (suggesting movement towards the speaker) but remains open at the end of 'go', implying departure, a contrastive pairing to be found, he pointed out, in a large number of languages.

Wallace is remembered less for his ideas about language than for the fact that he too had come up with a theory of evolution by natural selection about the same time as Darwin. Papers by the two naturalists had been read out at a meeting of the Linnaean Society (named after Carl Linnaeus) in London in 1858, but it was Darwin who was the first to publish his ideas. Although Wallace's view of evolution differed from Darwin's in doubting whether natural selection could account for the development of the human mind, they are now both credited with formulating a scientific idea which has influenced the study of the natural world ever since. Moreover, with proponents of the emerging science of language allying themselves to this giant scientific leap forward, Darwin and his contemporaries paved the way for the study of the *origin* of language to become the study of the *evolution* of language.

Finding fossils

Despite the craze for fossils in Darwin's time, findings had been mainly restricted to non-human species, so Darwin himself knew nothing about the specific stages of development between ape and man. Scientists discussed how modern humans might have evolved, and even considered how the adoption of an upright posture for walking on two legs might have been linked to the evolution of speech, but evidence was lacking. In 1856, just three years before Darwin published *On the Origin of Species*, some fossilised human-like bones had been found in the Neander Valley in Western Germany. The palaeontologists who examined the remains concluded that they belonged to a human adult who suffered from considerable deformity. Only later did the significance of the fossil remains become clear and the bones were identified as belonging to an extinct human species, the Neanderthals. The first fossil discovery of what is now believed to be one of our direct human ancestors, *Homo erectus*, was made on the Indonesian island of Java in 1891, nine years after Darwin's death.

Over three decades later, the Danish linguist Otto Jespersen, writing about the study of the origin of language, commented:

> With very few exceptions those who have written about our subject have conjured up in their imagination a primitive era, and then asked themselves: How would it be possible for men or manlike beings, hitherto unfurnished with speech, to acquire speech as a means of communication of thought? … If we are to have any hope of success in our investigation we must try new methods and new ways … (Jespersen, 1922, p. 413)

Even as Jespersen was writing this criticism of the speculative approach, however, a new opportunity for investigation was taking shape. The discovery of Java Man had been followed by further discoveries of fossils belonging to extinct human-like beings – **hominins**. The 1920s and 1930s saw a huge increase in finds from various parts of the world. At last, there was some substantial evidence that could lead to a fuller understanding of the process of human evolution and, in turn, perhaps throw light on the evolution of language.

Nowadays, that hominin fossil collection – consisting of bones and teeth from Europe, Asia and most significantly from East Africa, where modern humans originated – has grown to an impressive size and has enabled researchers, aided by far more sophisticated dating techniques and information provided by DNA analysis, to start piecing together the vast jigsaw puzzle that tells the story of our evolution. So far more than 20 extinct species of the **hominid** family (of which we are the only living descendants) have been identified (12 of them since 1987, with the most recent – *Homo naledi* – being announced in September 2015), although there is sometimes disagreement on how to assign fossil specimens to a particular species (depending largely on whether the emphasis is more on the similarities or the differences between specimens) as well as some debate as to which species are our direct ancestors. There are still many missing links, and, as more evidence emerges, classifications sometimes have to be amended.

The earth itself is now estimated to be about 4.5 billion (4,500,000,000) years old, a startling contrast to the 6,000 years or so calculated by early biblical scholars, and even to the 300 million years estimated by Darwin. Life, in the form of single-celled organisms, began around 4 billion years ago. The fossil record reveals that modern humans have probably existed for about 200,000 years, just 0.005% of the total span of life on earth. Our closest living relatives are chimpanzees, with whom we shared a common ancestor in Africa between 5 and 7 million years ago. Our hominid family developed from this ancestor. Around 2 to 3 million years ago, a new genus (or sub-group) emerged within the hominid family, characterised by a generally upright posture, a dome-like head with a vertical forehead but without pronounced eyebrow ridges, and a large brain. This was the *Homo* genus, to which modern humans belong and from which we get our species name, *Homo sapiens* ('wise man'). (The convention for labelling species in Latin, starting with the genus, goes all the way back to the eighteenth century and the *Systema naturae* of Linnaeus.) Figure 3.1 gives an approximate timescale for some of the members of the *Homo* genus. It is likely that our lineage is from *Homo habilis* ('handy man' – a user of tools) through *Homo erectus* (who stood fully upright) and then *Homo heidelbergensis* (whose remains were first discovered in Heidelberg, Germany, in 1907). The Neanderthals are our evolutionary cousins, as are the Denisovans, discovered only in 2010, in the Denisova Cave in Siberia. The Neanderthals and the Denisovans only became extinct about 35–40,000 years ago, and it is a sobering thought that we have not always been the only living human species inhabiting the planet.

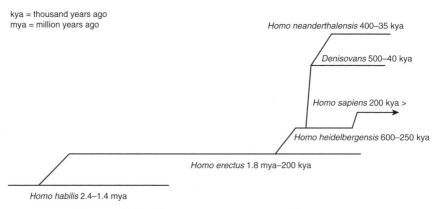

kya = thousand years ago
mya = million years ago

Homo neanderthalensis 400–35 kya

Denisovans 500–40 kya

Homo sapiens 200 kya >

Homo heidelbergensis 600–250 kya

Homo erectus 1.8 mya–200 kya

Homo habilis 2.4–1.4 mya

FIGURE 3.1   THE PROBABLE LINEAGE OF *HOMO SAPIENS*

Anatomical clues about the evolution of language

The vast collection of hominin fossils has revealed a great deal about our human ancestry. But can those silent bones provide any clues about the evolution of language? Anatomically, human language depends on both bones and soft tissue for its production and reception. Soft tissue – including the tongue, the **vocal tract**, the **larynx** (or voice box) and of course the brain – quickly decays after death, so researchers must rely on bones alone to make deductions about the emergent language capacity of our hominin ancestors.

Although relatively few specimens have been found, one bone that may provide such a clue is the tiny **hyoid** bone (shaped rather like a horseshoe) which sits just below the lower jaw to anchor the tongue, and is connected by ligaments to the larynx below it. So in fossil skeletons the position of the larynx can be deduced from that of the hyoid bone. In modern humans, the larynx is lower than in other primates, an important factor (along with the shape of the mouth cavity) in producing the range of sounds needed in our complex communication system. It is possible that the lowered larynx was caused by the skeletal changes that came about from being habitually upright, or possibly from a change of diet. A lowered larynx has been identified in *Homo erectus*, who lived from about 1.8 million to about 200,000 years ago and (as already mentioned) is probably one of our direct ancestors. This begs the question of whether some form of language had already developed at this stage of human development. However, the evolving brain is generally regarded as providing a better indication of language capability.

Despite a cutting remark made by Max Müller in a later lecture (from a series given in 1863) on the development of language that 'the science of language has nothing to do with skulls' (Müller, 1864/2013, p. 236), the brain case, or **cranium**, is of considerable interest to scientists for the clues it offers about the evolution of the human brain, in terms of both its volume and its shape. Although there is no precise correlation between the size of the brain and mental ability (elephants have the largest brains among mammals), the brain of *Homo sapiens* is large in proportion to body size, and about three times larger than that of a chimpanzee. (Modern research has also revealed how other primate species lack some of the pathways found in the human brain, and areas associated with language are less fully developed.) A comparison of craniums has shown that the oldest species of the *Homo* genus, *Homo habilis*, had an average brain volume of about 600 cc, less than half that of modern humans, whose brains are typically between 1200 and 1500 cc. By the emergence of *Homo erectus* about 1.8 million years ago, the volume had increased to about 800 cc. The fossil record then reveals a rapid increase to the 1200 cc of our ancestor *Homo heidelbergensis* by about 700,000 years ago. In addition, the changing shape of the hominid forehead (from sloping backwards to being more upright) suggests the development of the brain's frontal cortex, which is particularly associated with cognitive intelligence. Researchers strongly believe that there is a connection between dramatically increased brain capacity and the emergence of language as we know it.

Central to evolutionary research is the question of **adaptation** or **exaptation**, concepts which are also relevant to language and which are bound up with the complex nature of our language faculties. So in what ways did humans evolve particular traits as a direct response to communication needs (adaptation), and to what extent were existing features pressed into service for our developing language capacity (exaptation)? Researchers have calculated from the changing diameter of the spinal canal, for example, that at least 200,000 years ago hominids developed a better level of breath control, a necessity for sustained vocal articulation. This could well be an example of adaptation for language. By contrast, the changing shape of the hominid face, resulting in a less pronounced jawline, may have occurred to make the head more stable when running on two legs, but had additional benefits for speech by changing the shape of the mouth – a possible example therefore of exaptation. As for the brain, did it evolve (aided perhaps by a diet containing more protein) as a response to cognitive, communicative and linguistic needs, or did its development for other reasons (recent research suggests climate change in East Africa may have been an external factor) result in the additional benefit of language? The jury is currently out. However, if the brain and some capacity for language did indeed evolve together for the benefit of the species, that would be a remarkable example of natural selection at work.

Dating the emergence of language

The growing fossil record (along with various other archaeological discoveries) has yielded significant clues which have enabled current-day researchers to construct a tentative timescale for the emergence of language as well as a sketch map of the geographical settings for this extraordinary process. Like the *Homo* genus itself, our species originated in East Africa's Great Rift Valley about 200,000 years ago, and possibly earlier. About 140,000 years later, a steady migration 'Out of Africa' began, and *Homo sapiens* gradually populated the rest of the habitable world, following in the footsteps of other human species such as *Homo erectus* who had ventured out thousands of years before them but were destined to become extinct. On the simple basis that all living humans are descended from these African ancestors (as DNA analysis has shown) and all living humans have language, then language must have been fully developed in those early wanderers. That being so, there is good reason to believe that, long before their migration from Africa began, the earliest *Homo sapiens* were also in possession of language more or less as we know it. In fact, it is hard to imagine how those humans who lived so long ago could belong to the same species as we do and not share our language capacity. Having said this, some scholars, Noam Chomsky among them, believe that a sudden abundance of archaeological evidence for art and social ritual from about 50,000 years ago suggests that humans only became fully 'modern' – and fully 'linguistic' – relatively recently. This, it is proposed, could have been caused by a genetic mutation that dramatically accelerated cognitive and cultural development, and enabled complex thought and language (characterised by the mechanism of recursion mentioned in the previous chapter) to form at the same time. This alternative viewpoint is a salutary reminder that, while the 'gradual evolution' of language is an appealing and seemingly plausible idea, it can never be assumed that the development of language was smoothly incremental. In any case, researchers are by no means agreed on the complex sequencing of events that brought language into existence: tracking the production of anything in reverse is an enterprise that needs to be tackled with considerable caution.

Even before the idea of gradual evolutionary change became established as an explanation for the development of modern humans, and with it the development of the complex grammatical system that we now take for granted, many scholars, as we have seen, had proposed ideas about what language in its earliest guise might have been like. This incipient, primitive form has now come to be known as **protolanguage**, sometimes also called **pre-language** (and we will look at it more closely in the following section). So in seeking the beginnings of our fully-fledged language, we need to consider when protolanguage itself might have emerged, and in which of our ancestral species. Clearly, since none of our closest relatives – chimpanzees, bonobos, gorillas, orang-utans – possess even primitive language (whatever their potential to acquire limited elements of it from human teachers), its development must have started after the hominid family split from the evolutionary line which generated these living apes. The very early hominids can also be safely ruled out. One of the best specimens of these is an adult female known as 'Lucy' who was discovered in Ethiopia in 1974, with just under half of her bones present. Lucy belongs to the genus *Australopithecus*, which is considerably older than the *Homo* genus, and she probably lived about four million years ago. It is highly unlikely that Lucy had anything resembling human language in any shape or form. Although she walked some of the time on two legs like later hominins, the structure and position of her hyoid bone were similar to an ape's, so her range of vocal sounds would have been very limited. More significantly, her brain was similar in size to an ape's, suggesting her species lacked the cognitive skills to interact using even the simplest of linguistic forms.

The species with the most credentials for protolanguage is *Homo erectus*, our ancestor from around 1.8 million years ago. The significantly increased brain volume of these early humans, coupled with their tool-making skills and probable use of fire, as well as inferences we can make about their social behaviour, suggests a cognitive capacity sufficient for handling some degree of symbolic communication. The view that human language – in the form of protolanguage – began with *Homo erectus* is a persuasive one, and can possibly be supported with a small degree of genetic evidence in the form of the FOXP2 gene discovered in the late 1990s. (The full story is told in Chapter 10.) The human form of this gene has been shown to have a role in the comprehension and production of speech in living humans, but has also been found in the fossils of our Neanderthal cousins, suggesting it may have been inherited from *Homo erectus*, where it perhaps played a part in enabling the initial development of a linguistic faculty.

If researchers are indeed correct in their deductions that language evolved after the start of the *Homo* genus, but not before the advent of *Homo erectus*, then this begs the question of whether any later members of the *Homo* genus had language in a form which we might recognise. The obvious candidate for this is *Homo neanderthalensis*, who shared a common ancestor with *Homo sapiens* up to 500,000 years ago and existed alongside modern *Homo sapiens* in Europe for the last phase of their existence, only becoming extinct about 35,000 years ago. The evidence seems to be on their side: apart from the presence of the FOXP2 gene which has been shown to facilitate aspects of language, their lower jaws were a similar length to ours so the shape of their vocal tract was favourable for language, their larynxes seem to have been in the lower position, and they had the breathing power for sustained vocalisation. What is more, their brains were of a comparable size to ours. Based on evidence from archaeological sites, we know that the Neanderthals were like modern humans in some aspects of their behaviour, using tools and even burying their dead. It is an intriguing thought that *Homo sapiens* and *Homo neanderthalensis* may once have been able to communicate with each other linguistically. Based on DNA evidence, scientists know that there was interbreeding between the two species, so vocal interaction between us and our closest extinct relatives is a real – and rather appealing – possibility.

Of course, none of this is conclusive – more a best guess based on available information and current research. Although our modern capacity for language is generally regarded as innate, it is still not clear exactly what that means in either current-day or evolutionary terms, and we can only speculate about what kinds of genetic mutations or evolutionary changes might have led to the birth of some kind of language instinct. Also open to question is whether early language was relatively unified (population numbers are calculated in thousands) or how much diversity might already have existed before the Out-of-Africa migration began. There is certainly no agreement about whether it is possible to trace all existing languages back to a single source, as we shall see in the next chapter. Putting all the clues together, though, it seems likely that complex, grammatical human language as we now know it is at least 200,000 years old, and that its evolutionary origins in a simple protolanguage could have occurred hundreds of thousands of years before that. It is likely that *Homo erectus* possessed some ability to communicate linguistically, and possible that *Homo neanderthalensis* did too. When Herder commented in the eighteenth century that language is what makes us human he was, in a sense, correct, but not at all in the way we now understand it.

Protolanguage and grammaticalisation

When Otto Jespersen penned his criticism of speculative approaches to the origin of language in 1922, he proposed that 'the most fruitful source of information' (Jespersen, 1922, p. 416) was knowledge of changes that had taken place between known extinct languages (such as Old English or Latin) and their modern descendants. This provided an illustration of the process of change which could then be used to trace a 'backward path' to the very beginnings of language. This would enable scholars to 'arrive finally at uttered sounds of such a description that they can no longer be called a real language, but something antecedent to language' (ibid., p. 418). Although Jespersen did not use the term, it seems to be protolanguage that he was in search of, and the same might be said of some of the philosophers we considered earlier in the chapter.

Thoughts about protolanguage were also entertained by one of Darwin's most enthusiastic supporters, August Schleicher, who was a professor of **philology** (the historical and comparative study of languages) at the University of Jena, about 250 km south-west of Berlin. He had wasted no time in reading the German translation of *On the Origin of Species*, which became available a year after the English edition. Just three years later, Schleicher published an open letter to his friend and naturalist Ernst Haeckel, giving his response to Darwin's ideas about evolution. This letter was translated into English and published in London in 1869 (less than a year after Schleicher's death) as *Darwinism Tested by the Science of Language*. 'What Darwin lays down of the animal creation in general, can equally be said of the organisms of speech' (Schleicher, 1869, p. 15) is the confident assertion with which Schleicher begins. Not only did Darwin's ideas chime with his own view of existing languages having developed from shared, extinct ancestors, but he firmly believed that the process of change from one ancestral language to forms which increasingly deviated from it could be viewed as a convincing model for the evolution of species itself.

But Schleicher doesn't stop at ancestral languages. He sees them as reducible to cell-like 'radical elements' (ibid., p. 53) – sounds expressing meanings, but 'without any grammatical relation' (ibid., p. 54). For Schleicher, this provides an explanation for the presence of language among all humans, but equally for the existence of distinct, unrelated language families. Putting this in evolutionary terms, he compares the radical elements to 'incipient forms of organic life, that could neither be called animals or plants' but which 'developed themselves in various directions' (ibid., p. 55). We will look at language families and their 'evolution' more closely in the next chapter.

The idea of protolanguage was taken up with fresh vigour by the American linguist Derek Bickerton in 1990. To quote Bickerton in a more recent work, it is 'not true language, but it's made up of languagelike elements' (Bickerton, 2009, p. 40) and is an intermediate stage between animal communication and full language. In Bickerton's view, it would have consisted of simple proto-words which could not be broken down into component parts and these would only be combined, if combined at all, in a random way, without any structural rules. Interpretation of groups of words would have been on the basis of common sense rather than syntactic conventions. So everyday experience would lead a hearer to deduce the meaning of *bone eat animal* or *bone animal eat*. The word order would be immaterial. Nevertheless, unlike the meaningful elements of animal communication, the proto-words possessed **combinability** – the potential for forming new and longer messages – and this is what would have driven the next step.

The nature of protolanguage has prompted considerable debate among linguists. Many of Darwin's contemporaries were of the view that the emergent language of children might be used to hold up a mirror to the evolution of language in human beings, and some modern-day researchers still believe that children's language acquisition may provide clues: a child's first speech sounds may also be the first human speech sounds; the crucial leap from exercising the vocal apparatus to understanding meaning as the link between a sound and an object may replicate the formation of the earliest words; the repeated patterns of a child's first two-word utterances may echo the beginning of syntax. Some linguists reject children's language as a model for protolanguage but instead look for clues in contact languages – the pidgins and creoles which are born when speakers who share no common tongue create a new way to communicate. (Derek Bickerton is one of the linguists who has championed this approach.) For other linguists, gestures and song are regarded as important elements of protolanguage.

The next big question then must ask how protolanguage turned into language more or less as we know it, probably over 200,000 years ago. The theory of **grammaticalisation** may provide the answer. This essentially sets out to explain how grammatical word endings (namely, inflections) and grammatical words (such as pronouns and conjunctions) develop from existing content words like nouns and verbs. So, for instance, how would a combination like *animal eat bone* turn into *the animals are eating the bones*? Although formally conceptualised by French linguist Antoine Meillet in 1912, instances of grammaticalisation had been examined as far back as 1746 by Condillac in his *Essay*, and also by various nineteenth-century linguists interested in language change. The last three decades have seen a renewed interest in this approach, partly for its relevance to the study of language change per se, but also for what it can reveal about the vital transition from protolanguage to a fully-fledged grammatical system used by *Homo sapiens*.

A story with no ending

We have seen in this chapter how the quest for the origin of language has changed dramatically over the centuries to become the study of language evolution, and how the unfolding narrative of human development has provided it with a backstory. Over and above this, research has become rich and varied in a way which would have seemed unimaginable even 50 years ago. Much of this research is of course centred on language itself, as linguists seek to account for the development of all aspects of language – not just vocabulary and syntax, but morphology, phonology and semantics too. But, as Jespersen pointed out nearly a hundred years ago, these accounts can no longer be purely speculative. For linguists working today there is a burden of proof which did not exist for the early philosophers who pondered the emergence of language. A contemporary researcher must not only construct a hypothesis, but must also provide circumstantial or analogous 'evidence' which will demonstrate it to be, at the very least, scientifically plausible. Furthermore, interdisciplinary collaboration is crucial now if linguists are to make further headway in understanding language evolution, and few linguists would deny the debt they owe to researchers working in other disciplines. These include anthropologists, archaeologists, zoologists, neurologists, geneticists and biochemists. (Philosophers, though, have effectively left the building.) Scientific equipment and analytical techniques which have only become available in recent decades are also playing their part in the revitalisation of this age-old inquiry.

Fresh clues continue to arise from a variety of sources. The fossil record continues to grow, as excavations in various parts of the world reveal more hominin remains as well as artefacts which tell us more about early human society. The science of genetics is slowly unfolding the story of prehistoric populations and of our human brains, while the comparison of humans with other species provides useful material from which valid propositions about human development can be formulated. From monkeys to meerkats, and from songbirds to whales, any animal species is considered potentially worthy of study for the light it can throw on our own development and behaviour. In the previous section, we looked at protolanguage. Behind protolanguage lurk nagging but important questions about the mental state needed for the process of language development to begin. These are questions which are exercising psychologists and cognitive scientists, as is the requirement to define exactly what we mean when we talk about language as specific to, unique to or even innate in our species.

This epic story of the quest to find the origin of language may well have left readers wondering if all this effort is actually worth it. It is certainly difficult at the moment to believe linguists are within sight of their goal. Nevertheless, current researchers in the field would beg to differ with the view of Ferdinand de Saussure that 'the question of the origins of language does not have the importance generally attributed to it. It is not even a relevant questions as far as linguistics is concerned' (Saussure, 1916/1983, p. 72). Instead, they would have no difficulty defending their work. If the possession of language is what makes the *Homo sapiens* species what it is, then why would we wish to deny ourselves a greater understanding of our own nature? Curiosity-driven research can lead to unexpected discoveries, and in any case, thinking about the origin of language colours the way we think about language itself. As August Schleicher commented in his work on Darwinism and language, 'so long as we are ignorant of how a thing arose we cannot be said to know it' (Schleicher, 1869, p. 26). And that seems as good a reason as any for continuing the search.

Suggestions for further reading and research

On human evolution in general

Boyd, Robert and Joan B Silk (2014) *How Humans Evolved*, 7th edn (New York: W W Norton)

A standard textbook, covering all the elements relevant to human evolution, including the most recent work in genetics and ecology.

Maslin, Mark A et al. (2014) 'East African climate pulses and early human evolution', in *Quaternary Science Reviews*, vol. 101, pp. 1–17

A recent article which illustrates the kind of research being undertaken to understand the link between climate and the development of the human brain. Available at www.sciencedirect.com/science/article/pii/S0277379114002418 (accessed October 2015).

Stringer, Chris (2012) *The Origin of Our Species* (London: Penguin)

An authoritative survey of evolution in general by the leading researcher at London's Natural History Museum.

On the evolution of language in particular

Aitchison, Jean (1996) *The Seeds of Speech* (Cambridge: Cambridge University Press)

A highly readable exploration of the origins of language, piecing together ideas from a wide range of sources and disciplines.

Burling, Robbins (2007) *The Talking Ape* (Oxford: Oxford University Press)

An evolutionary account, taking our developing comprehension and the need to communicate with our fellow beings as the driving force behind the origin of language.

Di Scullio, Anna Maria and Cedric Boeckx (eds) (2011) The *Biolinguistic Enterprise: New Perspectives on the Evolution and Nature of the Human Language Faculty* (Oxford: Oxford University Press)

As the title suggests, this collection of articles brings together recent insights from biology and theoretical linguistics.

Fitch, W Tecumseh (2010) *The Evolution of Language* (Cambridge: Cambridge University Press)

This wide-ranging survey aims to bring together the many perspectives different disciplines have contributed to this complex subject.

Hurford, James R (2014) *The Origins of Language* (Oxford: Oxford University Press)

A 'slim guide' to the subject, providing a clear overview of current thinking about the process of language evolution.

McMahon, April and Robert McMahon (2012) *Evolutionary Linguistics* (Cambridge: Cambridge University Press)

A wide-ranging and interdisciplinary introduction, revealing to the reader the degree of consensus which has now been reached about the origin of language.

Mithen, Steven (2005) *The Singing Neanderthals: The Origins of Music, Language, Mind, and Body* (London: Weidenfeld and Nicolson)

As the title suggests, a rather different take on evolution, looking at music as a central attribute of the human species, and at its evolutionary relationship with language.

Pinker, Steven and Ray Jackendoff (2005) 'The faculty of language: what's special about it?', in *Cognition*, vol. 95, issue 2, pp. 201–36

An important article that responds to Chomsky's claim about the centrality of recursion and argues for the 'piecemeal evolution' of language as 'a complex adaptation for communication'.

Scott-Phillips, Thom (2015) *Speaking Our Minds* (Basingstoke: Palgrave Macmillan)

Pragmatics is at the heart of the theory presented here, looking at how new ways of communicating developed among our sociable species, leading in turn to the evolution of language.

Tallerman, Maggie and Kathleen R Gibson (2012) *The Oxford Handbook of Language Evolution* (Oxford: Oxford University Press)

An impressive collection of over 60 articles, representative of all the main areas of current interest.

Useful websites

Darwin Online
http://darwin-online.org.uk (accessed October 2015)

A useful resource for anyone wishing to know more about the work of Charles Darwin.

The Max Planck Institute for Evolutionary Anthropology/Department of Human Evolution
www.eva.mpg.de/evolution/index.htm (accessed 2015)

A useful site for finding out about current research projects and methods of analysis.

Natural History Museum, London
www.nhm.ac.uk (accessed October 2015)

A marvellous site for exploring up-to-date knowledge and developments in the field of human evolution.

National Museum of Natural History (Smithsonian Institution, USA)
http://humanorigins.si.edu (accessed October 2015)

A fun website with plenty of interactive features, ideal for getting to grips with human evolution.

Société de Linguistique de Paris (Linguistic Society of Paris)
www.slp-paris.com (accessed October 2015)

The society's website includes pages where you can find more information about its history.

4   Language diversity

Thinkers and researchers introduced in this chapter

Scholars thinking about language diversity prior to 1800:

Herodotus (c. 484–c. 425 BCE)	Greek historian
Plato (428–348 BCE)	Greek philosopher
Conrad Gessner (1516–65)	Swiss linguist
Georg Stiernhielm (1598–1672)	Swedish linguist
Marcus van Boxhorn (1612–53)	Dutch scholar
Gottfried Hensel (1687–1765)	German philologist
Sir William Jones (1746–94)	British philologist and orientalist

Some nineteenth-century philologists:

August von Schlegel (1767–1845)	German philologist
Thomas Young (1773–1829)	British philologist and scientist
Jacob Grimm (1785–1863)	German philologist
Rasmus Rask (1787–1832)	Danish philologist
August Schleicher (1821–68)	German philologist
Hugo Schuchardt (1842–1927)	German philologist
Johannes Schmidt (1843–1901)	German philologist
Karl Verner (1849–96)	Danish philologist/Young Grammarian

Modern thinkers interested in the opposing theories of monogenesis and polygenesis:

Alfredo Trombetti (1866–1929)	Italian linguist
Merritt Ruhlen (b. 1944)	American linguist
Johanna Nichols (b. 1945)	American linguist

Two scholars with different views about language diversity:

Claude Buffier (1661–1737)	French grammarian
Wilhelm von Humboldt (1767–1835)	German language scholar and philosopher

---

The world's many languages

No one is entirely sure how many languages are spoken worldwide. At the time of writing, Ethnologue, the American-based survey of the world's languages, states on its website that there are 7,102 known living languages. In another week or so, this figure could well have changed: a previously unrecorded language may be identified, or a known language may become extinct. In fact, languages are estimated to be dying at the rate of about 25 a year, and it is predicted that as many as half of the languages currently spoken across the planet could become extinct by the end of this century. In the last 50 years or so, not only have linguists been able to compile a more extensive catalogue of global languages, but – as we saw in Chapter 1 – they have also become increasingly concerned about the loss of languages across all the inhabited continents. In Europe alone, nearly 50 are under threat, and many more than that in Africa, where over 2,000 different languages are spoken. Just as any individual living language is constantly changing, so too is the state of human language in its entirety.

This overview of the global linguistic situation is of course something which was unavailable to early scholars, who were certainly unaware of the extent of the diversity in human language, and largely focussed their attention on just a handful of languages at any one time. Nevertheless, the status of individual languages and the relationship between languages has always been of interest. One of the earliest questions to be asked about the various known languages of the world was, which one was the oldest, the original language of humankind? Early Christian scholars believed that Adam, the first human created by God, was a speaker of Hebrew. Islamic scholars, by contrast, believed that Arabic was spoken in Paradise. The Greek historian Herodotus tells the story (in Book II of his *Histories*) of an experiment conducted in the seventh century BCE by the Egyptian pharaoh Psamtik I, who wished to discover which was the first race of human beings – the Egyptians or the Phrygians, who lived in what is now central Turkey. Language, he believed, would provide the answer. So two babies were placed in the care of a shepherd who was instructed to bring them up with his sheep and not allow them to hear any human speech. (A more gruesome version which Herodotus also reports is that the children were raised by women whose tongues had been cut out to prevent them talking.) Apparently, the infants' first unprompted language-like vocalisations resembled the Phrygian word for bread, *becos* (although it may simply have been an imitation of the sheep's baa-ing!), on the strength of which it was decided that Phrygian (which eventually died out in the fifth century) was the original language and the Phrygians therefore the oldest race. Occasional speculations about an original language continued into the medieval and Renaissance periods, and as late as the nineteenth century the French priest and scholar, Térence-Joseph O'Donnelly, declared (somewhat absurdly given other developments in linguistics taking place at the time) that the first language was in fact Ancient Egyptian, a claim based on his study of Egyptian hieroglyphs.

Early Western scholars were undoubtedly interested in languages other than their own, but could have had no real inkling of the diversity of global languages simply because they knew little of the world beyond Europe and certain parts of the Mediterranean. Not until the sixteenth century, with the increase in global exploration and colonisation, did scholars start to become more aware of languages which were distinctly unlike the Greek, Hebrew, Arabic and particularly Latin, which they regarded as classical languages of some status and significance. Knowledge about 'new' languages was accrued from various sources: merchants travelled by land and sea to places as remote as China and India, while Jesuit missionaries travelled not only to the Far East but also west to South America. Their work with the indigenous people they encountered there inevitably required them to study the previously unknown languages they heard. This initially commercial or religious interest in newly discovered languages gradually engendered an interest in them for their own sake.

With the discovery of new languages came the desire to codify them in dictionaries and grammars, just as many mainstream European languages were already being codified. Collections of vocabulary revealed the differences and similarities between the growing number of known languages. A nice illustration of this is provided by collections of the Lord's Prayer, a conveniently short and familiar text. The first such collection, compiled by the Swiss linguist Conrad Gessner in 1555, contains the prayer in 22 languages (although it also records over a hundred other languages and dialects, some of them extinct). A 1680 publication covers 80 languages, while a 1741 collection by German linguist Gottfried Hensel includes over a hundred examples, which Hensel believed to be all the known global languages at that time. This particular work, the *Synopsis universae philologiae*, is notable for the way he uses maps, inscribing the openings of the prayers onto the geographical area from which they originated (see Figure 4.1). By the beginning of the nineteenth century, similar publications contained over 500 examples, including both living and extinct languages. Nowadays, as the Ethnologue survey shows, the known number of living languages alone runs into several thousand.

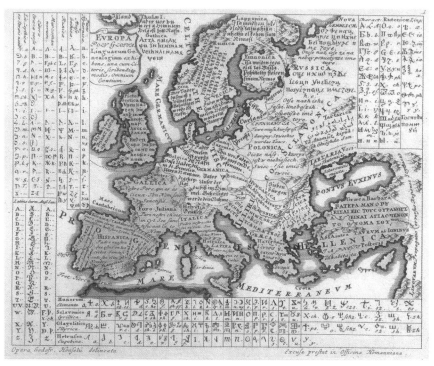

FIGURE 4.1 A PAGE FROM GOTTFRIED HENSEL'S *SYNOPSIS UNIVERSAE PHILOLOGIAE* SHOWING THE OPENING OF THE LORD'S PRAYER IN VARIOUS EUROPEAN LANGUAGES

The relationship between languages

Most thinkers of the ancient world, like Herodotus, saw languages very much as discrete entities, concomitant with national or racial identity, whereas linguists nowadays know a considerable amount about the intimate and complex relationship of languages with each other (although there is still much to discover). In his dialogue *Cratylus*, which we have discussed in the previous chapters, Plato comments on a handful of Greek words with similarities to their Phrygian counterparts and concludes that they must have been borrowed from that language. It would not have occurred to Plato that Greek and Phrygian might have derived from a single source, which we now know to be the case, just as we now know that Arabic, Hebrew and Ancient Egyptian all belong to the same Afro-Asiatic language group.

Even though some Roman scholars considered the possibility that Latin had derived directly from Greek (although it didn't!), it was not really until the Renaissance in Western Europe that scholars began to ask more searching questions about the relationship between European languages. As they studied texts written in older forms of existing languages (such as Old English) as well as extinct languages (such as Gothic or Latin), they were intrigued not only by the clear evidence of language change but also by the extensive similarity between languages, particularly in terms of their vocabulary. We saw in the previous chapter how the belief that language was a divine creation in some ways restricted scholars from inquiring about the origin of language itself. Religious belief also influenced thinking about why humankind possessed no common language. This derived from the biblical story of the Tower of Babel (told in Chapter 11 of Genesis), which tells how, after the massive flood survived only by Noah and his family, 'the whole earth was of one language' (Genesis 11.1). But the descendants of Noah displeased God by their attempts to build a tower that reached to heaven, so God punished them by throwing their language into a state of confusion 'that they may not understand one another's speech' (Genesis 11.7) and then dispersing them to different regions. However, linguistic evidence started to require far more than this simple account of how diversity came about. And similarities between languages also needed a fuller explanation.

More and more, the comparisons they made led scholars to propose that languages belonged in family groups and that certain similarities between languages revealed traces of a common ancestor from long ago. This was already apparent through the widespread knowledge of Latin, whose offspring included Italian, French and Spanish. As early as the fourteenth century the Italian poet Dante identified less obvious links between Greek and Latin and Germanic languages like English. One language that slowly became better known was Sanskrit, the classical and religious language of ancient India. This retained the same degree of status in India that Latin and Ancient Greek had in Europe. It had been discovered by Jesuit missionaries sent out from Europe to India in the sixteenth century. More than one of these missionaries commented on the similarity between Sanskrit and European languages: Filippo Sassetti observed a link with his native Italian, while the English priest Thomas Stephens noticed links with Latin and Greek. Isolated observations of this kind continued over the next 200 years or so. In the seventeenth century the Swedish scholar and poet Georg Stiernhielm attempted to prove that Gothic was the origin of all languages. The Dutch scholar Marcus van Boxhorn had noticed the similarity of Germanic languages (of which Dutch is one) to Latin, Greek, Persian and Turkish and proposed they were all derived from the extinct language Scythian, of which some scant evidence remains. Gottfried Hensel in his 1741 *Synopsis* mentioned above attempted to show that the collected languages in his volume had a common origin in Hebrew. The way was undoubtedly being prepared for what was to happen next.

A significant event in India

Linguistics has very few moments of real drama among its stories, unlike other branches of science, which have plenty. (Think of Neil Armstrong stepping down onto the surface of the moon in 1969, or the unexpected presentation in 1997 of the first cloned mammal, Dolly the sheep.) However, a gathering which took place in Calcutta in 1786 must have had a certain element of drama and excitement about it. The British lawyer and judge, Sir William Jones, who also happened to be a very proficient linguist and an expert on all things oriental, was delivering an anniversary lecture entitled 'On the Hindus' to the Asiatic Society which he had founded two years earlier for the study of Indian literature, culture and religion. Turning his attention to Sanskrit, he began by pointing out that it had 'a stronger affinity' with Latin and Greek than 'could possibly have been produced by accident' (Jones, 1786/1799, p. 26). This observation was not really anything new: the possible relationships between these languages had been recognised for some time, as we saw above. But Jones went on to make the confident assertion that this affinity was 'so strong indeed, that no philologer could examine all three without believing them to have sprung from some common source, which, perhaps, no longer exists' (ibid.). He went on to propose that Gothic and Celtic had also originated from this source. What was probably startling to his audience, and no doubt inspiring too, was the strength of Jones's evidence and the tantalising idea of a lost but maybe retrievable common ancestor from which a potentially vast family of languages had sprung. This 'flash of light from the east', as Professor R H Robins has described the Calcutta event (Robins, 1997, p. 168), heralded a new era in the comparative study of languages, and is often regarded as the dawn of modern linguistics.

The nineteenth-century philologists

And so began the search to discover the nature of this common source. Within 20 years, the impetus which Jones's lecture gave to language scholarship in Europe had become apparent, with Sanskrit being studied far more extensively in European universities. This in turn paved the way for a productive century of what was then called **philology** but is now termed **historical** or **comparative linguistics**. The comparative method adopted by the philologists who worked in the wake of Sir William Jones's claim was used for the purpose of establishing the exact relationship between the languages of Europe and the more far-flung languages, such as Sanskrit, which appeared to be related to them. This group of languages quickly came to be known as the **Indo-European** family, a term first used in 1813 by the English scientist and philologist Thomas Young, who had himself compared over 400 languages. The parent language of the Indo-European family – Jones's 'common source' – came to be known as **Proto-Indo-European**, which we now believe to have been spoken about 5,000, possibly as many as 10,000 years ago. The challenge to reconstruct this extinct ancestor also became a central occupation of the philologists. With not even the slightest scrap of written evidence of Proto-Indo-European to examine, deduction was the central strategy for these dedicated language detectives.

Extensive historical research into a wide variety of languages took place during the nineteenth century, much of it in Germany. Among the most renowned German researchers in the first half of the century were the brothers August and Friedrich von Schlegel, Jacob Grimm (who, together with his brother Wilhelm edited a famous collection of German fairy tales), Franz Bopp (another keen orientalist) and August Schleicher, the enthusiastic Darwinist who featured in the previous chapter. Their collective interests extended far beyond language into philosophy, oriental studies and many branches of literature – interests which inevitably fed their philological pursuits. One of their fellow philologists, the Danish scholar Rasmus Rask (whose last post was as Professor of Oriental Languages at the University of Copenhagen), is credited with an impressive mastery of over 25 languages, having studied these and many more during a lifetime spent travelling through Scandinavia, Russia, Persia, India and Ceylon.

This first wave of philologists pioneered the comparative approach by tracing patterns of language change and using them to make a best guess reconstruction of Proto-Indo-European. They established a systematic, evidence-based method for comparing languages and tracing their history – a striking contrast to the speculations so popular in the previous century about the beginnings of language itself. Much of their work was focussed on sound changes, although grammatical features were also of considerable interest to them (the irregular forms taken by the verb *to be*, for example). To identify family relationships and reconstruct the ancestral language it was necessary to formulate 'laws' which described the patterns of change. One of the challenges was to decide what constituted suitable evidence – borrowed words and random similarities had to be excluded, as did the inevitable exceptions to rules. (Languages, seen as natural phenomena, could not be expected to be completely regular!)

The following examples, a set of words for 'father', provide an illustration of the methods the philologists used to identify sound changes:

modern forms	English	Dutch	German	Portuguese	Spanish	French	Italian	
	father /fɑːðə/	vader /fɑːdə/	Vater /fɑːtəʳ/	pai /paɪ/	padre /padre/	père /pɛʳ/	padre /padre/	
older forms	Old English	Middle Dutch	Old High German	Latin				Sanskrit
	fæder	fader	fater	pater				pitah
The modern forms are given both in their current written form and in phonemic transcription. *The Sanskrit word is transliterated into the Roman alphabet.*								

Word groups like those above have to be assembled on the basis that the words collected appear to be **cognates**. In other words, they have a similarity in form and meaning which indicates they may share the same linguistic ancestor. The more closely related languages are, the more cognates they will share. Words drawn from core vocabulary (such as kinship terms, numbers from one to ten, animals and basic foods) make ideal data in that they will occur in most languages and be frequently used, so are therefore unlikely to have been borrowed. Having gathered some potential cognates together, attention is then turned to the pronunciation of the words. (For languages no longer spoken, this had to be deduced from the written forms.) The examples show clear similarities between Portuguese, Spanish, French and Italian: this would have confirmed what the philologists already knew about these languages being derived from Latin but having developed as independent offspring when Latin speakers spread into different parts of Europe. The Sanskrit word for 'father' also bears a striking similarity to the Latin. The remoteness of India from Italy begs the question of whether this similarity is merely coincidence. In order to strengthen the argument for Sanskrit and Latin being related, further correspondences are needed, which is exactly of course what Sir William Jones had lighted upon. The words from English, Dutch and German are similar, but do not seem so closely related from the evidence of their initial consonant sounds, with /f/ occurring rather than /p/. This could indeed be a coincidental similarity and although English, Dutch and German seem to be related to each other it is less clear that they share an ancestor with Latin or Sanskrit. However, much closer inspection of a wide range of examples reveals that not only is the /p,f/ correspondence a common feature across these languages, but also that /p/ often transmutes into /f/ but not the other way round. From this, it is possible to conclude that 'father' words with initial /p/ are older than those with /f/, and that the original Indo-European form therefore began with /p/. In fact the reconstructed Proto-Indo-European word for father is */pəter/ (An asterisk is used to indicate a reconstruction.) Sound correspondences and changes such as those between /p/ and /f/ were first noted by Rasmus Rask but later became part of Grimm's Law, a full account of a group of consonant changes affecting the Germanic languages as classified by Jacob Grimm.

One important aspect of the philologists' work, then, was to establish in which direction linguistic changes had taken place. A reconstruction of the common source would only be convincing if it could be shown that particular forms were older than others. This is why ancient languages such as Latin and Sanskrit were so useful as they were closer in time, and therefore in form, to the **protolanguage**. (Not to be confused with 'protolanguage' as used in the previous chapter – a term for the emergent form of human language.) Because sound changes proved to be generally consistent in terms of the direction of change, it was also possible to work out the ancestry of groups of languages. When it came to the grammatical structure of languages, however, there was considerable disagreement as to whether languages became simpler or more complex as they changed. Nevertheless, the philologists believed it was possible to make deductions about Proto-Indo-European grammar. After that, it was only too tempting not to compose a whole passage of reconstructed Proto-Indo-European, as August Schleicher did in 1868 when he produced what is known as 'Schleicher's Fable', a simple tale of 'The Sheep and the Horses'. Here it is, together with an English translation:

Avis akvāsas ka	*The Sheep and the Horses*
Avis, jasmin varnā na ā ast, dadarka akvams, tam, vāgham garum vaghantam, tam, bhāram magham, tam, manum āku bharantam. Avis akvabhjams ā vavakat: kard aghnutai mai vidanti manum akvams agantam. Akvāsas ā vavakant: krudhi avai, kard aghnutai vividvant-svas: manus patis varnām avisāms karnauti svabhjam gharmam vastram avibhjams ka varnā na asti. Tat kukruvants avis agram ā bhugat.	A sheep that had no wool saw horses, one of them pulling a heavy wagon, one carrying a big load, and one carrying a man quickly. The sheep said to the horses: "My heart pains me, seeing a man driving horses." The horses said: "Listen, sheep, our hearts pain us when we see this: a man, the master, makes the wool of the sheep into a warm garment for himself. And the sheep has no wool." Having heard this, the sheep fled into the plain.

Schleicher's fable was the first of its kind, but certainly not the last, and versions have continued to appear as recently as the twenty-first century. If this example leaves the reader wondering about the worth of such reconstructions, contemporary linguistics can attest to the value of these processes: the more we are able to produce plausible reconstructions of ancestral languages, the more we can learn about the history of living languages, the nature of language change and, ultimately, the origin of language itself.

While Schleicher was busy composing his Proto-Indo-European fable, the next generation of German philologists was growing up. Based largely in Leipzig, they were the jokingly named *Junggrammatiker* – or Young (sometimes Neo-) Grammarians. They too paid considerable attention to the study of sound changes, but based on the belief that there were essentially no exceptions to sound laws, just as there are no exceptions to the laws of physics. Verner's Law, formulated by the Danish philologist Karl Verner in 1875, was a demonstration of exactly that as he succeeded in accounting for apparent exceptions in Grimm's Law. The Young Grammarians wanted linguistic study to become far more scientific, so they even examined speech organs as part of their study of phonological change. They believed constraints needed to be integrated into the laws of linguistic change or else, in theory, anything could be derived from anything! They regarded (short-sightedly as it turned out) the attempt to reconstruct Proto-Indo-European as a fruitless, not particularly scientific activity. Instead of spending time on extinct, unrecorded languages, they believed their efforts would be better spent on living languages and dialects (the distinct varieties within languages – something we will explore in the next chapter). This was justified by their more enlightened belief that living languages were equal in status to their ancestors, which was not a view of the earlier philologists, many of whom saw language as being in a state of decline. The Young Grammarians effectively divided opinion about the study of language in Germany, although they had many supporters throughout Europe. However, by the end of the nineteenth century, philology in its existing guise had almost run its course.

Classifying the world's languages

In discussing the work of the nineteenth-century philologists, we have made use of vocabulary used primarily for human genetic relationships, such as 'ancestor', 'parent' and 'offspring'. The notion of related languages being like a family was one that the researchers slipped into very readily, especially as more and more relationships were identified. Just as a great-grandparent, for example, could be the ancestor of several children and many grandchildren and great-grandchildren, so Proto-Indo-European came to be regarded as the ancestor of many European and Asian languages, both dead and living. In the 1850s, August Schleicher formalised the idea of the language family with his concept of the *Stammbaum*, or family tree, a means of representation which was heavily influenced by Darwin's evolutionary ideas, by which one species may diversify and become the progenitor of newer species. Nowadays, we are very used to seeing this kind of branching diagrammatic representation, so Figure 4.2, which shows a simplified version of the ancestry of modern English, will no doubt seem very 'normal' to you.

In this particular tree, all the labels in capital letters are for languages which we know to have existed but for which we have no original evidence. These are all protolanguages. We know that the ancestry of English can be traced back to Proto-Indo-European, which is the 'parent' language of many offspring or 'daughters'. (Two of these daughters, Anatolian and Tokharian, have no living descendants and have therefore been omitted from this particular tree.) English descends from Germanic, and is a 'sister' to other living languages such as Dutch and German. Latin, incidentally, descends from the Italic line, while Sanskrit, which was so important to the early philologists, descends from the Indic branch of Indo-Iranian.

This diagrammatic form and the use of kinship terms certainly reflects some of our intuitions about language families, particularly in the way one language functions as the progenitor of another. The ramification also captures the fact that, although languages may belong in a 'family', they typically have only one parent. (There are some languages – **pidgins** and **creoles** – which are formed through the hybridisation of two highly dissimilar

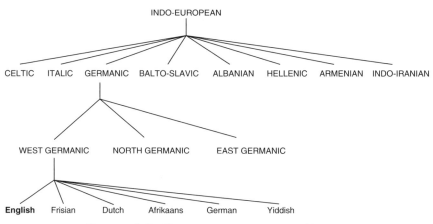

FIGURE 4.2 THE ANCESTRY OF MODERN ENGLISH

languages so these do effectively have two parents, not one. We will return to these hybrid languages later.) What the branching representation perhaps fails to suggest is that 'new' languages (and species for that matter), do not in fact appear relatively suddenly in the world but develop gradually over a period of time as a result of both internal and external changes to an existing language. The other difficulty with the *Stammbaum* representation is the suggestion that, having been 'born', languages are discrete entities, no longer affected by their close relatives or any geographically adjacent language. It also gives an impression that languages are uniform, whereas languages typically contain dialectal variation, to the extent that geographically adjacent dialects from supposedly different languages may in fact be mutually intelligible. As a contrast to the *Stammbaum* model, throughout the nineteenth century, philologists were also considering ways to classify languages which foregrounded their structural similarities rather than their family connections, as we will see in Chapter 6.

Despite the shortcomings of 'trees' of this kind, they remain a valuable means of plotting what is known about language families. Although there was a huge shift in the twentieth century away from the historical approach and towards a 'language as it is now' approach, the philologists had left a strong legacy for scholarly work on language families and the process of change to continue. Clearly, the construction of the Indo-European family tree on which they had concentrated their efforts seemed to account for a vast number of the known languages of Europe and Asia. Slowly, however, more language families were identified to include languages spoken in other parts of the world, or those languages of Europe and Asia which didn't seem to belong to the Indo-European family. This work continues today on a global scale and, rather like the classification of hominin fossils we talked about in Chapter 3, the picture continues to change as more evidence comes to light. We now have a much fuller picture of the world's languages than the nineteenth-century philologists could have dreamed of. The 7,000 or so living languages of the world have been or are in the process of being classified into family groups. This is no easy task for languages about which little is known, so it is no wonder that the lists of language families vary within the region of 150–200 families (although the number of languages in each family varies dramatically, as does the size of the family). This figure excludes extinct families (of which there are a frightening number – something like a quarter of all known families), pidgin and creole languages (as they are hybrid formations) and also language **isolates** – languages which seem to have no relatives at all, such as the European language Basque. Needless to say, the assignment of some languages to a particular family is disputed (the Indo-European family tree is not entirely agreed upon), and in the case of others, not enough is currently known about them to make an assignment. Often this is because they have very few speakers and/or no written records. What may have amazed the early philologists is the size of some language families and the fact that Europe is now known to have considerably less linguistic diversity than other continents. For example, the Austronesian family, found mainly in South-East Asian and Pacific islands, accounts for over 1,200 of the world's languages, roughly three times more than Indo-European.

As more and more language families have been identified, the challenges of classification have become greater not less, despite strategies for the assignment of languages to families having become more sophisticated, even to the extent of applying mathematical probability analyses to linguistic data. In the last 50 years or so, attempts have been made to identify linguistic 'super-families'. One proposal, for example, which gained considerable attention was for a Nostratic family incorporating Indo-European with the Afroasiatic family and various Asian families including Uralic, Kartvelian and Dravidian. No convincing evidence for this connection has been found. This is perhaps unsurprising since inevitably it becomes more and more difficult to reconstruct the early forms of language the further back you attempt to go. The chances of a vocabulary item surviving at all or in a recognisable form over more than a thousand years, for example, are relatively modest, and a historical linguist will find, sooner or later, that the trail goes cold.

An ancestral world language?

If, in tracing the ancestral forms of the languages we use now, we could go back hundreds of thousands of years instead of a mere 5,000–10,000 years, would we discover that the world's surviving language families share a common source, possibly an ancestral world language from which all diversity sprang? Undoubtedly, this idea of a '**Proto-World**' is a very appealing one. The biblical account of the Tower of Babel, which we looked at earlier in this chapter, is testament to the dream of all human races being united in some way by a common tongue. As we have seen, the idea that all languages do indeed come from the same source has been around for some time, and has never really gone away. A theory of **monogenesis** (this single source for all human languages) was proposed at the beginning of the twentieth century by the Italian linguist Alfredo Trombetti. He first published his ideas in 1905, but calculated in a later work that the first language could be dated to about 100,000–200,000 years ago, a striking correlation with what we now know to be the age of the *Homo sapiens* species. More recently (in 1994), the

American linguist Merritt Ruhlen has attempted to demonstrate the exist
ence of cognates across seemingly unrelated language families – although
many linguists are sceptical about his claims.

Thinking about monogenesis invites us to peer again into the mists of
time – or at least return to the previous chapter – and to reconsider how
language might have originated among our human ancestors. We know that
modern humans evolved around 200,000 years ago in Africa and that about
60,000 years ago (maybe earlier) they began to migrate out of Africa. As
Figure 4.3 shows, they gradually moved north into the Middle East, then
west to Europe, and east towards Asia. Some groups crossed into Australasia.
(During this geological period, sea levels were lower and land bridges therefore exposed, enabling migrants to cross more easily from one continent
to another.) Eventually, migrant groups moving north-east through Siberia
reached the Bering Strait and travelled across to the American continent, the
last stage of this extraordinary diaspora.

As the human population dispersed, and the various groups lost contact
with each other, so shared language must have slowly diverged and new
languages emerged, a process repeated as geographical distances widened. Is
it possible that all these languages came from an ancestral language that was
well established before this migration began? The fact that all global races
and populations share the ability to acquire language suggests that the answer
to this question may be yes: fully-fledged language – entailing biological and
genetic adaptations for language learning by new generations – must have
been in place before the dispersal from Africa began. So there may well have
been a time when, somewhere in Africa's Rift Valley, the earliest members of
our species shared an essentially uniform means of communicating with each
other linguistically. If evidence is lacking, this is due to the passage of time.
Not even the most assiduous philologist could expect to find living traces of
this ancestral language after so many millennia.

However, the American linguist Johanna Nichols was doubtful about the
single ancestor theory, which presupposes a relatively small and coherent
human population for its speakers, and has spent the last 20 years working on an alternative approach – **polygenesis**. In contrast to philological
research, which traditionally begins with the languages themselves, Nichols'
approach begins with global populations. She argues that prior to the start of
the migration out of Africa, the earliest speakers, though possibly only about
30,000 in total, would already have been living in separate tribal groups
across an area approximately the size of Northern Australia, which is known
to have supported a considerable variety of languages for thousands of years.
Her contention, based on a geographical perspective, is that diversity existed

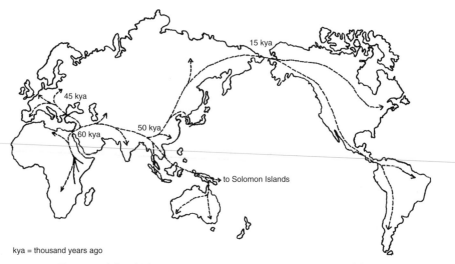

15 kya

45 kya

50 kya

60 kya

to Solomon Islands

kya = thousand years ago

FIGURE 4.3   WORLD MAP SHOWING THE MIGRATION OF *HOMO SAPIENS* OUT OF AFRICA (ROUTES AND TIMES ARE APPROXIMATE)

in human language long before the migration from Africa, and probably even when our human ancestors were still at the protolanguage stage, so the first fully-fledged languages would have sprung from diverse beginnings. Nichols' work has led her to the clear conclusion that 'There was no single ancestral language' (Nichols, 2012, p. 572). Knowledge about population distribution seems to confirm this, as, for her, does the structural diversity of existing languages. Linguists who wish to support any monogenesis account of language origin face the challenging task of demonstrating that there are universal properties that unite languages, no matter what family they belong to. We will look at one linguist's attempt to do this in Chapter 6.

Languages in contact

Over the centuries, linguists have clearly paid a considerable amount of attention to the way in which languages diversify, giving rise within a particular family to a new linguistic generation. However, as we saw when discussing the pros and cons of representing a language family as a tree (August Schleicher's *Stammbaum*), it is naïve to treat speakers of a particular language as immune to the influence of any other language whose speakers they may come into regular contact with. In fact, it was two of Schleicher's own students who realised that some linguistic features in a particular language or dialect could not be explained by inheritance because they were the result of contact with a neighbouring language or dialect. This led these students, Hugo Schuchardt and Johannes Schmidt, to formulate a 'wave theory' to identify features which had spread out from a point of origin like the concentric waves from a stone dropped into water. Nowadays, this approach has developed into what is known as **areal linguistics**, which focuses on features occurring across neighbouring but unrelated languages. In other words, they form a **linguistic area**. The benefits of this approach are significant. Comparative linguists have long been wary of vocabulary items that have been borrowed from other languages, but areal linguistics identifies structural borrowings – aspects of the phonological and grammatical systems – which are the result of diffusion rather than inheritance. In this way, linguists are able to build up a far more comprehensive picture of the type of changes that have occurred in a particular language as well as make more accurate family group attributions.

Contact between languages and what might result from that contact is, then, an important aspect of studying linguistic diversity. Language contact is the crucial starting point for **pidgins** and **creoles**. As mentioned earlier, these are languages which, unlike most of the world's languages, effectively have two parents, not one. A pidgin language comes into existence when speakers who do not share a common language but need to communicate with each other form a hybrid means of communication using elements of their respective languages, although one language usually predominates as the provider of vocabulary. This means that very often the pidgin is the offspring of languages from different families. If the pidgin develops and becomes extensively used to the point where it is then taught to children as their native tongue, then it is classified as a creole.

A host of interesting stories accompany pidgins and creoles because of the circumstances in which they spring up. Some have come about due to global trade and exploration, while others, sadly, are the result of slavery or war. One such pidgin, for example, developed in Saigon during the Vietnam War (1955–75) between American soldiers and local Vietnamese people. Pidgins and creoles have been studied extensively since at least the nineteenth century, often by explorers or missionaries as well as by linguists. Because they are structurally less complex than their parent languages, they have traditionally been treated as primitive or inferior, although this is not a view held by contemporary linguists. On the contrary, because their origins are often known, they can provide helpful insights into human linguistic behaviour and language development and change. There are millions of pidgin and creole speakers worldwide and the large numbers of languages they represent is a significant part of the global picture as a whole.

Attitudes to diversity

The attitudes that scholars have adopted towards the various languages of the world form a thread that runs through the story of linguistic diversity. Opinions go back as far as the study of language itself. These attitudes are primarily concerned with the status of individual languages and with the question of whether the changes which have been observed to occur in languages are a matter of 'progress or decay' to use Otto Jespersen's terms (Jespersen, 1922, p. 319). The original language of humankind was, for instance, regarded as perfect (and perfectly logical) by those who believed it was a divine creation. Despite many earlier views to the contrary, linguists nowadays regard all languages as equal no matter what family they belong to, what specific linguistic features they possess or how many speakers they have.

This egalitarian approach was adopted by the grammarian Claude Buffier in the early eighteenth century but not everyone shared his opinion. A scholar as eminent as Wilhelm von Humboldt (born in Berlin in 1767) considered languages with inflectional systems (such as a range of verb endings to indicate person and tense) as considerably more sophisticated than those without them. Sanskrit, for Humboldt, was a perfect language, while Chinese and the indigenous American Indian languages were looked down upon as more primitive than their inflected counterparts. Languages which were less well-known were often regarded as primitive by nineteenth-century philologists because their sounds were allegedly too imprecise to be examined, an apparent problem only because they were not familiar enough with the languages to classify the sounds. Perhaps surprisingly, it didn't occur to the philologists that their own languages might have seemed just as imprecise to these supposedly 'primitive' speakers or that, if the languages truly were primitive, then it was rather surprising that the speakers were able to communicate with each other as effectively as they did! The fitness of all global languages as effective communication systems for the people who speak them is in fact one of the reasons why modern linguists have no truck with language inequality.

The same can be said of language change: to modern researchers, change is the constant condition of language and is inherently neither good nor bad. Again, this is an opinion linguists have not always held. Although change was seen as inevitable and even natural, fears that language change was for the worse were often prevalent, especially if the process of change involved the loss of inflections – a feature frequently observed by the early philologists when scrutinising languages such as English and the various descendants of Latin. Many even viewed the aim of their work as a reconstruction of language in its best and purest form.

Linguists nowadays are not inclined to fret over the changes they observe in the languages they study. Decades of research have taught them that at any one moment in its history, a language exhibits new features resulting from recent change, but equally many other features that speak of its age and history. Diversity and change are not to be feared, but to be welcomed, since they reflect the way in which speakers – consciously or subconsciously – adapt language so it remains fit for purpose, both as a communicative tool and as a means of maintaining and promoting social identity, as we will see more fully in the next chapter. What cause linguists sleepless nights, however, are the endangered languages we considered at the start of this chapter. We do not know at what point in human history the greatest number of languages were spoken on our planet or how many languages that entailed, and, sadly, we will never know just how many languages have been lost to human knowledge altogether. We do know that, in startling contrast to the increasing global population, the number of global languages is decreasing, and that this trend will continue as globalisation makes our planet a place where languages like English, Spanish, Chinese and Arabic have international currency. The quest to seek out and record endangered languages before it is too late has now become even more important. It is probably no exaggeration to suggest that the story of linguistic diversity has become an urgent account of life and death.

Suggestions for further reading and research

On the nature of diversity and change

Aitchison, Jean (2001) *Language Change: Progress or Decay?* 3rd edn (Cambridge: Cambridge University Press)

A highly readable exploration of attitudes and evidence relating to language change.

Deutscher, Guy (2005) *The Unfolding of Language* (London: Arrow Books)

An entertaining account of how languages change and develop over time, with plenty of fascinating examples to consider.

Janson, Tore (2002) *Speak: A Short History of Languages* (Oxford: Oxford University Press)

Beginning with a consideration of the origin of language, this sweeping account considers the coming and going of languages as part and parcel of their historical context.

Nichols, Johanna (1992) *Linguistic Diversity in Space and Time* (Chicago: University of Chicago Press)

A highly acclaimed take on the study of language diversity based on population science.

Sebba, Mark (1997) *Contact Languages: Pidgins and Creoles* (Basingstoke: Palgrave Macmillan)

A detailed account of contact languages, including a range of interesting case studies.

On the study of language diversity and change

Campbell, Lyle (2004) *Historical Linguistics: An Introduction*, 3rd edn (Edinburgh: Edinburgh University Press)

An excellent, detailed introduction to this complex subject.

Crowley, Terry and Claire Bowern (2010) *An Introduction to Historical Linguistics*, 4th edn (New York: Oxford University Press)

A well-regarded, systematic account of all the key areas of language change, including the many reasons for change.

Lehmann, Winfred P (1967) *A Reader in Nineteenth Century Historical Indo-European Linguistics* (Bloomington: Indiana University Press)

An anthology of extracts which gives the reader the opportunity to sample some of the most important works written by nineteenth-century philologists.

Available at www.utexas.edu/cola/centers/lrc/books/readT.html (accessed October 2015).

On the disappearance of languages

Crystal, David (2000) *Language Death* (Cambridge: Cambridge University Press)

A clearly argued and balanced account of what causes languages to die out, and what can be done to preserve and maintain endangered languages.

Harrison, K David (2008) *When Languages Die* (New York: Oxford University Press)

Written by an American linguist with first-hand experience of endangered languages, this book explores precisely what is lost to human knowledge when languages become extinct.

Nettle, Daniel and Suzanne Romaine (2002) *Vanishing Voices* (New York: Oxford University Press)

This account of language extinction considers the ecological impact of language death as well as the cultural and linguistic consequences.

Useful websites

The Atlas of Pidgin and Creole Language Structures (APiCS) Online
http://apics-online.info (accessed October 2015)

A fascinating resource for anyone interested in learning more about these hybrid languages.

Ethnologue
www.ethnologue.com (accessed October 2015).

An online survey of the world's languages.

The Foundation for Endangered Languages
www.ogmios.org/index.php (accessed October 2015)

The online newsletters provide an interesting insight into the kind of work being done to protect endangered languages.

UNESCO Atlas of the World's Languages in Danger
www.unesco.org/languages-atlas/ (accessed October 2015)

This interactive atlas enables you to search languages by country or by degree of endangerment. Current information about their status is also provided.

5 Language variation

Mapping regional variation

In 1897, the French dialectologist Edmond Edmont was sufficiently dedicated to the study of language variation to set out on a four-year cycling trip
around France gathering data for a proposed *Atlas linguistique de la France*.
This survey of linguistic variation across the country was the brainchild
of the Swiss linguist Jules Gilliéron, who had already conducted similar
fieldwork on a hiking holiday in the Rhone Valley in 1880. Discovering
Edmont's abilities as a phonetician, Gilliéron commissioned him to visit
over 600 localities to collect examples of regional speech, something
Edmont did with impressive care and accuracy, using phonetic symbols
to transcribe what he heard and filling nearly a thousand notebooks with
information about the localities he visited. Notwithstanding the immense
popularity of cycling in France, his journey was a considerable undertaking
and an extraordinary contribution to the success of the *Atlas*, which was
published in full between 1902 and 1910. It reflected a new direction that
language study had been moving in for some time, based on the recognition
that any language as it was actually spoken was far from uniform and there
was considerable variation across speakers, particularly in relation to their
geographical distribution.

Gilliéron was not the first linguist to collect examples of variation on
such a wide scale. The German philologist Johann Schmeller, for instance,
had published a detailed study of the Bavarian dialects in 1821, based on
extensive data collected specifically for the purpose. Nor was Gilliéron the
first to use maps to record linguistic information. We saw in Chapter 4,
for example, how Gottfried Hensel used a map to present the opening of
the Lord's Prayer in different languages. A cartographical project similar
to Gilliéron's had been undertaken in Germany between 1877 and 1887,
where linguist Georg Wenker had obtained data by sending out questionnaires to schools, asking for regional dialect versions of 40 Standard
German sentences. He received over 45,000 replies and the maps he published showing the distribution of regional dialect features (both phonetic
and grammatical) were met with great acclaim. Gilliéron, however, was the
first to combine cartography so extensively with the face-to-face collection
of data.

Slowly, linguists started to see evidence that, in terms of geographical distribution, dialects were rather more complex than they had realised. One of
the most important revelations to come out of this fieldwork was the discovery that there were no clear boundaries between dialects. This was revealed
by the mapping of **isoglosses** – dividing lines between the use of a feature in
one area and its equivalent in an adjacent area. (Isoglosses for English might

show, for example, the regions where /h/ is not normally pronounced at the beginning of *house* and *hat*, where alternative dialect words for 'splinter' or 'silly' are used, or where different forms of personal pronouns occur.) What quickly became apparent was that the various isoglosses of any particular dialect did not coincide with each other, as might have been expected. Instead, there were areas where the denser criss-crossing of boundaries suggested a geographical region of transition between one dialect and another. Variation studies of this kind continued throughout the twentieth century, and are still undertaken by linguists today. Portable sound recording equipment has enabled researchers to make even more accurate phonetic transcriptions and collect long passages of spoken material, while cars and trains have generally replaced bicycles as their main mode of transport. More noticeable than these technological changes, however, is the way in which many regional dialects are being subsumed by standard language forms, their speakers becoming something of a rarity. This doesn't necessarily mean that a language will be any less varied, however, as we shall see.

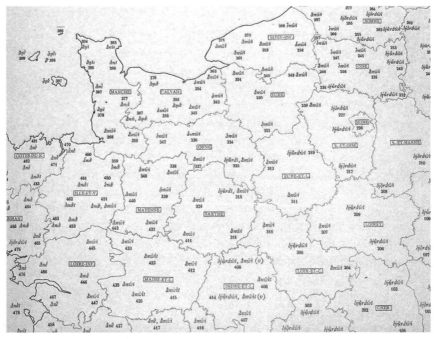

FIGURE 5.1   PART OF A PAGE FROM THE *ATLAS LINGUISTIQUE DE LA FRANCE* SHOWING VARIANTS OF *AUJOURD'HUI* ('TODAY')

Real speakers come to the fore

The Young Grammarians we discussed in the previous chapter used regional dialect studies to help them understand more about the patterns of sound changes that occur in all living languages. For them, regional dialects captured the essence of a living language. They rejected the idea that a language somehow existed in its own right (a widely held view in the nineteenth century, with supporters of evolution even regarding language as a kind of independent living organism), and believed instead that 'language … has its true existence only in the individual, and therefore all changes in the life of a language can originate only with individual speakers', according to Hermann Osthoff and Karl Brugmann (1878, p. xii) in what is now known as the 'Neogrammarian Manifesto' but was actually the preface to a new journal they had founded. The compilation of dialect maps reflected something of this belief by revealing variation as being aligned with the geographical distribution of speakers. But maps could not provide the complete picture, and the data collectors were already paying attention to other factors connected to linguistic variation.

The data which Edmond Edmont had collected for Gilliéron was supported by additional notes he made on the profession, age and sex of the respondents. This demographic information accompanied the published *Atlas linguistique* in a separate volume. Around the time of the atlas's publication, linguist Louis Gauchat, who had already done a considerable amount to promote the study of the French dialects spoken in his native Switzerland, carried out a detailed survey of the remote village of Charmey in the Swiss Alps, a two-hour walk from the nearest town of Bulle. Even here, variation within the dialect could be detected. Comparing the generations, Gauchat observed that the young people were distinguished from their parents not only 'in their habits and dress' (Gauchat, 1905, p. 28), but in specific aspects of their pronunciation, which he goes on to describe. Three decades later in the USA, the *Linguistic Atlas of New England* (edited by Hans Kurath and published between 1939 and 1943) supplemented the mapping of phonetic variation among speakers native to different localities with information about not only their ages but also their level of education.

The early dialectologists, as we have seen, focussed their attention on rural districts. Edmont and Gilliéron, for example, made a conscious decision not to include Paris – where a standard form of French predominated – in their survey. However, urban areas were not completely overlooked. The industrial Magdeburg region of Germany, for instance, was studied at the end of the nineteenth century by the dialectologist Philipp Wegener, who described how rural workers migrating to the towns and cities for work were adopting aspects of local speech in recognition of the prestige they associated with urban life. His observations foreshadow the work of a later researcher, William Labov, as we will see in the next section.

Through both rural and urban studies like these, the multidimensional nature of language variation was slowly being revealed, and with it the individuality of speakers. Clearly, it was no longer going to be possible to ignore real speakers if linguistic variation and change were to be fully understood. Age, sex, education, profession and lifestyle were all factors that needed to be considered: variation was not just a regional phenomenon, but a personal and social one too.

Watching change happen

The next part of our story takes us to the East Coast of the United States. Here, in the 1960s, the American linguist William Labov undertook some pioneering research that threw an exciting new light on linguistic variation, the starting point for permanent changes in a language. The philologists of the previous century had studied change largely by drawing on any available written evidence of earlier forms of languages as well as information they found in grammars and dictionaries. They were comparing these sources in order to identify changes that had taken place within languages and that had led to the 'birth' of new languages. However, they did not believe it was possible to observe language change as it happened. Labov's studies on the fishing island of Martha's Vineyard, a popular and fashionable holiday resort off the coast of Massachusetts, and later in the buzzing department stores of New York City, showed that, by collecting data from real speakers in situations where there was variation in the local language, the process of change could indeed be observed. The nineteenth-century philologists centred their attention on linguistic diversity over long periods of time and across different languages, but Labov's interest in diversity (not unlike the interests of Gauchat and Wegener) centred on the variation to be found within a small geographical area at any one time, or at least over a relatively brief period. Furthermore, whereas the philologists focussed on *how* change happened, the work of Labov and his successors was able to cast more light on *why* language changed.

Clearly, some linguistic changes were the result of internal processes relating to the nature of language itself. But what of external influences? The Young Grammarians had used these to explain exceptions they encountered to their strict sound change rules, since an exception might be the result of a sound being copied in some way from another language. (Similarly, differences in vocabulary could also be explained as borrowings from another language.) Other explanations had been both speculative and generally unconvincing. Some scholars had attributed changes to climatic conditions: one suggestion was that speakers who lived in foggy regions preferred to keep their mouths closed and so were less likely to have open 'o' sounds! One of the explanations offered to account for the change from /p/ to /f/ in Grimm's Law (see Chapter 4) was that it was caused by living in mountainous regions where you would frequently have to puff your way uphill! Jacob Grimm himself suggested that the sound changes he had identified were due to the Germanic race seeking a means to assert their national identity through distinct linguistic features. You might like to consider how plausible this is once you have read more about Labov's work.

Labov was interested in external conditions which might bring about sound changes but they had nothing to do with the weather. Instead, he focussed his attention on the social contexts in which he believed change to be taking place. His research (published in 1963) began in the early 1960s on Martha's Vineyard, where he was intrigued by some variable forms he had identified there, namely the pronunciation of the vowels in words such as *house* and *night*. The vowels in these words are **diphthongs** – complex sounds in which the mouth glides from one position to another. Labov noticed a clear difference in the pronunciation of these vowels between the fishermen who worked on the west side of the island and the rest of the locals who lived and worked on the east side, where most of the summer tourists came. Labov was able to consult the *Linguistic Atlas of New England* (mentioned above), which recorded that around 1930 the traditional island pronunciation of these vowels was dying out. Now, however, the fishermen seemed to be leading the way in reviving and even exaggerating it, a change which Labov attributed to their determination to maintain the island's identity in the face of increased (and, for them, unwelcome) tourism.

Labov then turned his attention to New York City, where he wanted to investigate variation in the New York accent. One of the variables he examined was the presence of /r/ in the pronunciation of words such as *floor* and *fourth* – what is known as **rhotic** pronunciation. Although this feature had scarcely existed after World War II, it now seemed to be reappearing among a significant number of the population. In November 1962, Labov undertook some research in three large department stores of varying degrees of prestige. Adopting the role of a genuine customer, he would ask assistants to tell him the location of goods that he knew could be found, conveniently, on the fourth floor. (And on the fourth floor itself, his inquiry would be 'Excuse me, what floor is this?'.) Their replies of course enabled him to calculate the extent to which the rhotic pronunciation was being used – and where. His findings showed that it was most common among the assistants of the two more prestigious stores, Saks Fifth Avenue and Macy's, suggesting that prestige and social aspiration were driving linguistic change (Labov, 1972a). What was also revealing was that Labov cunningly pretended not to hear the assistants the first time, obliging them to repeat their answers. In all three stores, the /r/ occurred more frequently in the more careful second responses, which seemed to lend support to the notion that this was becoming regarded as a standard pronunciation. This finding was confirmed in 1986 when the researcher Joy Fowler repeated Labov's study and found the use of the rhotic pronunciation to have increased, as predicted.

Labov had drawn his conclusions from his work on Martha's Vineyard and in New York by collecting spoken data and calculating the percentage of usage by different groups of speakers. This **quantitative** approach to exploring variation was to be hugely influential because it was able to plot the degree of change in progress and also demonstrate statistically that social concerns such as identity and prestige could exert a significant external influence on speakers. The geographical context was clearly not unimportant for observing and understanding variation and change, but – as Labov demonstrated – the social context offered many more perspectives. 'The point of view of the present study', he wrote in his paper on the Martha's Vineyard research, 'is that one cannot understand the development of a language change apart from the social life of the community in which it occurs … social pressures are continually operating on language … as an immanent social force' (Labov, 1963/1972, p. 3). His commitment to this approach led to him being instrumental in the formal recognition of a new branch of linguistics, as we are about to see.

The birth of sociolinguistics

The dialectal studies which began during the nineteenth century were the first indications that practical steps were being taken to pay more attention to ordinary language in use and, as we have seen, there was a growing recognition that real speakers (as opposed to dictionaries, grammars and other texts written in idealised standard varieties) could be an important source of information about language variation and change. This developing appreciation of language as a social phenomenon is reflected in the views of the American linguist William Dwight Whitney, who, while supporting the principle of evolution and natural selection as an analogy for how language change occurred, put emphasis on the means by which this was brought about, entailing speakers' linguistic behaviour within the communities to which they belonged. As he observed in an often-quoted passage from his 1867 work *Language and the Study of Language*:

> Speech is not a personal possession, but a social: it belongs, not to the individual, but to the member of society. No item of existing language is the work of an individual; for what we may severally choose to say is not language until it be accepted and employed by our fellows. The whole development of speech, though initiated by the acts of individuals, is wrought out by the community. (Whitney, 1867, p. 404)

Whitney's comments here could be seen as prophetic of what would happen a hundred years later, when a group of American linguists (including William Labov) would stake a claim for the primacy of the social context in understanding language and warn of the dangers of neglecting communities of actual speakers when describing and accounting not just for linguistic change and variation, but for the nature of language itself.

At the start of the twentieth century, this developing interest in social aspects of language was eclipsed somewhat by the posthumous publication in 1916 of Ferdinand de Saussure's *Course in General Linguistics*. (We explored this in some detail in Chapter 2.) Although he by no means dismissed the notion of language as a 'social institution', Saussure's central interest was in linguistic structure – 'internal linguistics' – rather than 'external linguistics', which, for him, was concerned largely with the way a language's history is tied up with racial, national, cultural and political history. Speakers themselves, and what their personal and social circumstances reveal about language in use, were effectively overlooked by Saussure.

A potential division, then, was opening up in linguistics between the study of language as an essentially self-contained, idealised system and the study of language as explicable only in terms of speakers and communities. Although many linguists came under the influence of Saussure, the social aspect of language was certainly not being neglected in linguistic thinking and research. In the USA, urban areas became the location of dialectal data collection for the first time. Researchers quickly realised how very different this undertaking was from the study of rural dialects. Instead of collecting data from a small population where the speech of the inhabitants was relatively (although certainly not entirely) uniform, they were faced with the challenge of how to collect a representative sample from a much larger and more diverse population. The correlation between speech forms and social class also came under the spotlight. The American linguist Leonard Bloomfield in his 1933 work *Language* offers some specific examples of class pronunciation differences in

Chicago, noting that, notwithstanding the geographical diversity within the United States, 'the most striking line of cleavage in our speech is one of social class' (Bloomfield, 1933, p. 48).

In Europe, linguists were looking at similar aspects. The Dutch dialectologist Gesinus Kloeke was one of the leading lights. His 1927 study of Dutch dialects (much admired by Bloomfield) combined geographical, historical and sociological approaches to explain how the Dutch words for 'mouse' and 'house' (*muis* and *huis*) had come to have different vowels in some parts of the Netherlands but retained their rhyme in other parts. This study, as well as much of his later work, focussed on social differentiation as an explanation for language variation. One of the most influential early works on language and society was that of the Danish linguist Otto Jespersen, who wrote in his 1925 *Mankind, Nation and Individual from a Linguistic Point of View* about 'the linguistic crossplay of the individual and of the community to which he belongs' (Jespersen, 1925, p. 204). Referring not to the followers of Saussure, but back to the 'language as organism' view of the nineteenth century, Jespersen welcomed the social direction being taken by many of his fellow linguists:

> The most notable advance that has been made in the theoretical conception of the nature of language since the serious study of language first began consists in this, that we no longer do what was so frequently done in earlier times, that is, conceive language as a self-existent thing or substance, or – to use an expression frequently employed – as an organism, that lives and dies like a plant or any other organism, but have learnt to see that language in its essence is a human activity, an effort on the part of one individual to be understood by, or at least come into relation with, another individual. (ibid., p. 4)

Interestingly, Jespersen rejects what he perceives as the sentimentality of some philologists towards regional dialects, and sees their gradual decline as part of a natural social development. By way of compensation, he sees the spreading 'common language' as just as full of variation, recognising that individuals will adapt their speech as appropriate to the 'particular linguistic community' to which they belong.

Despite the amount of sociologically driven linguistic research taking place and the fact that universities had started to introduce courses on sociology and language, even by the 1950s there was as yet no formal recognition that the work of these researchers and academics constituted a linguistic subdiscipline in its own right. The theoretical approach to language prompted by Saussure gained a further boost in 1957 when Noam Chomsky published his groundbreaking work *Syntactic Structures*. (We considered this in Chapter

2 and will return to it in Chapter 6.) Chomsky's ideas certainly had the power to divide the linguistic world, as we will see. Within ten years of this publication, although its effects were being seen on linguists who were attracted by its theoretical dynamism, others rejected an approach which took no account of the social contexts in which language was used. For this new wave of linguists, the study of an idealised, even sanitised version of language was inferior to the study of language through the unpredictable and rough spontaneity of everyday speech.

This was the strongly-held view of William Labov, who is now regarded as preeminent among the founders of **sociolinguistics**. Interestingly, Labov had spent ten years working as an industrial chemist before moving into linguistics in 1961, something he attributes to his interest in studying 'the everyday world'. Writing in 1972, he reflected on this time: 'In spite of a considerable amount of sociolinguistic activity, a socially realistic linguistics seemed a remote prospect in the 1960s' (Labov, 1972b, p. xiii). Nevertheless, Labov's intention was to 'gather data from the secular world' (ibid.), which, of course, is exactly what he did on Martha's Vineyard and in New York City. Fortunately, other researchers shared Labov's intentions. In 1964, a group of these linguists, Labov among them, gathered for the summer event of the Linguistic Institute being held at the Bloomington campus of Indiana University. The Social Science Research Council had agreed to fund a seminar on what was already becoming known as 'sociolinguistics'. This was to be an important development in the crystallisation of this field. For the first time, researchers interested in language and society (some of them linguists, some of them sociologists) were able to meet formally as a group and share ideas. The final report of the 1964 gathering contains the names of various attendees and their affiliations, and from this list it is possible to pick out academics who would become household names in sociolinguistics over the next few decades. The report also includes a complete list of the lectures organised by the Linguistic Institute, and these hold up a mirror to the divided linguistic interests of the 1960s. The series opened with a set of four lectures in the first week on 'Topics in the Theory of Generative Grammar', given by none other than Noam Chomsky.

The Bloomington event enabled those working in the field of language and society to establish themselves as a working group. In a general sense, they shared common goals, although it was to prove difficult to reach agreement as to how exactly the aims of sociolinguistics should be defined, or even precisely what was meant by the term 'sociolinguistics'. However, Labov's view – that 'sociolinguistics' was effectively a redundant term insofar as all linguistic study should contain a social element – continues to resonate with many researchers.

Variation studies take off

We have already seen the kind of work Labov undertook in the 1960s, around the time of the summer meeting in Bloomington in 1964. The now officially recognised field of sociolinguistics expanded quickly and its influence was soon evident in Europe as well as the United States. The first British linguist to follow in Labov's footsteps was Peter Trudgill, whose first professorship was at the University of Essex. Only ten years after the Bloomington event, he wrote:

> ... language is very much a social phenomenon. A study of language totally without reference to its social context inevitably leads to the omission of some of the more complex and interesting aspects of language and to the loss of opportunities for further theoretical progress. One of the main factors that has led to the growth of sociolinguistic research has been the recognition of the importance of the fact that language is a very variable phenomenon, and that this variability may have as much to do with society as with language. (Trudgill, 1974a/1983, p. 32)

Trudgill's own research was carried out in the early 1970s in his home town of Norwich (Trudgill, 1974b). Here, he used Labov's quantitative method to explore how the stratification of society was mirrored in the extent to which speakers used local features such as *she like* and *she's walkin'* (as opposed to *she likes* and *she's walking*), with the regional variants used increasingly on the gradient between the middle middle class and the lower working class.

The commitment to exploring the complex relationship between language and society inspired many linguists to devise effective (but at the same time ethical) methods for gathering data. It was well understood that speakers will not speak 'normally' if they think their speech is being scrutinised. Labov had overcome this difficulty in New York by posing as a regular shopper. In Norwich, Trudgill asked his respondents to participate in formal data gathering activities, such as reading a passage aloud. The most useful material, however, came from the recordings made after the 'formal' interview, when Trudgill chatted informally to the participants as if the business of collecting the data was already complete. Other researchers adopted the strategy of long-term observation by getting to know their respondents and being accepted to some degree within the social groups they were studying. In Belfast, Lesley Milroy's introduction to family and friendship groups as a 'friend of a friend' enabled her to compare the dialects of three working class **social networks** in different parts of the city (Milroy, 1980), while in Reading, Jenny Cheshire took advantage of her youthfulness to engage with a group of children and teenagers who had effectively dropped out of mainstream culture and spent a lot of their time hanging out at local adventure playgrounds (Cheshire, 1982). Establishing a **vernacular culture index** based on their attitudes to fighting, swearing, carrying weapons and committing minor offences, she was able to demonstrate which non-standard features in their speech were the strongest markers of their loyalty to the subculture they belonged to.

These sociological studies by Trudgill, Milroy and Cheshire are representative of the kind of studies being carried out in the 1970s and which continue to this day. The fact that society is constantly changing means that sociolinguists are unlikely to run out of opportunities for new research! What is interesting is that all three researchers, while focussing primarily on social groupings such as class, local network or subculture, also included in their findings some consideration of the sex of the respondents as a factor in their linguistic behaviour, and in all three instances, there were notable differences between male and female speech. This attention to the speakers' sex was not merely incidental, but part of the increasing interest in this aspect of language variation.

Male/female language variation

In 1658, the French cleric Charles de Rochefort published (at first anonymously) his extensive study of the Antilles Islands where he had lived and worked for many years. Within a decade it had been translated into Dutch, English and German. Although some of the historical facts were disputed by his contemporaries, scholars interested in language were intrigued by his account of the language spoken by the Carib people who lived there. According to Rochefort's work, which also includes a vocabulary list compiled by fellow Frenchman and missionary Raymond Breton, a significant number of lexical items were sex-differentiated pairs: one form used by women, one by men. They related particularly to lexical sets such as body parts and kinship terms: the women, for example, would use the form *noukóuchili* if referring to their fathers, while the men would use *youmáan*. Differences like these required some explanation. Raymond Breton claimed that the invasion and conquest of the islands by the Caribs, who had come from the South American mainland, had all but wiped out the Arawak-speaking natives who had previously lived there, but the Caribs had spared the lives of the women and married them. Although obliged to adopt the Carib language, these women had managed to retain a significant percentage of their Arawak vocabulary.

Interest in the differences between the way men and women speak clearly goes back a long way – there are many passing observations about it by various (male) writers down the centuries – and the story of the Carib women has fascinated many linguists. Otto Jespersen, for instance, discusses it in some detail in his influential 1922 work *Language* (mentioned in previous chapters), although he is not entirely convinced by Breton's explanation of how the sex-differentiated variants came about. Sex-differentiated languages are relatively unusual in that male/female choices are determined by the language's internal make-up. However, various instances have been catalogued, and modern Japanese is an often-quoted example. In a grammar or dictionary of Japanese, there would need to be some indication of the forms that are regarded as 'male' or 'female' (even if they are not used exclusively by the designated sex). This would not be the case in English, since, in theory, any speaker can use any form. But in practice this is not so, and it is the features male and female speakers select as a result of social conventions and expectations that have come to be of particular interest to linguists.

Jespersen's discussion of female speakers can be found in a chapter designated for the purpose, simply entitled 'The Woman'. Occupying 18 of the book's 448 pages, it is a matter of opinion whether the singling out of the female of the species in this way is a good thing – a recognition that potential differences in female and male speech are worthy of inclusion in a standard textbook – or whether this approach simply reinforces some implicit notion that language norms are established by reference to male usage. Many of his remarks will doubtless have modern readers throwing up their hands in horror: for example, 'women much more often than men break off without finishing their sentences, because they start talking without having thought out what they are going to say' (Jespersen, 1922, p. 250). Jespersen does, however, attribute many of the disadvantageous features of women's language he identifies to social circumstances, recognises a recent 'rise of the feminist movement' (ibid., p. 248) and prophesies a change in the future: 'great social changes are going on in our times which may eventually modify even the linguistic relations of the two sexes' (ibid., p. 254).

In 1973, a lengthy article devoted entirely to language used by 'the woman' was published in the American journal *Language in Society*. Two years later, and with some additions, it appeared as a separate volume. With its clearly provocative title, Robin Lakoff's *Language and Woman's Place* was to become the cornerstone of a new wave of interest in women's language, not least because it was the first substantial text about language and gender actually to be written by a woman. Within the relatively new field of sociolinguistics, research was already starting to reveal a correlation between sex and preferences for standard or non-standard linguistic forms, as we have just seen. Approaching language partly as a linguist and partly as a feminist, Lakoff wanted to demonstrate the connection between language and the view that women were 'systematically denied access to power' (Lakoff, 1975/2004, p. 42). However, she focussed her attention not on standard or non-standard features but on other linguistic choices made by women, which she claimed were examples of 'powerless' language, reflecting women's social position. These included features such as **hedges** – expressions such as *kind of, sort of, I guess* which convey an element of uncertainty or an unwillingness to be more definite. Lakoff's claim was that hedges were used more by women than by men 'because they are socialized to believe that asserting themselves strongly isn't nice or ladylike, or even feminine' (ibid., p. 79).

Lakoff's ideas, although criticised later for being intuitive rather than based on empirical data, were to have far-reaching effects. Reflecting on her book's publication nearly 30 years later ('Language and Woman's Place *Revisited*'), Lakoff herself commented on how 'the original essay was situated at a revolutionary moment, in both linguistics and women's history' (Lakoff, 2004, p. 15). This revolutionary effect was quickly seen as more and more researchers (the vast majority of them women) began to explore the various ways in which men and women's language differed, and the social implications behind those differences. All kinds of contexts and uses were considered, and conversational interaction became particularly prominent. Theoretical positions evolved as research expanded. Lakoff's 'deficit' model of women's language as 'powerless' developed into a 'dominance' model, where the primary cause of linguistic variation between the sexes was attributed to a subordinate position occupied by women in relation to men. It was not long before researchers reacted against this model, which presented women as weak and lacking confidence in themselves, as well as being based on the assumption that men's language did indeed provide a linguistic norm from which women's language deviated. So the dominance approach was superseded in the 1980s by the 'difference' model with the aim of presenting women's language as culturally equal to men's, whatever the reason for the variation. In fact, many studies started to reveal how power and status were determining factors in linguistic behaviour, irrespective of sex.

In her 2004 retrospective Lakoff also comments:

> It is hard to remember just how different the world was when *Language and Woman's Place* was first published in 1975 and harder still to return (even in imagination) to that world. (ibid., p. 15)

and

> The inclusion of gender as an area of linguistic investigation was less obvious thirty years ago than it seems today. (ibid., p. 18)

More than a decade on, the study of sex (or gender) variation in language has continued to move away from the world Lakoff describes when it was not yet clear how it should be incorporated into linguistic research. Now, however, a range of methodologies and theories abound, applied across a range of languages and cultures. The focus on female language has also been counterbalanced by some illuminating studies of male language. In 2003, for instance, the British linguist Jennifer Coates published *Men Talk*, a detailed study of men's narratives in all-male conversations.

While Lakoff was preparing *Language and Woman's Place*, another aspect of male/female variation was starting to attract some attention, namely the study of language and sexual orientation, particularly in relation to homo-sexuality. The beginnings of this can be traced back to the 1930s, and a very different climate for publishing research in this field. In 1941, the American physician George Henry published a study – 'prepared for the use of the medical and allied professions only' – on *Sex Variants*. The main part of the book consists of personal accounts and analyses of subjects who volunteered to take part in the research (in New York City), but it also contains seven appended items. The last of these is a glossary of over 300 items compiled by writer and lexicologist Gershon Legman. 'The Language of Homosexuality' lists and defines words used specifically by homosexual men as well as those used about them. But it was to be many decades before such studies were to be available beyond the medical sphere, with just a handful of articles on the language of homosexuality starting to appear in the journals of the 1960s and 1970s. An important collection of essays on language and sexual orientation published in1997 – Anna Livia and Kira Hall's *Queerly Phrased* – indicates how much the field of gender studies has grown, as well as the theoretical approaches that have developed around it. Thankfully, the twenty-first century has begun with a commitment to understanding more fully the connection between language variation and gender identity already well established.

Cultural variation

Most people who have learned a foreign language and then tried to use their newfound knowledge among native speakers have quickly discovered that there is more to successful cross-cultural communication than simply a good grasp of grammar, vocabulary and pronunciation. A native speaker of English attempting to communicate with French speakers, for instance, has to develop some sensitivity with regard to the second person pronoun 'you' – either *tu* (the grammatical singular) or *vous* (the grammatical plural) in French. The selection of the appropriate pronoun is not a simple matter of how many people you are speaking to, however. In French, *tu* and *vous* also have dimensions of intimacy and politeness, so it would generally be considered rude to address another adult you didn't know well as *tu*. This is so embedded in the culture of French speakers, that there is even a verb – *tutoyer* – which speakers use to invite others to start using *tu* to address them once they become better acquainted.

Linguistic customs like these exist among all groups of speakers, whatever their language, and affect many aspects of language use. Across speech communities throughout the world, all kinds of cultural variation can be found. In some communities, for instance, it is acceptable in conversation for everyone to speak at once, while others frown on overlapping talk and interruptions. Specific types of speaking – or **speech events** – also carry with them customary expectations as to how those events should be constructed. So different conventions may affect, for instance, the telling of jokes, public narratives, greetings and farewells, telephone conversations, religious rituals, and insults and compliments, to name just a few.

These kinds of variables were of considerable interest to the American sociolinguist Dell Hymes, a contemporary of William Labov. Hymes had a keen interest in anthropology and particularly in the languages and cultures of the indigenous populations of the United States in the region around Oregon, where he grew up. Early in his career, Hymes came under the influence of another American linguist/anthropologist, Edward Sapir, who devoted much of his life's work to the study of the Native Americans and their languages. (We will return to Sapir's work in Chapter 8.) For Hymes, language was all about communication: he was interested in real speakers in real contexts. We saw above how the field of sociolinguistics developed side-by-side with the theoretical work inspired by Chomsky, in which language was treated as a phenomenon detached from any instances of its actual use. In other words, the focus was on what Chomsky called competence – our internalised rules for generating well-formed sentences of our language – as opposed to performance, which was of marginal interest. Hymes became a fierce critic of this approach, arguing that speakers had to acquire not only the grammatical rules of a language but also the social and cultural codes which enabled them to use language appropriately in any particular context. To neglect what he termed **communicative competence** was to give only a partial account of a speaker's linguistic abilities.

Hymes first set out his ideas on the study of cultural linguistic variation – an **ethnography of speaking** – in 1962. He describes it as 'concerned with the situations and uses, the patterns and functions, of speaking as an activity in its own right' (Hymes, 1962, p. 45). Over the next decade, Hymes was to develop a systematic framework for the study of what he renamed as the **ethnography of communication**, a framework he devised largely for the benefit of field linguists and anthropologists working within communities and cultures very different from their own. To understand cultural linguistic differences, Hymes believed, it was essential to analyse speech events in relation to aspects such as purpose, genre, the roles of the participants, and the settings in which the events takes place. His advice to fellow anthropologists was that they should make use of linguistics to answer ethnographic questions about different types of spoken interaction. Systematic comparison of speech events across cultures was something akin to the comparative study of religious beliefs or of the values enshrined in the laws of different communities.

Ethnographic studies of language have yielded many interesting findings, and any one of them could provide an interesting example to conclude this section. But as part of our exploration into language variation, a consideration of silence, or the deliberate choice to refrain from speech, provides some interesting food for thought. A study by the American anthropologist Keith Basso published in 1970 attracted a lot of interest and spin-off studies, and also illustrates how not all sociolinguistic-type studies are based on statistics, but some instead on close observation leading to a classification and explanation of the social conditions in which certain choices are made. Basso had spent a total of 16 months observing a Western Apache community living on an Arizona reservation. He identified a range of situations when, from his own cultural point of view, speech would have been expected but did not occur. These situations included strangers meeting for the first time (it usually took several meetings before they decided whether or not they would like to speak to each other), children returning home after a period away (when the parents waited for the children to re-open communication channels) and being in the presence of someone who was recently bereaved (when speakers remained silent out of consideration for the person's intense grief as well as from a degree of wariness about their mental state). Overall, Basso concludes that 'keeping silent among the Western Apache is a response to uncertainty and unpredictability in social relations' (Basso, 1970, p. 227), something that may well seem unnatural to a speaker from a more talkative culture.

The individual speaker

In the mid-1960s, the Swedish linguist Jan Svartvik was asked to assist in a public inquiry into a murder conviction for a crime that was committed in London in 1949. The victims – a young woman, Beryl Evans, and her one-year-old daughter Geraldine – were believed to have been murdered by Beryl's husband Timothy John Evans, who was hanged in 1950. Three years later, the appalling discovery of other victims at the property where Evans and his family had lived led to the arrest of another former tenant, John Christie, who confessed to the murder of several women, including Beryl Evans. Christie was hanged in July 1953. Over a decade later, Svartvik was able, through a linguistic analysis of the statements that Evans had made over a period of three days in the winter of 1949, to show that significant parts of his confession (transcribed by the police officers who conducted the interviews) were unlikely to be the words of the accused but must have been formulated by the officers themselves (Svartvik, 1968). The evidence for this was the fact that the transcriptions contained both standard and non-standard forms (such as regularised past tenses or multiple negation, which Evans used consistently in his trial), as well as formal expressions (such as *in a fit of temper* and *made my way*) and multi-clause sentences which were unlikely stylistic choices for the uneducated Evans. A difference was particularly noticeable in the sections in which the murders themselves are described. This, coupled with the realisation that the whole investigation had been carelessly handled, had led to a man being hanged eighteen years earlier for a crime he did not commit. Following this shocking revelation, Timothy Evans was granted a posthumous pardon.

Svartvik's analysis drew on something which linguists had known for some time – that every individual is linguistically unique, making it possible in theory to determine the authorship of disputed texts. Long before Labov adopted his quantitative method for exploring language variation, the British mathematician Augustus de Morgan (a contemporary of Charles Darwin) had proposed that statistics could be used to characterise a person's language use. (He suggested applying statistical analysis to the New Testament letters attributed to St Paul.) De Morgan's proposal was that average word length would prove a suitable indicator, an idea that was taken up and then developed by various scholars of the time who also looked at factors such as word frequency and average sentence length. Some scholars busied themselves with examining the authenticity of literary works, especially of some of Shakespeare's plays, a question that still occupies researchers. In 1890, the Polish philosopher and writer Wincenty Lutoslawski published his 'Principes de Stylométrie', the first work on this new practice of **stylometry**. A few years later, he applied his analytical methods to the works of Plato, using changing language features as a means of tracing the development of the philosopher's thinking and placing some of his key works in chronological order.

The study of linguistic individuality has not been limited to writers or to those who unwittingly find themselves in the public eye. Nor has the study of individuality been confined to written texts. Among sociolinguists there has been an increasing recognition of the many factors that contribute to each person's distinctive way of using language – their **idiolect**. In addition to our personal grammatical and lexical preferences, we are all subject to a complex mix of social and cultural influences, and personal aspects such as age, sex and status also help to shape our idiolects. Even our size and physical make-up contribute, since each human voice is unique. And, to add to all these strands, no one individual speaks (or writes) in the same way all the time, but adjusts their style according to purpose and context. Jenny Cheshire's study of young people in Reading (which we considered earlier) provides a fascinating example of this. Primarily, her 'playground' study looked at the **sociolect** of her respondents – the shared way of talking that set them apart and gave them a distinct socio-cultural (or subcultural) identity. But even within this group, individual differences could be observed, and Cheshire used both statistics and background knowledge to explain these. Her accounts of some of the respondents certainly bring them to life: one boy, Barney, a long-term truant, significantly increased his use of vernacular forms in school as a marker of his rejection of its values and his strong dislike of the teachers, while a fellow pupil, Ricky, reduced his use of them when talking to a teacher that he liked and respected, especially because the teacher was happy to talk to him about racing cars and motorbikes.

In this chapter, then, we have seen how linguists and other scholars have approached the many layers of variation that can be found among speakers. In the 50 years that have elapsed since that summer meeting in Bloomington, sociolinguistics has continued to thrive, encompassing more and more aspects of society and in an increasingly wide range of languages and contexts. Language variation has been extensively studied in relation to social class, social groups and networks, education, occupation, ethnicity, bilingualism (a vast number of people speak more than one language), age, gender, sexual orientation … The list goes on. And it is quite probably true to say that whatever social encounters a speaker has in a typical day – a chat with a friend, a phone call to a colleague, buying a ticket at the railway station, paying a visit to the doctor – someone has studied it! The orientation of some linguists towards geographical, social, cultural and individual variation is in stark contrast to the preferences of other linguists who try to extract and distil from all this variation what it is that unites all speakers of a particular language – or of any language, for that matter. In the next chapter, then, we will move into the rarefied world of the theoretical linguists and take a look at language from their more abstract perspective.

Suggestions for further reading and research

On the study of dialects

Chambers, J K and Trudgill, Peter (1998) *Dialectology*, 2nd edn (Cambridge: Cambridge University Press)

A standard work on the development of this field in the late twentieth century.

Dollinger, Stefan (2015) *The Written Questionnaire in Social Dialectology: History, Theory, Practice* (Philadelphia: John Benjamins)

Exploring the history of the use of questionnaires for data collection, this new study also looks at more recent research and gives practical guidance on current methods for collection and analysis.

On sociolinguistics

Coupland, Nikolas and Adam Jaworski (eds) (1997) *Sociolinguistics: A Reader and Coursebook* (Basingstoke: Palgrave)

As well as containing helpful articles on the development and definition of 'sociolinguistics', this is an excellent introduction to all the strands that make up sociolinguistics today.

Wodak, Ruth, Barbara Johnstone and Paul Kerswill (eds) (2011) *The Sage Handbook of Sociolinguistics* (London: Sage)

A wide-ranging collection of essays, including a useful section devoted to the history of sociolinguistics.

On social, cultural and individual variation

Giles, Howard and Peter F Powesland (1975) *Speech Style and Social Evaluation* (New York: Academic Press)

An important theoretical work from the 1970s focussing on the interplay between speaker and listener, and its effect on linguistic choices.

Hymes, Dell (ed.) (1964) *Language in Culture and Society: A Reader in Linguistics and Anthropology* (New York: Harper and Row)

A fascinating collection of 69 articles, covering topics discussed in this chapter and much more.

Mather, Patrick-André (2012) 'The social stratification of /r/ in New York City: Labov's department store study revisited', in *Journal of English Linguistics*, vol. 40, no. 4, pp. 338–56

An even more recent replication of Labov's original study, with findings showing further changes in the use of /r/.

Mendenhall, T C (1887) 'The characteristic curves of composition', in *Science*, vol. 9, pp. 213–49

A demonstration of Augustus de Morgan's ideas about individual style applied to a selection of literary works. Available at https://archive.org/details/jstor-1764604 (accessed October 2015).

Sherzer, Joel (1983) *Kuna Ways of Speaking: An Ethnographic Perspective* (Austin: The University of Texas Press)

An intriguing ethnographic study of the language and customs of the Kuna people of South America.

On language and gender

Coates, Jennifer and Pia Pichler (2011) *Language and Gender: A Reader*, 2nd edn (Chichester: Wiley-Blackwell)

An excellent collection of primary sources which includes classic as well as more recent papers on language, gender and sexuality.

Johnson, Sally and Ulrike H Meinhof (eds) (1997) *Language and Masculinity* (Oxford: Blackwell)

A collection of articles on aspects of men's language, redressing the balance after more than 20 years of focus mainly on women's language.

On attitudes to variation

Cameron, Deborah (1995) *Verbal Hygiene* (Abingdon: Routledge)

An open-minded assessment of attitudes towards various types of language variation and use.

Meyerhoff, Miriam (2011) *Introducing Sociolinguistics*, 2nd edn (Abingdon: Routledge)

A useful textbook in general, this title includes a substantial chapter on 'Language attitudes' as well as an interesting chapter on 'Multilingualism and language choice'.

Saville-Troike, Muriel (2003) *The Ethnography of Communication: An Introduction*, 3rd edn (Oxford: Blackwell)

Another generally useful textbook, this study of communication in different cultural contexts also contains an interesting section on 'Attitudes toward Communicative Performance'.

Useful websites

The Atlas of North American English

www.atlas.mouton-content.com (accessed October 2015)

The online version of this extensive atlas, focussing on phonology and including interactive maps with sound recordings, as well as specific information about the speakers who were recorded.

Linguistic Atlas Project

www.lap.uga.edu (accessed October 2015)

A useful site for information about research into the dialects of American English, with a large amount of data available online.

Survey of English Dialects

http://sounds.bl.uk/accents-and-dialects/survey-of-english-dialects (accessed October 2015)

A sound archive, based at the British Library, of recordings made during the 1950–61 dialect survey conducted by a team from the University of Leeds.

6   The structure of language

Thinkers and researchers introduced in this chapter

Some early grammarians and their key works:

Pāṇini (c. 520–460 BCE)	*Eight Books*
	(Ashtadhyayi)
Dionysius Thrax (c. 160–85 BCE)	*The Art of Grammar*
	(Tekhne grammatike)
Marcus Terentius Varro (116–27 BCE)	*On the Latin Language*
	(De lingua Latina)
Priscian (active c. 500)	*Grammatical Foundations*
	(Institutiones Grammaticae)
Thomas of Erfurt (active 1300–25)	*On the Modes of Signifying or*
	Speculative Grammar
	(Tractatus de modis significandi seu
	Grammatica speculativa)
Sanctius (1523–1600)	*Minerva, or the Underlying Principles*
	of the Latin language
	(Minerva sive de causis linguae Latinae)
Arnauld, Antoine (1612–94) ⎱	The Port-Royal Grammar
Lancelot, Claude (c. 1616–94) ⎰	
Beauzée, Nicolas (1717–89)	*General Grammar*
	(Grammaire Générale)

Some of the more recent scholars who have contributed to our understanding of language structures:

August von Schlegel (1767–1845)	German philologist
Franz Boas (1858–1942)	German–American anthropologist
Leonard Bloomfield (1887–1949)	American linguist
Joseph Greenberg (1915–2001)	American linguist and anthropologist
and	

Noam Chomsky (b. 1928) makes a further appearance

Some of the scholars who have explored the structure of speech:

Jan Baudouin de Courtenay (1845–1929)	Polish linguist
Henry Sweet (1845–1912)	British phonetician and philologist
Nikolai Trubetskoy (1890–1938)	Russian linguist
Roman Jakobson (1896–1982)	Russian–American linguist

A medieval perspective

If you lived, say, at the beginning of the thirteenth century and had been lucky enough to receive an education, then (assuming you were male) you may have found yourself as a student at one of the relatively new seats of learning, a university. The University of Oxford was one of these. Although the precise date of its foundation is unknown, teaching was certainly taking place there from as far back as 1096, so its claim to be Britain's oldest university, preceding Cambridge (founded in 1209) by at least a century, is a valid one. Elsewhere in Europe, only the University of Bologna in Italy is likely to be older, predating Oxford by about a decade. Modern images of Oxford often show the panorama of 'dreaming spires' that the city is famous for, but in the early 1200s very few of the now famous college buildings had been constructed. Instead, students congregated in medieval halls, the only one to survive as an educational establishment being St Edmund Hall, located at the heart of what was then a much smaller, quieter English town – nothing at all like the bustling tourist attraction it has become.

The thirteenth century was an exciting time then for scholarship and there was plenty for the medieval scholars to study. Their curriculum, however, bore little resemblance to that of contemporary students. Teaching and learning styles were very different. With no printed books (the printing press was not invented until the mid-1400s), the handwritten copies of canonical works on which scholars relied were expensive and scarce. There was considerable dependence, therefore, on the oral transmission of knowledge, so students needed a good memory and no doubt a very good level of concentration! As for the range of subjects, this bore only slight comparison to modern-day choices, and a great deal was prescribed by the teachers in any case. Of particular importance were three interconnected disciplines (known as the **trivium**) with a lineage from ancient Greece: rhetoric (the art of public speaking), dialectic (the art of logical, reasoned argument) and last, but certainly not least, grammar. The three 'liberal arts' of the trivium – and grammar in particular – were regarded as the foundation of learning and knowledge, and the means by which students could progress to the study of the other four liberal arts – arithmetic, geometry, astronomy and music. Beyond these, scholars could move on to study philosophy, theology and medicine.

'Grammar' is a slippery label. The word itself comes from the Greek for 'letter' – '*gramma*' – a root which also crops up in medieval words associated with magic and the occult, and again in the word 'glamour' – originally a magic spell. For many people nowadays, 'grammar' functions as a blanket term for correctness in language use – correct spelling, correct punctuation and the supposed superiority of standard over non-standard forms (such as

I'm not over *I ain't*). For contemporary linguists, however, grammar is the set of internalised rules (relating to inflections and syntax) that enable us to produce and understand well-formed sentences in the language we speak. (So, for example, native English speakers know implicitly that *I gave Martin a cup of tea* is a well-formed sentence but *I gave a cup of tea Martin* is not.) Indeed, for many theoretical linguists, the study of grammar is central to the discipline of linguistics, not least because it can illuminate the nature of human language by exploring what it is that all language systems share. In turn, this commonality can perhaps reveal something of the complex workings of the human mind. 'Grammar' can also be used for a reference book containing a description of those mental rules, or to label a theory about how they operate, such as the theory of transformational grammar. In medieval times, however, the mention of grammar to our imaginary Oxford scholar would have brought to mind the study of Latin, which formed a substantial part of his studies.

Latin, the language of ancient Rome and the vast empire that grew up around it in the early centuries of the common era, has played a pivotal role in the study of the structure of language, even though it has now been consigned to a more modest status in linguistics. From the first century BCE, Latin began to grow in importance, and even to supersede Greek as the language of culture and learning, and also as a *lingua franca*. As the Roman Empire expanded, the need to speak Latin for administrative, legal and commercial purposes prompted scholars to produce grammars for teachers and their students, although the Latin described in them was the prestigious literary variety, not the colloquial Latin spoken by the average Roman in the street. In fact, for many early scholars, a grammatical understanding of Latin (and Greek before it) was crucial for a full appreciation of the literature of the ancient world – particularly of the legendary Greek epic poet Homer and his Roman counterpart, Virgil. As Christianity slowly established itself throughout the Western world, with Rome as its centre, Latin extended its influence by becoming the language of Christian ritual, and of seminal works of theology. Latin was revered by scholars everywhere. In the twelfth century, for example, Geoffrey of Monmouth, who spent most of his career as a teacher and canon of the church in Oxford, wrote his history of the kings of Britain, *Historia regum Britanniae*, in Latin, and as late as the end of the seventeenth-century scientists throughout Europe were still using it to write their treatises. So for our Oxford scholar, expertise in Latin was crucial if he was to gain access to the great works of Western civilisation. For him, the study of Latin grammar was probably viewed chiefly as a means to a fairly immediate end. From a modern perspective, the study of language structure that would lead to the inventive and sometimes mind-boggling theories of grammar that abound today was already under way.

Early grammarians

The earliest grammarians we know about lived in Mesopotamia (an area of modern-day Iraq) over 3,500 years ago. Based in the ancient city of Babylon, they described and recorded the ceremonial and literary language of the Sumer region of Mesopotamia. With the Sumerian language fast being overtaken by a local rival, Akkadian, their purpose was to ensure that the literature would remain accessible to future generations. These 'grammars' were inscribed on clay tablets and mainly consisted of lists of Sumerian words with their Akkadian equivalents. Another grammarian whose purpose was essentially the preservation of a culturally important language was the Indian scholar Pāṇini, who recorded Sanskrit in the fourth century BCE in his substantial *Eight Books* (*Ashtadhyayi*). As we saw in Chapter 4, a growing knowledge of Sanskrit among Western scholars from the sixteenth century onwards eventually led to it being established as belonging to the same family as Latin, Greek and other European languages.

The oldest known grammar of Greek, *The Art of Grammar* (*Tekhne grammatike*), was written by Dionysius Thrax around 100 BCE (although there is some doubt as to whether the entire work is his). At this time he was living in the Egyptian city of Alexandria, the hub of Greek influence in that area of the Mediterranean. He wrote his grammar as a guide to classical, literary Greek for his pupils, who spoke a modern, regional variety of the language. The *Tekhne* is a very short work in 25 sections and its most important purpose, as proclaimed by Dionysius, is the 'criticism of poetical productions', which he declares to be 'the noblest part of grammatic art' (Dionysius, c. 100 BCE/1874, p. 4). Nevertheless, his brief outline of the component parts of the Greek language has had long-lasting influence, as we will see in a moment.

Dionysius Thrax's Roman counterpart and approximate contemporary was Marcus Terentius Varro, who wrote an extensive account of Latin – *De lingua latina*. Varro was known to be prolific, but most of his works shared the fate of countless other ancient texts – to have left no trace apart from the mentions made of them elsewhere by other writers. *De lingua latina* survives in just one damaged manuscript from the eleventh century originating from the Monte Cassino monastery in Southern Italy. Of the 25 books that make up this grammar, only six are undamaged, but there is enough here to demonstrate Varro's insights as a grammarian. His observations on morphology are especially remarkable: he assigns words to particular groups (such as nouns or verbs) based on their distinctive morphological features (such as marking for tense on verbs and for possession on nouns), and on the different functions of morphological elements. To use an English example, the

-*ness* in *kindness* must be distinguished in terms of function from the -*er* in *kinder*. The former results in the creation of a new word (*kindness* is distinct from *kind*), while the latter is a modification of the same word (*kinder* is the comparative form of *kind*). As far as we know, Varro was the first to point this out, and it is has remained a central principle for the classification of words, as has the distinction he made between 'fruitful' and 'unfruitful' words – those which can be inflected to generate new forms and functions (like *kind*), as opposed to those whose form never changes (like *as* and *to*).

The grammarian likely to have been most familiar to our Oxford scholar was Priscian, who lived in the sixth century. Born on the North African coast in what is now Algeria but was then a province of the Roman Empire, Priscian later moved to Greek-speaking Constantinople (modern-day Istanbul) where he became a teacher of Latin. Three of his grammatical works survive, but most important is his *Grammatical Foundations* (*Institutiones grammaticae*), which flourished when it was first written, enjoyed a revival in the eighth century, then remained a standard Latin grammar throughout the medieval period. The *Institutiones* is a formidable work in 18 books, running to nearly 1,000 (smallish) pages. Written in Latin, it also contains many comparative examples from Greek, as well as illustrative quotations from a wide range of Roman writers and poets.

Establishing a metalanguage

Linguistic analysis is impossible without a **metalanguage** – here a set of dedicated terms for the purpose of identifying and categorising the structural components of language and their functions. By the time Priscian was composing his *Institutiones*, a metalinguistic framework was already well established among grammarians, and much of that framework has survived into contemporary linguistics, although it has been adapted and extended in ways that Priscian could never have anticipated. Its construction, however, had begun in ancient Greece in the last few centuries BCE. Originally intended only for Greek, the first metalinguistic concepts were transferred by the Roman grammarians to Latin, and, over time, have been applied to more and more languages across the whole range of language families. To what extent this metalanguage is a good fit for certain non-Indo-European languages has been a matter of some debate, and we can only imagine how different our modern metalanguage might be had it been derived from the study of a language bearing little structural resemblance to Greek or Latin.

As it happens, many of the first metalinguistic terms were not used primarily for the analysis of language *per se* but as instruments for the study of logic, philosophy, rhetoric and literature. Aristotle, for example, employs metalinguistic terms in two of his works. One of these is the *Poetics*, where he uses both literary and linguistic terminology to establish the distinguishing features of dramatic and poetic genres. The other is *On Interpretation*, one of the six works he wrote on logic.

Probably the most salient contribution that the Greeks and Romans made to the later study of linguistic structure was in establishing what are traditionally known as **parts of speech** (from the Latin *partes orationis*) but are now usually known as **word classes** (a term introduced by the linguist Leonard Bloomfield in 1914). Here, the Greek or Latin terms are given with their English equivalents.

c. 100 BCE Dionysius Thrax *Tekhne grammatike*	c. 500 CE Priscian *Institutiones grammaticae*	contemporary linguistics
noun *onoma*	noun *nomen*	noun
verb *rhema*	verb *verbum*	verb
participle *metokhe*	participle *participium*	
		adjective
adverb *epirrhema*	adverb *adverbium*	adverb
pronoun *antonumia*	pronoun *pronomen*	pronoun
preposition *prothesis*	preposition *praepositio*	preposition
conjunction *sundesmos*	conjunction *coniunctio*	conjunction
article *arthron*		determiner (includes articles)
	interjection *interiectio*	(interjection)

The table above begins with Dionysius Thrax although it is unlikely that he introduced these terms himself: they are more likely to be a reflection of the parts of speech already in general use at the time. The middle column lists the parts of speech used by Priscian, which were mostly inherited from the Greeks, and have largely remained in use ever since, with a degree of modification. The noun is a central part of speech (or word class). Some of the early Greek grammarians recognised two noun types – **proper** and **common** – but these are now treated as subdivisions of the same class. The verb is also central. In Greek and Latin grammars, the **participle** (a form like *winning,* or *defeated* in *they were defeated*) is treated as a separate part of speech because it shares properties with both nouns and verbs, but it is generally now treated as a verb form. Similarly, the **article** (*a/an* and *the* in English), which is absent from Latin, has been subsumed into the larger class of determiners. **Interjection** appeared with the early Latin grammars but has only marginal status in contemporary grammar since interjections (like 'ouch'!) do not normally enter into linguistic structures. In Latin and Greek, there was no separate class of adjectives, which were grouped instead with nouns because they shared their sets of inflectional endings denoting gender, number and function.

The definitions of the various parts of speech in the early grammars make for interesting reading although space doesn't allow for more than a brief examination of them here. The ancient grammarians tended to draw on both semantic and formal aspects in their descriptions. For instance, Priscian's definition of a noun (using the translation of Professor R H Robins) is essentially a semantic one:

> The property of the noun is to indicate a substance and a quality, and it assigns a common or a particular quality to every body or thing. (Robins, 1997, p. 71)

His definition of a verb, however, begins with its semantic properties but moves on to its formal properties:

> The property of a verb is to indicate an action or a being acted on; it has tense and mood forms, but is not case inflected. (ibid.)

These 'mixed' definitions make an interesting contrast with contemporary ones. This definition of a verb, for instance, is taken from the *Oxford Dictionary of English Grammar*:

> A member of a word class that is normally essential to clause structure and which inflects and can show contrasts of aspect, number, person, mood, tense, and voice.

Here the use of formal features alone enables a word's class to be identified purely on the basis of its inflectional and syntactic properties (although the simplistic notion of a verb as a 'doing' word has persisted to this day).

Although the early grammarians did consider the morphological make-up of words, they tended to concentrate on the word in its entirety as the basic unit of a sentence. On syntax – the principles by which words are combined to create sentences – they were almost silent. Dionysius Thrax devotes a section to 'The sentence' in the *Tekhne* but it is brief to the point of negligence. He describes the sentence as 'a combination of words, either in prose or verse, making complete sense' (Dionysius, c. 100 BCE/1874, p. 8). He is unlikely to have got very far as a contemporary theorist with this definition of what has now become the predominant unit of grammatical analysis! However, it would be a misrepresentation to say that the early thinkers ignored sentence structure altogether. Plato, for instance, considered the relationship between sentence form and function for rhetorical purposes. For instance, what form could a question take, or a command? And in terms of logic, both Plato and Aristotle concerned themselves with the relationship between the two essential parts of a logical proposition such as *Socrates is a wise man*. The division between *Socrates*, the **subject** of the proposition, and its **predicate** (*is a wise man*), found its way into the study of grammar in medieval times and has played a prominent part in contemporary linguistic theory.

Looking back at the work of grammarians up to and including Priscian, it is possible to see an emerging framework for analysing the structure of language, but hard to identify any unifying theoretical concepts. For thirteenth-century scholars of grammar, this was all about to change. To all intents and purposes, grammatical study up to this point had been motivated by the need to teach Latin and Greek, but now the study of grammar started to take on a more philosophical, theoretical quality.

The speculative grammarians

A survey of scholarly works of the mid-thirteenth century onwards reveals a crop of titles whose similarity can hardly be a matter of chance. These scientific and theological titles all include the Latin word for 'mirror', *speculum*: *Speculum astronomiae*, *Speculum perfectionis*, *Speculum humanae salvationis* to name just three. For medieval thinkers of this period, a mirror had mystical properties in the way it reflected truths about both the physical world and the status of humanity within it, perhaps even revealing greater truths than could be seen by gazing directly at these things. Not surprisingly, therefore, the image of the mirror came to stand as offering a fuller perspective on whatever it reflected, and *speculum* came to have connotations of a panoramic survey, or a view from which nothing is hidden. This idea, sharpened by a renewed interest in Aristotelian philosophy, quickly found its way into the study of grammar, and the scholars who explored these ideas came to be known as **speculative grammarians**. Their awareness of themselves as a coherent group is signified in the title of an early-fourteenth-century work by Thomas of Erfurt, *De modis significandi seu grammatica speculativa – On Modes of Signifying, or Speculative Grammar.*

So how exactly did this new wave of grammarians hold a mirror up to the world around them? Their ideas were born out of a frustration with grammar being treated largely as a pedagogical tool. Their belief was that grammar could and should provide a reflection of the physical world and of human thought, something that was constrained by the attention to one language alone, even if that language did have the intellectual status of Latin. They were interested in a grammar which would be applicable to any language and, by being universal, would in turn reflect universal truths about the world. In seeking this, they turned their attention to Priscian's parts of speech to see if they could be elevated to this status. They found, for instance, that the world contains objects which are in a state of seeming permanence: this 'truth' was embodied in the noun. By contrast, other aspects of the world were not static but in the process of 'becoming' something, a process embodied in the verb.

So powerful were these ideas that the natural truths were all assigned their own *modus essendi*, or 'mode of being' – such as permanence or becoming. A human being's conceptual grasp of the various *modi essendi* led to the *modi intelligendi*, or 'modes of understanding'. These concepts were then translated into signifying words through the parts of speech – or *modi significandi* (as referred to in Thomas of Erfurt's title). In other words, the parts of speech no longer merely helped a language scholar to distinguish one grammatical form from another: rather, they stood as signs of the natural truths they reflected. The focus on the different modes (with echoes of Saussure's later theory of the sign) provides the name for this particular group of speculative grammarians – the *modistae* (or **modists**). For them, the structure of language was not only a reflection of the world itself but the means to express our human understanding of it.

The Port-Royal Grammar

The speculative grammarians were not without their critics, but rather than pursue the ideas of their dissenters, we leap forward now in time to seventeenth-century France, to the Abbey at Port-Royal des Champs, about

35 km south-west of Paris. From the late 1630s, this religious community became an important centre of education, and attracted various intellectuals and teachers to its confines. By this time, printed books had been in circulation throughout Europe for well over 150 years, allowing a speedier and more widespread dissemination of new ideas, and providing a very different climate for scholarly pursuits. Highly valued among the Port-Royal thinkers was the principle of rationalism found in the philosophy of fellow countryman René Descartes. Descartes's opinion that reason and deduction, not the impressions of the senses, were the key to knowledge and understanding seemed to find its way into much of the thinking at Port-Royal, and in particular to a work on language which was to have a remarkable long-term influence.

Published in Paris in 1660, this *General and Rational Grammar* (*Grammaire générale et raisonnée*) was the result of a collaboration between two men. Claude Lancelot was a teacher and linguist, who had already written grammars of Latin, Greek, Italian and Spanish. Antoine Arnauld was a theologian, mathematician and philosopher with a strong interest in logic. The book's title page summarises its contents as: 'the foundations of the art of speaking', 'the reasons for what is common to all languages, and the main differences between them' and 'various new observations on the French language'. Behind the first item lies the authors' pedagogical purpose of providing their readers with a greater appreciation of language in general, while the third is a nod to the fact that the readers may be particularly interested in knowing more about their native tongue. The second item, however, reveals a wider perspective. The authors (who were not in fact named in the publication) intend not only to illuminate what it is that languages share and how they differ, but to offer an *explanation* for their common features.

This interest in the universal properties of language was not, of course, entirely new. We have already seen how the speculative grammarians hoped for an account of grammar which would mirror the universal truths of the world itself. Arnauld and Lancelot were heavily influenced by the Spanish scholar, Francisco Sánchez de las Brozas, known generally as Sanctius, who published a highly influential work on the underlying principles of Latin (*Minerva, sive de causis linguae latinae*) in 1562, with a further edition in 1587. *Minerva* (the book is named after the Roman goddess of wisdom) was also written in a rationalist vein: Sanctius aimed to provide a reasoned explanation for the grammatical features and structure of Latin rather than simply compose an educational manual. The authors of the Port-Royal Grammar (as it came to be known) were also interested in explaining rather than describing. After all, if language is the product and expression of a rational mind, as Descartes claimed, then it should be possible to provide a rational account of its properties. They hoped to go further than Sanctius, however, by comparing a range of languages, although in actual fact French remained the focus of their discussion.

A simple example will serve to illustrate the rationalist cum universalist approach of the Port-Royal Grammar, and is drawn from a chapter on nouns (Lancelot and Arnauld, 1660, pp. 27–30). You may remember that, in classical categories, adjectives were treated as nouns. The same is true of the Port-Royal Grammar, which makes a distinction between a *nom substantif* (what we would now simply term a noun) and a *nom adjectif* (a modern-day adjective). The difference between them is explained in terms of the way the human mind works when we consider the things around us or the 'objects of our thoughts' (ibid., p. 27). Our thoughts focus first on 'substance' – the Grammar gives *the earth*, *the sun*, *water* and *wood* as examples. But we may also consider the 'manner' of these things, such as being *round*, *red*, *hard* or *wise*. The substances exist in their own right, but their characteristics only exist because the substances do, and we think of them therefore in relation to the substances. As in the mind, so in language. Substances are signified by nouns, their characteristics by adjectives, which are dependent on nouns. This explanation of the workings of the mind can therefore provide us with one of the universal features of language: '… that it is not possible to have an adjective which has no reference to a substantive noun' (ibid., p. 129).

The Port-Royal Grammar contains many examples like this where a grammatical feature is described and then its occurrence explained. The majority of the Grammar's 30 chapters are devoted to such analyses of parts of speech and several chapters are given over to phonological considerations. Syntax, however, is yet again given minimal treatment, taking up just one brief, final chapter. The opening comment of this chapter is particularly striking to a modern reader: 'It remains to say a word about syntax … of which it will not be difficult to give some general notions, following the principles we have established' (ibid., p. 127). In brief, the chapter provides some remarks about different types of inflections and when they come into operation, a handful of general maxims about language, including the observation about adjectives given above, and some comments about four figures of speech which are as much stylistic as they are syntactic. To read this chapter on syntax is to appreciate how very differently it is regarded now, having been brought out from the grammatical wings and into the limelight.

This is not to detract from some of the syntactic insights to be found in the Port-Royal Grammar, however. A particularly interesting piece of analysis is to be found in the chapter on **relative pronouns** (like *who*, *which*, *that*) that 300 years after the book's publication was to catch the eye of that master syntactician, Noam Chomsky. The passage in question (ibid., pp. 58–9) relates to the meaning and structure of the sentence *Dieu invisible a créé le monde visible – Invisible God created the visible world*. (The authors' preference for examples with a theological twist is a nice reflection of their affiliation with the abbey at Port-Royal.) For Lancelot and Arnauld, this statement contains not one proposition but three:

God is invisible   God created the world   The world is visible

Relative pronouns can be used to link these three ideas together and express the three propositions fully:

God, <u>who</u> is invisible, created the world, <u>which</u> is visible

This, in turn, can be reduced to give the original example:

Invisible God created the visible world

For Chomsky, this example was evidence of thinking about the difference between **deep** and **surface structure** in language, an idea that was to become central to his own theory of syntax. What is more, Chomsky declared a strong affinity with the writers of the Port-Royal grammar, seeing himself as an inheritor of the Cartesian rationalism they espoused (Chomsky, 1966). Although the grammar had remained influential well into the nineteenth century, thanks to Chomsky it was now truly destined for linguistic immortality.

In search of more universals

The essential premise of the *General and Rational Grammar* from Port-Royal – that languages are united by universal features which reflect the workings of the human mind – inspired many other grammarians to adopt this approach. The influence of Descartes remained strong, but the interest in the common properties of language was also fuelled by an increased knowledge of the world's languages (as we saw in Chapter 4) and the gradual decline of Latin and Greek as the languages of European scholarship. These factors meant that the study of grammar effectively came to have two distinct purposes – the description of a specific language and/or an account of the way in which human reason is manifested through language.

Over a hundred years after the Port-Royal grammar was first published, the French grammarian Nicolas Beauzée published his own *Grammaire Générale* (1767), which is also underpinned by Cartesian rationalism. In his detailed preface, Beauzée reconciles the dual purposes of grammar, making a distinction between '*la grammaire générale*' and '*une grammaire particulière*'. The former he defines as 'the rational science of the unchanging and general principles of language' in contrast to a particular grammar, which is the practical 'art' of relating the 'arbitrary and customary' features of any one language to these principles (Beauzée, 1767, p. x). He is at pains, however, to point out that his distinction here between the 'science' of one approach and the 'art' of the other does not mean the study of grammar should be divided. On the contrary, they are both instrumental in enabling the grammarian to arrive at a more secure understanding, and Beauzée places considerable emphasis on the interdependency of the two approaches.

There is no doubt that by the eighteenth century a more theoretical approach to the study of language structure was taking shape, driven by the underpinning principle of universals. Beauzée's work intersects with the growing interest in languages (both living and extinct) from beyond Europe which we explored in Chapter 4. Among the grammars of the 17 specific languages that Beauzée says he has consulted are listed Syriac and Chaldean (both classical languages of the Middle East), Japanese, Chinese and Peruvian. Less than 20 years later, Sir William Jones was to present his paper in Calcutta which sparked the golden age of philology, and the interest in universals was to be swept aside by the new historical approach to language study.

Structural differences

Successful classification requires a delicate balance between similarity and difference. The study of the structure of language has certainly demonstrated this. We have seen how, in the approaches to grammar up to the eighteenth century, considerations about what languages had in common – the universal properties of language – came to the fore. By the start of the following century, as the classification of far more diverse languages drew linguists' attention and the view of the Romantic movement that languages reflected the individual essence of different peoples and cultures became more widespread, the balance began shifting towards the ways in which linguistic structures differed.

We have already seen in Chapter 4 how, in the nineteenth century, linguistic study was dominated by philology, and how scholars were chiefly concerned with the history of languages, especially if this could enable them to construct family trees and reconstruct ancestral languages. Their chief vehicle for this historical approach was the phonological aspect of languages, for which they formulated a vast body of sound laws. It was the structure of words – their morphological properties – that provided some alternative ways of looking at language classification, and particularly the perplexing question of the direction of linguistic change.

Morphology, then, provided the material for the early development of what has come to be known as **linguistic typology**, which is concerned with classifying languages according to structural features, irrespective of whether or not they are genetically related. The first wave of philologists (we met several of them in Chapter 4) used the differences they observed in the word formation of the languages they compared to develop a three-way distinction between morphological types. August von Schlegel is usually credited with pioneering this approach.

To illustrate the three types, we will use some examples from English. (Some languages exhibit features of more than one type, even though they are regarded as belonging to one of the three.) Here are three sentences to compare:

1. *The late train must now try to pick up speed*

2. *Fairness can minimise inequality*

3. *She strikes me as the kindest of children*

In Sentence 1 the words used are all morphologically indivisible: they cannot be broken down into smaller units of meaning. This principle of one **morpheme** (unit of meaning) per word is typical of an **isolating** language such as Vietnamese or Yoruba. In Sentence 2, three of the words are divisible, with the added morphemes having distinct functions. So *-ness* turns *fair* into a noun (and *-ity* does the same to *equal*), *-ise* is a verb affix (contrast *minim-al*), while *in-* provides the opposite of *equality*. Languages that rely heavily on 'glueing' words together in this way are **agglutinative**. Swahili, Korean and Japanese belong to this type. In the third sentence, there are several inflected forms, inflection being a means of providing grammatical information. For example, the pronoun *she* is third person, singular, and of feminine gender, while the *-s* inflection on the verb *strikes* denotes a singular, third person subject, as well as the present tense. Languages that are highly inflected in this way use inflections to provide more than one piece of grammatical information, while the addition of an inflection often results in changes to the word's stem (as in *child* and *children,* where the vowel sound is affected). These **inflecting** languages include Russian, Arabic and Navajo. English itself, although somewhat mixed, is usually regarded essentially as an isolating language since it has very few inflections and a consequent dependence on word order to relay some of its grammatical information.

These typological groups provided the philologists with plenty to think about in terms of how morphological structure could provide clues about language relationships and language change. One key topic of debate was whether typology could shed light on the direction of change. Those who promoted evolution as a model for language change tended to believe in a desirable progress from the simplicity of the isolating type to the complexity of the inflecting type. Others noted how change could also happen in the opposite direction (as in fact has happened in English, which has lost most of its earlier inflections) and saw the shift towards an isolating type to be indicative of linguistic decay. Another question related to the interplay between the typological approach to language classification and the genetic one. Could languages belong to the same family and yet not be of the same morphological type? Conversely, one could not assume that common typological features are evidence of genetic relationship. Over time, the tripartite system was remodelled as a continuum between an analytic (i.e. isolating) tendency at one end and a synthetic (highly inflected) tendency at the other. Comparative linguists use this now as a way of mapping morphological change, but with the proviso that change can occur in both directions, and – of particular importance – that changes can be taking place in both directions at the same time.

Structural similarities

The preoccupation of the philologists and their early-twentieth-century successors with linguistic diversity meant that, for a time, the focus on differences caused by language change eclipsed the search for the universal features of language. Only in the 1960s did the interest in universals resurface, not as a means to reveal truths about the world around us or even, initially, the workings of the human mind, but as a way of exploring language structure for its own sake. This was due to the interests and insights of linguistic anthropologist Joseph Greenberg, who was born in New York in 1915.

As you may have already noticed, many linguists are sponge-like in their ability to soak up new languages, whether they experience them directly or study them in reference books. Greenberg was one of these. At university he studied anthropology (departments of linguistics were virtually non-existent at that time) – and came to linguistics as a subdivision of that discipline. It was through his anthropological pursuits that Greenberg became increasingly aware of the diverse structures of world languages (he carried out an extensive project in Africa, for instance) but his inclination was to look for similarities, and to see beyond apparent irregularities: 'natural language did not seem to be so irregular and complicated that it could not be described', he remarked in his 1986 career retrospective (Greenberg, 1986, p. 9).

In 1953, Greenberg attended a summer seminar at the University of Indiana organised for linguists and psychologists in the hope they might find some common ground for future research. This occasion was to determine the rest of his academic career after a chance remark became his lifelong mission statement. Greenberg's task at the seminar was to present some sessions explaining the method used by American linguists at this time to analyse and record indigenous languages. (More of this in the next section.) When the sessions were over, Greenberg was approached by one of the other delegates, who complimented him on his delivery but explained that, as a psychologist, he would be far more interested in learning something which was true of *all* languages. This remark touched a nerve with Greenberg in relation to his recent research. Suddenly he saw an alternative approach to the many languages he had encountered: 'typology, by assigning languages to different types, seems to emphasize their differences, while the study of universals emphasizes their uniformity' (ibid., p. 16). The features languages share became uppermost in Greenberg's mind. The problem, though, was how to identify and present these universals convincingly, and how to avoid simply stating the obvious, such as 'all languages contain vowels'. Nevertheless, Greenberg knew the direction he wanted to go.

By 1961 a conference on universals had taken place and in 1963 Greenberg published his tentative but seminal paper on 'some universals of grammar' in which what he believed to be 'a considerable measure of orderliness' is presented (Greenberg, 1963, p. 58). Thirty languages from across the globe are used as the sample for the 45 statements included in the paper. The universals relate to word order, some other aspects of syntax such as question structure, and to morphology. For any readers coming to universals for the first time, the findings are a revelation. The statements themselves take three different approaches. Some make absolute statements about features that have no exceptions. For example, this one relating to pronouns:

> Universal 42. All languages have pronominal categories involving at least three persons and two numbers. (ibid., p. 75)

Others have a more statistical aspect and use qualifications such as 'almost always' or 'with greater than chance frequency' to express tendencies:

> Universal 18. When the descriptive adjective precedes the noun, the demonstrative and the numeral, with overwhelmingly more than chance frequency, do likewise. (ibid., p. 68)

There are also implicational universals, which seem particularly powerful. These are expressed through conditions, such as in Universal 12, which connects the order of the verb (V), subject (S) and object (O) in a 'normal' sentence to question formation:

> Universal 12. If a language has dominant order VSO in declarative sentences, it always puts interrogative words or phrases first in interrogative word questions; if it has dominant order SOV in declarative sentences, there is never such an invariant rule. (ibid., p. 65)

Greenberg's work laid the foundation for a new field of inquiry into universal aspects of language based on as much empirical evidence as possible. The Stanford Project on Language Universals which was established in 1968 produced, in its eight-year lifespan, enough findings to fill four volumes, which were edited by Greenberg and published in 1978.

The work to explore structural similarities continues, its most recent incarnation being the World Atlas of Language Structures (WALS), a huge database generated by a team of 55 specialists, and, at the time of writing, covering 2,679 languages. Sadly, the first edition of this database wasn't published until 2005, four years after Greenberg's death. But its impressive scope (as well as its online availability) is testament to the research trend started by his determination to say something significant about what languages share.

Leonard Bloomfield and the descriptivists

In the early stages of his academic career, Greenberg had been fortunate enough to work with many of the distinguished linguistic thinkers of the time. As an undergraduate at Columbia University, he had studied Native American languages under Franz Boas, the most influential figure in that field, and Greenberg recalls how he read Boas's vast 1911 *Handbook of American Indian Languages* in its entirety. After graduating, he spent two periods at Yale University (which actually boasted its own linguistics department!) and it was here in the late 1930s that Greenberg met Leonard Bloomfield, who had himself been a pupil of Franz Boas. However, Greenberg and Bloomfield were destined for different paths in American linguistics. As we have just seen, Greenberg was prompted to go in search of universal features, while Bloomfield embraced a belief in the unlimited variety of natural languages.

Descriptivism had grown out of Boas's work on the indigenous American languages. The aim of the descriptivists was to record as many of these endangered languages as possible. Their diversity, and their striking differences from European languages, led the descriptivists to reject the traditional grammar based on Latin and Greek as a default framework for analysis and instead to devise a new methodology applicable to any language. By the 1920s, Leonard Bloomfield had become their leading light.

In 1933 Bloomfield had published his seminal work entitled, simply, *Language*. Its contents reveal several influences – in addition to that of Boas – which shaped Bloomfield as a linguist. Early in his career he had studied philology and (even though the heyday of philology had already come and gone) several chapters of *Language* are devoted to the comparative method and historical change. The influence of Saussure's *Course in General Linguistics* (published posthumously in 1916 – see Chapter 2) can also be detected, placing Bloomfield within the structuralist movement as well as the descriptivist. Moreover, there is the influence of behaviourist psychology. This branch of psychology was in the ascendant at this time, and its methodology demanded that research be based on observable data, not on intuition or preconceived ideas. (We will explore more of its influence on Bloomfield when we look at children's language acquisition in Chapter 9.) Above all, Bloomfield wanted linguistics to be recognised as a science, and he adopted what he believed to be a scientific approach to language by his empirical methods. In the chapters that cover language structures, he is at pains to establish strategies for the identification of linguistic forms – what are sometimes termed **discovery procedures**. He describes language features in detail and these sections are dense with examples from a wide range of languages.

Of particular interest is the notion that Bloomfield introduces of the **constituent**, which makes up part of any complex linguistic form. This can apply to words – for instance, *blackberry* is a complex form, divisible into the constituents of *black* and *berry* – but also to phrases and sentences. Of central concern to Bloomfield is the importance of avoiding a purely linear analysis. He gives the example of *Poor John ran away* (Bloomfield, 1933, p. 161), which is made up of a string of what he calls **ultimate constituents**: these cannot be broken down into smaller structural elements (apart from *a-* + *way*, but we will ignore this morphological division for now). So his example, as a word string, is made up of *poor* + *John* + *ran* + *away*. This, however, reveals nothing about the internal structure of the example, nor would it enable the linguist (particularly when working with an indigenous American language) to distinguish the function of different elements within it. Instead, Bloomfield introduces the concept of the **immediate constituent**, one of two parts into which a complex linguistic form can be divided. So *black* and *berry* are the immediate constituents of *blackberry*. This doesn't seem particularly startling or productive until you apply the principle to more complex linguistic forms, when a hierarchical structure begins to emerge. Thus, *Poor John ran away* is made up of the immediate constituents [*poor John*] and [*ran away*] (an intuitive division, although in fact based on the traditional division between subject and predicate), while [*poor John*] may then be further divided into [*poor*] and [*John*]. This uncovering of a form's constituent structure was an idea that was to blossom over the next few decades, as we are about to see.

The coming of the generative age

Leonard Bloomfield and his teacher Franz Boas were descriptivists who believed every natural language had a unique structure and there was effectively no limit to the different features that might occur in languages, nor could any feature be assumed to be universal. In 1957, the American linguist Martin Joos edited and published a collection of *Readings in Linguistics* which charted 'the development of descriptive linguistics in America since 1925', as its subtitle announced. This makes interesting browsing, particularly appearing as it did in the same year as Noam Chomsky's *Syntactic Structures* – the short work which was to transform the way linguists viewed language structure. Joos's collection provides a snapshot of the context in which Chomsky's ideas entered the linguistic world, heralding the start of the **generative** age.

We have seen in previous sections how grammarians were interested in morphology, but less so in syntax. That is to say, words were given more attention as structural units than sentences. (Of course, we have so far not dealt with phonology, but this will be covered in the next section.) Only with the arrival of *Syntactic Structures* was syntax elevated to a position of much greater importance. The majority of papers in Joos's *Readings in Linguistics*, then, are concerned with phonology and morphology. But syntax is clearly exercising the minds of some of the contributors and Bloomfield's idea of constituent structure is the framework for this thinking.

One of the papers in the collection (by Rulon Wells) grapples with a crucial question in syntactic analysis: when you divide units into their immediate constituents, how do you ensure your procedure is correct and that incorrect analyses are excluded? Wells discusses the example of *The King of England opened parliament* (Wells, 1947/1957, pp. 187ff). What strategy would guarantee that this was divided into [*The King of England*] and [*opened parliament*], and not [*The King*] and [*of England opened parliament*]? Wells's solution is to think in terms of expansion from a comparable but more basic structure, and he demonstrates how this example can be correctly analysed if seen as an expansion of a 'fundamental' sentence type such as *John worked*. The collection also contains a paper by Charles Hockett (the anthropologist whose design features we explored in Chapter 2), who considers the hierarchical structures revealed by immediate constituent analysis as a useful means of explaining ambiguity, thus accounting for the two possible interpretations of *The old men and women stayed at home*. (Are the women old, or is it just the men?) (Hockett, 1954/1957, p. 391.)

Examples such as these illustrate the growing interest in syntactic analysis by 1957. The very title of Chomsky's *Syntactic Structures* seemed to be announcing that it was high time syntax was granted the full amount of attention it merited. Over the next 30 years or so, Chomsky was to provide plenty of ideas about syntax and its status at the core of language. He began, in *Syntactic Structures*, by introducing a productive, dynamic approach to syntax, a contrast to the static descriptive methodology of Bloomfield. He does this by formulating rules whereby the immediate constituents of [*poor John*] and [*ran away*], to use Bloomfield's example, are not only refined by the addition of phrase structure labels – [*poor John*] is a Noun Phrase (NP) and [*ran away*] a Verb Phrase (VP) – but can be connected by a **phrase structure rule**:

Sentence → NP + VP

Similarly, to simplify one of Chomsky's own examples, [*the man*] (NP) [*hit the ball*] (VP) would need an additional rule to account for the internal structure of [*hit the ball*], namely:

VP → Verb + NP

where [*hit*] is the verb and [*the ball*] is the NP. Finally, NPs have a phrase structure rule:

NP → Determiner + Noun

These structures and relationships can also be represented as a tree diagram, as Figure 6.1 illustrates. Chomsky offers a range of phrase structure rules and explores their potential to *generate* any possible grammatical sentence in a language. However, he is also aware of the limitations of such rules – chiefly, that they do not show the relationship between structures. How, for example, is a statement related to a question, or an active sentence (*the police brought in the criminal*) to its passive counterpart (*the criminal was brought in by the police*)? A grammar that fails to capture these relationships is unnecessarily

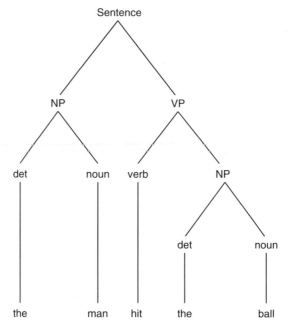

FIGURE 6.1   TREE DIAGRAM OF *THE MAN HIT THE BALL*

cumbersome and it is the business, therefore, of the linguist to look for the means by which one structure is *transformed* into another. **Transformational generative grammar** had been born.

Chomsky's next major publication, *Aspects of the Theory of Syntax* (1965), refined his theory by positing the concept of deep and surface structures, whereby transformational rules act on the former to produce the latter. It is in this respect that we can detect the possible influence of Descartes and the seventeenth-century Port-Royal Grammar on his thinking. In later works, he set about defining the aspects of the transformational grammar that would inhibit the production of ungrammatical sentences. Chomsky has continued to refine his transformational approach, and this has resulted in a series of modifications and new theories. The most recent project is the **minimalist program**, effectively a search for the most efficient, economical design possible of what Chomsky refers to as **universal grammar**, our innate mental capacity for language learning and production. Here again, in his belief that the universal grammar models the workings of the human mind, we see the influence of the Cartesian tradition to which Chomsky claims to belong. We will explore universal grammar further in Chapter 9, when we consider language acquisition.

The seeds of many of Chomsky's ideas can be traced back to earlier scholars but he has undoubtedly taken thinking about language structure in a new and exciting direction, injecting extraordinary vigour into linguistic theory. No theoretical linguist working now, whether they agree with Chomsky or not, can ignore his transformational-generative framework. In Chapter 10, we will return briefly to Chomsky's influence in this area to consider where syntactic theory might be headed in the future, but for now we will turn our attention to a different aspect of language structure.

The structure of speech

So far in this chapter our attention has been given to the internal structure of words and sentences, and we have seen how syntax has gradually accrued the level of importance it now holds in linguistic theory. But the structural picture is incomplete without some consideration of the primary mode by which human beings express language, namely speech. Over time, a branch of linguistics has developed which is entirely concerned with the production and reception of speech. This is the field of phonetics and phonology. (Phoneticians concentrate on the production and reception of the distinct sounds which are used to transmit language, while phonologists look at the patterns which exist in the set of speech sounds for any particular language, and across languages in general.)

Speech has been of interest to scholars from earliest times, and there is plenty of evidence of the analysis of speech sounds in terms of both their properties and their distribution. In fact, the first indications we have of phonetic analysis is to be found in ancient writing systems, and we have examples from about 5,000 years ago. For instance, everyone has seen – and no doubt wondered at – the intricate hieroglyphs used by the ancient Egyptians, including images of animals, birds, parts of the body, tools, natural phenomena and so on. Although this writing was intended for religious and administrative purposes, substantial linguistic analysis must have been involved in the devising of such a complex system, where some symbols represent whole words while others represent either single sounds, or combinations of two or three sounds. It is little wonder that hieroglyphs were not deciphered until early in the nineteenth century.

Whatever its purpose then, devising any writing system where symbols stand for speech sounds is a phonological activity since it requires the identification and classification of the discrete sound segments of the language in question. This is also the starting point for an accurate description of a language's phonological system, and many of the works of earlier centuries that have already been mentioned in this chapter contain such phonological material. Pāṇini's grammar of Sanskrit, for instance, includes detailed information for the correct pronunciation of the sacred texts. Observations about vowels and consonants (and syllables) are to be found in the *Tekhne grammatike* of Dionysius Thrax and in Priscian's *Foundations*. Both the Port-Royal Grammar and Beauzée's *General Grammar* also contain detailed sections on these elements of speech.

Aristotle was one of the first to outline the nature of sounds (what he called letters, although this had a wider meaning for him than it has for us) by establishing the crucial idea of sound segments being indivisible. In English, this would mean that /br/ is not a discrete sound because it can be divided again into /b/ and /r/. But /b/ and /r/ are indivisible sounds. Furthermore, he distinguished between indivisible sounds made by animals and those which belong to human language. Only the latter are 'letters' because they combine into groups to form words. (An early awareness of the double articulation system which characterises human language.)

For the only time in this book, our journey takes us to Iceland, where, in the twelfth century, an unidentified scholar wrote a treatise on Icelandic orthography in the wake of a move from using the Runic alphabet to the Roman one. Essentially this treatise is about spelling reform: its author is proposing an adaptation of the Roman alphabet to suit the needs of Icelandic pronunciation. In doing so, he presents a comprehensive inventory of Icelandic speech sounds using what we now call minimal pairs. This method establishes the existence of independent speech segments by pairing words which differ by one element only. In English, for example, it can be demonstrated that /t/ and /d/ are distinct segments as they distinguish pairs such as *to/do*, *bet/bed*, and *writer/rider*. Sadly, the manuscript for what is now known as the 'First Grammatical Treatise' (due to its position in a thirteenth-century collection) received little attention and remained unpublished until 1818. The techniques of this obscure writer, however, were to become important hundreds of years after his death, as we will see in a moment.

In Chapter 4 we observed how important the study of speech sounds became in the nineteenth century when philologists (working mainly in Germany) used them as their central tool for understanding language diversity and identifying family relationships. In 1877, the English philologist and phonetician Henry Sweet published *A Handbook of Phonetics*. The preface opens with his declaration that:

The importance of phonetics as the indispensable foundation of all study of language – whether that study be purely theoretical, or practical as well – is now generally admitted. (Sweet, 1877, p. 5)

He goes on to celebrate the fact that the study of phonetics has recently expanded in his own country, which can 'now boast a flourishing phonetic school of its own' (ibid., p. viii), and he praises the work of some of his contemporaries. Also evident is his excitement about the boost that new technology has given to the study of speech: he mentions the invention of the laryngoscope and the benefits it has brought to phonetic research. Sweet himself saw phonetics as particularly important in the learning of foreign languages, and there was a strong movement at this time in an educational direction. In 1886 this led to the founding in Paris of what was to become, in 1897, the International Phonetic Association, which flourishes to this day. One of its chief contributions to the scientific study of phonetics has been the compilation of the **International Phonetic Alphabet**, containing a symbol for every known distinctive speech sound in any natural language.

Although speech has traditionally been treated as central to the study of language, its relationship to the other aspects of language is problematic. On the one hand, it is through the spoken medium that young children normally acquire language, so it plays an important role in the transmission of language through the generations. On the other hand, speech is not the only medium that can 'embody' or transmit language. For a significant number of people, signing is the primary mode of communication. It is perfectly possible for two people to have a conversation using gestures rather than speech. Despite Sweet's view that phonetics was central to the study of language, language is arguably neither sound nor gesture – they are merely the vehicles for making language 'real'. This was an argument made by Saussure, who pointed out that someone could lose their powers of speech but this would not deprive them of their language faculty (Saussure, 1916/1983, p. 14). Language was not speech, nor was speech language, despite the close relationship between the two. Saussure, who was fond of analogies, likened language to a symphony, which exists separately from any performance which an orchestra might give of it (ibid., p. 18). So from Saussure's point of view, phonetics is not a part of linguistics.

Nevertheless, the study of phonetics and phonology continued to thrive at the start of the twentieth century. While the descriptivists developed their work in America, a group of Eastern European linguists formed themselves in 1926 into the **Prague Linguistic Circle**. Two of their members were to prove particularly influential in the study of phonetics and phonology. These were Prince Nikolai Trubetzkoy and Roman Jakobson, both born in Moscow in the 1890s. By this time, a new dimension to the individual speech segment had been recognised – its psychological reality. This idea allowed for variation in pronunciation of individual sounds (resulting from speaker variation or differences in the phonological environment), yet with the 'intended' sound remaining identifiable. For instance, you can hear a difference in the pronunciation of /l/ in *line* and *nail* but it would be surprising if you thought of them as distinct elements of the English sound system since they do not occur in a minimal pair. This phenomenon was accounted for by the concept of the **phoneme**, which was defined at the very end of the nineteenth century by the Polish philologist Jan Baudouin de Courtenay as a 'unitary concept which exists in the mind' (Baudouin, 1894/1972, p. 152).

Both Trubetzkoy and Jakobson developed the concept of the phoneme by identifying the features that characterised individual sounds. (Although speech sounds are indivisible as a linguistic unit, this is not so say they are one-dimensional in themselves.) Trubetzkoy devised a way of distinguishing phonemes based on contrasts between them: for instance, /p/ is distinguished from /t/ by being articulated at the lips not on the alveolar ridge behind your upper teeth, while /k/ is distinguished from both of them by being articulated against the soft palate at the back of the mouth. In all other articulatory respects, these three phonemes are identical. Trubetzkoy was also interested in how pronunciation would vary according to position, so in English you could account for the variation of /l/ in *line* and *nail* by a rule which states that /l/ becomes **palatalised** when it occurs at the end of a word. (In Trubetzkoy's native Russian, /l/ is always palatalised, so no such rule would be needed.) Jakobson developed Trubetzkoy's methods for classifying phonemes by using a binary approach. This consisted of a set of possible features of all phonemes: each phoneme would then be identifiable by whether it carried a positive or negative value for each feature. The concept of binary features was to prove a very productive one, not least because it provided a neat way of expressing phonological rules. In 1968, the approach was taken up and given the generative treatment by Chomsky and his colleague Morris Halle in *The Sound Pattern of English*, which demonstrated how this theoretical approach could be applied to phonology, not just to syntax.

While works like this show how phonology had moved into more theoretical territory, the practical aims of phonology, particularly in recording endangered languages, have not been abandoned. Furthermore, phonology has had a significant part to play in the discovery of language universals. The UPSID project based at the University of California (UCLA Phonological Segment Inventory Database) is a good example of this. First published in 1984, it gives findings for a survey of 451 languages worldwide and provides some intriguing statistics – for example, about the number of speech segments found in languages as well as their frequency of occurrence. For instance, /m/ occurs in 94% of the languages surveyed, while /s/ – perhaps surprisingly to English speakers – only occurs in 44%. Whatever the views of linguists about the relationship of phonetics and phonology to the rest of linguistics, it remains one of the remarkable features of language that a small set of sounds which have no inherent meaning should be able to convey the millions of diverse messages which we humans generate every day.

Suggestions for further reading and research

On grammar and grammar teaching before 1600

Bursill-Hall, Geoffrey L (1971) *Speculative Grammars of the Middle Ages* (The Hague: Mouton)

A critical examination of the theories of the speculative grammarians, looked at through the lens of modern linguistics.

Copeland, Rita and Ineke Sluiter (eds) (2012) *Medieval Grammar and Rhetoric: Language Arts and Literary Theory, AD 300–1475* (Oxford: Oxford University Press)

A detailed survey of many of the works on grammar and on literature which would have been studied by medieval scholars.

Covington, Michael (1984) *Syntactic Theory in the High Middle Ages* (Cambridge: Cambridge University Press)

A study of the grammatical theory of the modists, not only tracing its origins, but also considering the aspects that have survived into modern linguistics.

Donatus, Aelius (4th century) *Ars Minor*
Available at www.intratext.com/IXT/LAT0192/ (accessed October 2015)

This short work by the fourth-century Latin grammarian on parts of speech (composed in a question and answer format) was a standard text for teaching grammar throughout the medieval period.

Law, Vivien (1997) *Grammar and Grammarians in the Early Middle Ages* (London: Longman)

The status of Latin as the medium for teaching grammar, and the development of a grammatical metalanguage are just two of the topics covered in this interesting examination of the period in question.

Law, Vivien (2003) *The History of Linguistics in Europe: From Plato to 1600* (Cambridge: Cambridge University Press)

Also recommended in Chapter 1, this is an excellent study of the period up to 1600.

On the modern treatment of linguistic structure

Christiansen, Morten H, Chris Collins and Shimon Edelman (eds) (2009) *Language Universals* (Oxford: Oxford University Press)

A collection of articles illustrating the direction that the study of universals has taken since Greenberg, and examining new insights in the field.

Harris, Zellig S (1951) *(Methods in) Structural Linguistics* (Chicago: Chicago University Press)

A standard textbook of its time, also available at https://archive.org/details/structurallingui00harr (accessed October 2015).

Hawkins, John (ed.) (1988) *Explaining Language Universals* (Oxford: Basil Blackwell)

A variety of contributors argue for the different possible explanations of the common features which languages have been found to share.

Matthews, P H (1993) *Grammatical Theory in the United States: From Bloomfield to Chomsky* (Cambridge: Cambridge University Press)

An overview of American linguistics from 1910–90, concentrating on its two most influential figures.

Moravcsik, Edith A (2012) *Introducing Language Typology* (Cambridge: Cambridge University Press)

An accessible introduction to the study of similarities and differences across languages, offering both linguistic and non-linguistic perspectives.

Song, Jae Jung (ed.) (2011) *The Oxford Handbook of Linguistic Typology* (Oxford: Oxford University Press)

A collection of essays providing a detailed overview of current work and theory in the field of typology.

Tallerman, Maggie (2015) *Understanding Syntax*, 4th edn (Abingdon: Routledge)

An introduction to the central concepts of syntax, with examples drawn from a range of languages and some helpful exercises to try.

On the study and structure of speech

Anderson, Stephen R (1985) *Phonology in the Twentieth Century* (Chicago: University of Chicago Press)

A history of phonology during the twentieth century, including chapters on the Prague Linguistic Circle, the theory of distinctive features and the development of generative phonology.

Clark, John, Colin Yallop and Janet Fletcher (2007) *An Introduction to Phonetics and Phonology*, 3rd edn (Malden, MA: Blackwell)

A useful handbook, which also includes sections on the history of phonology.

Toman, Jindrich (2003) *The Magic of a Common Language: Jakobson, Mathesius, Trubetzkoy, and the Prague Linguistic Circle* (Cambridge, MA: MIT Press)

A very readable account of the linguists who founded this circle, the work they did, and why the group was so influential.

Useful websites

Corpus Grammaticorum Latinorum (Collection of Latin Grammars)
http://kaali.linguist.jussieu.fr/CGL/index.jsp (accessed October 2015)

A French website based on a nineteenth-century collection of early Latin grammars edited by Heinrich Keil. It includes over 70 works by 40 different grammarians, and is well worth a browse even for the non-Latin reader.

International Phonetic Association (IPA)
www.internationalphoneticassociation.org (accessed October 2015)

The website of the world's oldest organisation for phoneticians, founded in 1886.

The Noam Chomsky Website
www.chomsky.info/index.htm (accessed October 2015)

An excellent source of information about Chomsky's life and work.

Syntactic Structures of the World's Languages (SSWL)
http://sswl.railsplayground.net (accessed October 2015)

Originating at New York University's Department of Linguistics, this database can be searched by language or by linguistic property.

UCLA Phonological Segment Inventory Database (UPSID)
http://web.phonetik.uni-frankfurt.de/upsid.html (accessed October 2015)

This URL is an interface to the UPSID website at the University of California via Frankfurt University.

The Universals Archive
http://typo.uni-konstanz.de/archive/intro/index.php (accessed October 2015)

Run by the University of Konstanz, this is an extensive database of over 2,000 language universals, including examples, counterexamples, sources and comments.

World Atlas of Language Structures (WALS)
http://wals.info (accessed October 2015).

The 2013 online version is edited by Matthew S Dryer and Martin Haspelmath under the auspices of the Max Planck Institute for Evolutionary Anthropology in Leipzig.

7 The construction of meaning

Thinkers and researchers introduced (or reintroduced) in this chapter

From the seventeenth century:

John Wilkins (1614–72)	English theologian and natural scientist
John Locke (1632–1704)	English philosopher

Some key contributors to ideas about meaning from the late nineteenth century onwards:

Michel Bréal (1832–1915)	French philologist
Gottlob Frege (1848–1925)	German philosopher and mathematician
Gustaf Stern (1882–1948)	Swedish philologist
Jost Trier (1894–1970)	German linguist
Louis Hjelmslev (1899–1965)	Danish linguist and structuralist
Richard Montague (1930–71)	American mathematician and philosopher
Jerrold Katz (1932–2002)	American linguist
Jerry Fodor (b. 1935)	American philosopher and cognitive scientist
Eleanor Rosch (b. 1938)	American psychologist
Barbara Partee (b. 1940)	American mathematician and linguist
George Lakoff (b. 1941)	American linguist

Some thinkers particularly interested in meaning in real-life contexts:

Ludwig Wittgenstein (1889–1951)	Austrian philosopher
John L Austin (1911–60)	British philosopher
Paul Grice (1913–88)	British philosopher
Norman Fairclough (b. 1941)	British linguist
Deirdre Wilson (b. 1941)	British linguist and cognitive scientist
Dan Sperber (b. 1942)	French psychologist

Also reappearing in this chapter:

Leonard Bloomfield (1887–1949)	American linguist
Noam Chomsky (b. 1928)	American linguist

'Colorless green ideas sleep furiously'

We begin this chapter not in a particular place or with a particular event, but with a now famous quotation: *Colorless green ideas sleep furiously* is offered by Noam Chomsky in his 1957 *Syntactic Structures* as an illustration of a sentence that is nonsensical but nevertheless grammatical (Chomsky, 1957, p. 15). He uses it to make the point that the grammatical acceptability of an utterance cannot be based on a semantic judgement, only on a syntactic one, and this leads to his rather startling conclusion 'that grammar is autonomous and independent of meaning' (ibid., p. 17). Whether this is truly the case is something we will return to later in this chapter. For now, though, Chomsky's example can provide an interesting starting point for our consideration of meaning and the way it is constructed in human language, a topic which has exercised the minds of a vast array of scholars.

A few comments about this example give some indication of the complexity involved in determining how meaning works. Although Chomsky calls it 'nonsensical', this doesn't mean that the sentence is completely meaningless. We can start with the individual words. These of course all carry distinct meanings, although *green* stands out by being **polysemous** – it has several meanings. How do we know which one is intended here? Does *colorless* (we will retain the American spelling) give a clue about the meaning we should select, or do we find ourselves searching for an alternative meaning that might make the sentence less 'nonsensical' – for example if 'green' referred to the Green Party in politics? This of course is a relatively new meaning – not applicable in 1957 – and is a useful reminder that word meanings are not fixed but change over time, another aspect of meaning that linguists need to consider. And while we're thinking about words more or less in isolation, we need to take account of the fact that some words are divisible into smaller indivisible elements of meaning, or **morphemes**. *Colorless*, for instance, is divisible into *color* and *-less*, the suffix providing the sense of 'without'. In fact, if we substituted *-less* with *-ful*, would we have gone some way, with *colorful green ideas*, towards making the sentence less nonsensical?

This brings us to the question of the semantic relationship between the words in a sentence and how they work together to produce something meaningful, providing, that is, that the sentence is also grammatical. It is clearly not the case that any word can combine freely with any other word. But can we explain the restrictions in a systematic way? And would these restrictions allow any exceptions? For example, can *ideas sleep* if we think of this metaphorically rather than literally? Could an angry person *sleep furiously*? A poet certainly might think so and we would understand what they meant. (In fact, there is a 2007 film – not about Noam Chomsky! – with this exact title.) It seems, then, we have a will to understand surprising combinations if we possibly can, even if our interpretation is not entirely satisfactory. However, could a situation ever arise in which this entire sentence was readily meaningful, and would that imply that in some sense it was also true? Chomsky himself admitted the sentence could possibly be uttered and understood in a 'sufficiently far-fetched context' (ibid., p. 16). So to what extent must we rely on context to interpret meaning, and is it even possible to study linguistic meaning satisfactorily without some reference to the non-linguistic world in which we use language?

These considerations reveal how meaning is not restricted to one particular aspect or level of language, but pervades every corner of linguistic structure – morphemes, words, phrases, sentences – and we could add the phonological aspects of language to this list, the way we add emphasis or even attempt to suggest meaning with certain sounds. (Does the initial fricative sound of *furiously* suggest anger?) Furthermore, if meaning cannot be fully determined without some consideration of context, we must conclude that it has both linguistic and non-linguistic properties. In this chapter we will see how linguists have tackled the many challenges that an explanation of meaning presents, and why a comprehensive account of how meaning works has remained elusive.

The undeniable importance of meaning

Without meaning being conveyed and understood, language is futile. Communication is the *raison d'être* of language, the reason for its very existence. So it is entirely reasonable to expect that semantics – the study of meaning – will play some part in all linguistic research, and in general this has been true. However, although some have fought for the centrality of meaning in the study of language, others have taken it somewhat for granted, and there have also been dark days when it has been neglected or marginalised. Unlike the rags-to-riches Cinderella story of syntax that we traced in the previous chapter, semantics has arguably still not attained the royal status in linguistics that it demands.

This is perhaps surprising when we consider how much human investment there is in conveying and understanding meaning. In everyday life, we all scurry for our dictionaries or to the internet when we encounter an unfamiliar word, and in our various interactions we are usually at pains to make our own meanings clear as well as to comprehend our fellow beings with remarks such as 'what I'm trying to say is…' or 'are you trying to tell me…?'. Many professionals – lawyers, doctors, teachers, politicians – rely heavily on linguistic clarity and accuracy in their work. Scholars of various disciplines – anthropology, semiotics, psychology – find themselves exploring meaning as part of their research. This is particularly the case for philosophers, for whom the nature of meaning has always been an important consideration. And it is from philosophy in particular that linguistics has drawn many of its ideas about the study of meaning. So do not be surprised to come across quite a few more philosophers (including one or two you will have met already) as the story of semantics unfolds.

To begin this story at its very beginnings, we would once more need to go back over two millennia to the philosophers of ancient Greece, but instead we will mainly be focussing our attention on the last hundred years or so. This is partly because you will probably, by now, have already gained some sense of how much linguistics owes to thinkers of the distant past, but also due to the cyclical, reiterative way in which thinking about meaning has developed. Many of the ideas we will be exploring can be found not once, but several times in the course of linguistic history, handed down from age to age, subtly changing in keeping with the intellectual climate of the times. To track the evolution of every idea would be impossible in one short chapter, although we will occasionally make an excursion into this linguistic backstory. But you should read about the modern scholars of semantics with an awareness that, just over their shoulders, linger the many philosophers who first sought to uncover the mysteries of meaning.

Exploring word meanings

We move, then, to the closing decade of the nineteenth century when philology – the comparative and historical study of languages – had long established itself as the chief pursuit of language scholars. On the whole, semantics was not of particular interest to philologists, beyond the identification of cognate words that would hopefully provide clues for a fuller understanding of language family relationships. Their primary focus, as we saw in Chapter 4, was on sound changes. But in Germany, the heartland of philology, the philosopher and mathematician Gottlob Frege had turned his attention to semantics. In 1892 he published a paper 'On sense and reference' ('Über Sinn und Bedeutung') to tackle a problem with which many philosophers had been grappling, namely the relationship of the two elements in a statement where one thing is said to be another, such as *the Nile is earth's longest river*. In logical terms, because *the Nile* and *earth's longest river* both refer to the same stretch of water, then in theory you could just as well say *the Nile is the Nile* (or *earth's longest river is earth's longest river*), although it is highly unlikely that any speaker would want or need to do that (except, perhaps, for emphasis). In essence, Frege's concern was the same as that of earlier philosophers like Aristotle who struggled with the untidiness, so to speak, of natural language as a means of expressing 'tidy', coherent arguments. Clearly, though, in natural language, logic is not paramount, but conveying information is. And speakers know that *the Nile* and *earth's longest river* actually convey different types of information, even if they refer to the same geographical feature. Frege's solution to the problem therefore was to make a distinction in natural language between the actual thing being referred to – the **reference** (here, a particular stretch of water in Africa) – and any possible way of referring to it – the **sense**. Frege's idea – which captures something central about how meaning works – has proved influential and useful in modern semantics, although terms like **denotation** and **connotation**, or **cognitive** and **affective meaning** are sometimes used instead.

Frege, then, sought to explain the way meaning is constructed in a word (or expression) by making the distinction between reference and sense. As we saw in Chapter 2, the structuralist ideas of Ferdinand de Saussure, introduced in 1916 in his posthumous *Course in General Linguistics*, offered another angle on this issue by looking at the composition of the linguistic sign, made up, as you may recall, from a mental concept (the signified element) and the sound image or signifier. In his framework, the meaning of signs is delimited by their relationship to each other. In the field of **lexical semantics**, this idea has often been explored by looking at **sense relations**, such as those found in **antonyms** – opposites such as *big* and *small*, *rich* and *poor* – and in word group membership, where a hierarchical structure exists. *Carrot* for example is a member (or **hyponym**) of the category *vegetable* (its **hypernym**). **Synonyms** also provide some interesting food for thought. In everyday terms, synonyms are words of equivalent meaning (as crossword puzzlers know), but from a linguist's point of view there are no true synonyms in a language. Why would you have two words occupying exactly the same position in the language's lexical system? Instead, synonyms may be defined as words that are sometimes, but not always, interchangeable. For instance, *faith* and *trust* could both occur in *They put their ___ in their leader*, but only *trust* can fill the gap in *The leader betrayed their ___*. Explaining and categorising these subtle differences between word meanings present considerable challenges for lexicographers and theorists alike.

This shift towards looking at words not in isolation but in conjunction with related words was also expressed in the notion of the **semantic field**, usually attributed to the German linguist Jost Trier who published a paper on the subject in 1931. Trier proposes that the lexicon (the set of words in a language) is divided into semantic fields, and it is within these that conceptually related words acquire their precise meanings. For linguists, semantic fields provide a useful way of comparing languages since a specific word may have no counterpart in another language but the semantic field to which it belongs almost certainly will. Here is a nice example given by the Danish linguist and structuralist Louis Hjelmslev (1943/1961, p. 54) in which he compares words in the semantic field of trees (and you may like to consider how the English words *tree*, *wood* and *forest* would line up in this comparison):

Danish	German	French
skov	Wald	forêt
	Holz	bois
træ	Baum	arbre

Our understanding of word meanings, it is argued, is enhanced by our knowledge of such categories: we think of words in groups rather than as random, isolated entities. Anthropologists have also found this approach useful when studying the languages of indigenous populations. A comparison of colour terms, for instance, has provided some interesting data for the claim that our language shapes our view of the world (something we will explore in the next chapter).

The components of meaning

Word meanings may be best illuminated when related words are placed side by side but there is a long tradition of defining words by analysing whatever it is they actually refer to. Medieval scholars were taught to define words in this way as part of the all-important discipline of logic. Only through such careful analysis of meaning could clear, logical argument proceed. Definitions were therefore based on identifying similarities and differences, starting by assigning the entity to which the word referred (its **referent**) to its type, or genus, and then determining what distinguishes it from other members of the same genus. So *human* and *pig* were similar in being 'animal' and 'mortal', but distinguished by the fact that a human is 'rational' and 'capable of laughter', while a pig is 'irrational' and 'able to grunt'. This method of analysis was employed for many centuries and was valued by philosophers. However, the seventeenth-century philosopher John Locke was somewhat sceptical. In his *Essay Concerning Human Understanding* – where he writes extensively about meanings – he is dismissive of the attempts by fellow philosophers to organise linguistic signs in such a way as to reflect their perception of an organised and hierarchical world. He sees no point in 'this whole mystery of genera and species' (Locke, 1690, III.iii.9) and offers the common-sense observation that 'languages are not always so made according to the rules of logic' (ibid., III.iii.10).

Nevertheless, by the twentieth century linguists were still seeking a systematic method to analyse word meanings and to give semantics scientific credibility. A new approach emerged in what has come to be known as **componential analysis**. In this approach a word is broken down into its **semantic components** and these are used to establish its meaning by comparison with the components of other words. We saw in the previous chapter how members of the Prague Circle used distinctive features to analyse and classify phonemes. The basis of this approach was a binary analysis, in which a feature was marked to be either present or absent for a particular sound. In this method, the phoneme was characterised as the sum of its distinguishing features. It was not difficult to transfer this principal from phonemes, then to inflectional features (the *-s* in *she walks*, for example, is [+singular, +present tense, +third person]) and then finally to word meanings. Here is a simple illustration of how some related words might be presented:

	human	adult	male	female
girl	+	−	−	+
boy	+	−	+	−
child	+	−	+/−	+/−
woman	+	+	−	+
man	+	+	+	−

The semantic features of 'human', 'adult' and so on, are sufficient here to define and distinguish the five related words. The approach fits neatly with Saussure's structuralist theory of linguistic signs as part of a closed system where the meaning of one sign is defined by its relationship to other signs, and demonstrates how that closed system might operate. Several advantages have emerged from this approach. One of the benefits is as a means of explaining nonsensical combinations. To draw again on Chomsky's example, something cannot be both *green* and *colorless* because of the +/– conflict in the semantic feature of 'colour'. (You might like to think about how the other apparent contradictions could be explained using this method of analysis.) Linguists working in the field of foreign language teaching have also found this method helpful for explaining some of the subtle differences between apparent equivalents. (And even before linguists started using it, the semantic component approach had already been employed by anthropologists to help them understand cultural differences, for example in kinship relations.)

Of course, it is not difficult to identify some of the possible shortcomings of this model. For one thing, despite the mathematical aspect of plus or minus, it still utilises words as a means to define words – a perennial problem in semantics. (This is why some linguists and philosophers have resorted to symbols to express observations about meaning and meaning relations.) Furthermore, the method lends itself to content words like nouns, verbs and adjectives, but is less amenable to grammatical words such as *if*, *because*, *since*, although this method has been applied to them. Binary features like these were originally intended for the analysis of phonemes, of which any language contains only a limited, fixed number. (English has about 45, depending on which accent you take as your benchmark.) Distinguishing between 45 phonemes is possible. Making distinctions between thousands and thousands of words seems virtually impossible, however careful your taxonomy. A binary feature of '+/– animate' could provide a useful starting category but imagine the difficulty of identifying semantic features for all inanimate things. However, this difficulty has not prevented some linguists from proposing the existence of universal semantic features (again, an idea which can be traced back through the centuries as the medieval example reveals), a possible way of uniting all human languages.

Fuzziness proves useful

Dictionaries tend to lull us into believing that all words have clearly defined meanings, possibly determined by an analysis of their semantic components, but is this exactly how our minds store word definitions? Are our minds really like dictionaries? For a possible answer to this question, linguists looked to an idea that became prominent among mathematicians in the 1960s, that of fuzzy logic. Fuzzy logic rejects the use of binary, plus-or-minus analysis in favour of a gradation from 0.0 to 1.0. This concept was first taken up by philosophers and scientists, the latter developing many practical applications inspired by this idea. (Even washing machines benefited from it!) For linguists, grading seemed to deal effectively with the 'fuzziness' of words like *tall*, *happy*, *talented*, whose meanings are relative rather than absolute. Those who were particularly interested in this approach were **cognitive linguists**, who were chiefly concerned with how the linguistic categories we create reflect our understanding and perception of the world around us. Word meanings are therefore very fertile territory for this group of researchers.

A fascinating paper of 1973 by the American linguist George Lakoff provides some insights into how 'fuzziness' works in natural human language. He begins by observing that:

> students of language, especially psychologists and linguistic philosophers, have long been attuned to the fact that natural language concepts have vague boundaries and fuzzy edges and that, consequently, natural language sentences will very often be neither true, nor false, nor nonsensical, but rather true to a certain extent, true in certain respects and false in other respects. (Lakoff, 1973, p. 458)

Lakoff acknowledges his debt to Azerbaijani mathematician Lofti Zadeh and his fuzzy set theory (1965), and builds on the (unpublished) 1971 research of the American psychologist Eleanor Rosch, who demonstrated how members of a set are not equal but are members to differing degrees. For instance, through an experiment based on the perceptions of her own students she showed that robins are central members of the set of birds, followed by eagles, then chickens, ducks and geese, next penguins and pelicans, and lastly bats, who are very marginal members (ignoring their zoological status as mammals). Lakoff is concerned in his paper with hedges – expressions we use to qualify propositions, such as *sort of*, *largely*, *actually* – and he shows how these are used systematically to express a speaker's perceptions about set membership. Here are just two of his examples:

1. *A robin is sort of a bird*
2. *A penguin is sort of a bird*

Example 1 would seem to be a false proposition since a robin is clearly a bird, while Example 2 feels true because a penguin is a less central example of the bird set. Of course, a speaker's perception of the truth or otherwise of these examples depends on their own perception of the bird set hierarchy. Lakoff's findings led him also to propose the existence of **semantic prototypes** – typical set members against which we judge the degree of membership for other members in our mental fuzzy sets.

Semantic change

The nineteenth-century philologists may not have been particularly interested in semantic change but in 1897 an attempt was made to rectify this situation by the French philologist, Michel Bréal, who is generally regarded as the founder of modern semantics. His *Essay on Semantics* (*Essai de Sémantique*) is a response to any false notion that semantic change, in contrast to phonological change, is random or unmotivated. Bréal sets out to find the universal principles underpinning semantic change and even formulates laws just as the philologists had done, although these laws were applicable to language in general, not to a specific language or family of languages.

The continuing influence of Bréal during the following decades is reflected in the degree of interest in semantic change still evident in the early 1930s when the Swedish philologist Gustaf Stern published his *Meaning and Change of Meaning*. With the aim of establishing 'a theoretically tenable and practically workable system of classification comprising all known types of sense-change' (Stern, 1931, p. 4), this substantial work identifies a core set of seven processes by which semantic change occurs. Stern makes a clear distinction between his first process – **substitution** – and the other six on the basis that this is caused by external rather than linguistic factors. Stern offers an example of substitution, which takes on a new dimension over eighty years on:

> The word *ship*, at present, may have meanings that were unknown at a time when *steam-ships*, *motor-ships*, *airships*, etc., were not yet invented; and it will no doubt go on gathering new meanings in future, as new types of ship are built. (ibid., p. 166)

As for Stern's other six categories, these changes are not caused by external factors but are the result of intentional or unintentional linguistic behaviour on the part of the speakers in question. Examples include **shortening** (*private soldier* becomes simply *private*) and **transfer**, a metaphorical use which takes place on the basis of similarity 'as when *bed* is used for the foundation of a steam-engine or other machine, because it supports the machine as a bed supports a person lying on it' (ibid., p. 168).

Categories of semantic change like these are characteristic of other discussions of semantic change from this period. Leonard Bloomfield's 1933 book *Language*, for example, contains a short chapter on the subject in which he lists nine processes of meaning change identified by 'earlier students' as well as reviewing the work of some of his colleagues. This list begins with **narrowing** (*meat*, for example, used to refer to food in general) and **widening** (the Middle English *bridde* – 'bird' – referred only to a baby bird, but now refers to any bird) (Bloomfield, 1933, p. 426). Bloomfield recognises the difficulty of studying semantic change because it is difficult to identify the instances of use in which change occurred. This is particularly true for older examples, where supposition must play a large part in trying to determine how change came about, so the task for the linguist is made somewhat easier when dealing with more recent examples of semantic change.

After this flurry of activity in the first few decades of the twentieth century, semantic change seemed to be overlooked for a while, partly perhaps because of the difficulty of tracing it accurately, but almost certainly because the interest in historical linguistics was eclipsed by the growing concern with structural and therefore synchronic linguistics, ushered in by the ideas of Saussure. The study of semantic change has now been revitalised by contemporary researchers in the field of historical linguistics, who regard it as a central part of their research. What is more, perhaps prompted by other developments in linguistics which we will consider later, the need to consider the context in which semantic change occurs has been fully embraced. As John Lyons points out in his substantial 1977 work on semantics, a central principle is that 'the history of vocabulary cannot be studied independently of the social, economic, and cultural history of the people' (Lyons, 1977, p. 620). Those philologists who recognised the influence of external aspects in their own work on sound changes would have approved.

Meaning is left out in the cold

Although Leonard Bloomfield was happy enough to write about aspects of semantic *change* in his 1933 work *Language*, when it comes to incorporating meaning into a model of how language works he sees nothing but difficulty. This is because, whatever we might assume about meaning based on the effect of an utterance upon the person who hears it, very little can actually be verified through observation, a principle very dear to Bloomfield's behaviourist heart. In other words, the study of meaning is not a scientific undertaking, and for this reason cannot be dealt with convincingly as part of the science of linguistics. 'The statement of meanings is therefore the weak point in language-study', remarks Bloomfield, 'and will remain so until human knowledge advances very far beyond its present state' (Bloomfield, 1933, p. 140). Bloomfield's position was enough to deter many of his colleagues from attempting to tackle meaning, and it was left out in the cold by theorists for the best part of three decades.

When Noam Chomsky published *Syntactic Structures* in 1957, he too was clear about the position of semantics within language theory, although he defined the problem differently from Bloomfield. Providing an interesting comment on the status of semantics at the time, he remarked:

> There is no aspect of linguistic study more subject to confusion and more in need of clear and careful formulation than that which deals with the points of connections between syntax and semantics. (Chomsky, 1957, p. 93)

For Chomsky, however, the question was not, 'How can you construct a grammar with no appeal to meaning' but simply 'How can you construct a grammar?' (ibid.). Although Chomsky goes on to offer some thoughts on the dependency of grammar on meaning which had been claimed by others, he maintains his assertion (which we considered at the start of the chapter) that 'grammar is autonomous and independent of meaning' (ibid., p. 17) and proceeds to construct a model with syntax as its core component.

A turning point for meaning as a crucial element in a theory of grammar came in 1963 when the American scholars Jerrold Katz and Jerry Fodor published a paper entitled 'The Structure of a Semantic Theory'. Katz and Fodor, like Chomsky, were based at the Massachusetts Institute of Technology, so they were familiar with *Syntactic Structures* and the effect it had had on the linguistic community. Like Chomsky, they adopted the position that the aim of any theory of natural language is to account for what they term the **projection problem**: how can a speaker produce and understand an infinite number of possible sentences? In the previous chapter we saw how Chomsky offered an answer to this problem by proposing a generative grammar based on transformations. Since semantics played no significant part in Chomsky's theory, for Katz and Fodor this meant that the projection problem had only been partly solved. Only the inclusion of a semantic element would complete the picture: 'semantics takes over the explanation of the speaker's ability to produce and understand new sentences at the point where grammar leaves off', they wrote (Katz and Fodor, 1963, pp. 172–3). They also lamented the neglect of semantics by theorists in general. Although meanings and meaning relations had received plenty of attention (as we saw in an earlier section), semantics was suffering from 'the lack of an adequate theory to organize, systematize, and generalize these facts' (ibid., p. 170). Not only this, but it was the meaning of sentences, not just words, that needed accounting for.

To illustrate the need for a semantic theory to complete the theoretical account of natural language, the authors present an unlikely, but nevertheless revealing scenario (ibid., p. 175) in which various people – some being fluent speakers of English, the others having only a knowledge of its grammatical structures – are sent anonymous letters containing one simple sentence only, such as *The paint is silent*. (It is hard not to imagine that Chomsky's *colorless green ideas* was in their minds when they composed this example.) Those recipients who possessed grammatical knowledge alone would recognise that the sentence was grammatically acceptable, but only the fluent speakers, who possessed semantic knowledge too, would be able to identify this as an anomalous, nonsensical sentence. This illustrates, then, why a semantic component is necessary to make any theory of language complete: linguistic competence could only be fully understood if a speaker's semantic knowledge is accounted for.

Linguists at war

Katz and Fodor's paper was not a theory itself, but an explanation of why a semantic theory was needed and what it should be able to account for. When they wrote it, they probably had little inkling of the rivalry and dissent it was about to unleash in the linguistic community. Chomsky's next major work, *Aspects of the Theory of Syntax*, published in 1965, included (rather reluctantly, one senses) a semantic component, which was applied once the syntactic structure of an utterance had been generated. This did not satisfy many of his fellow linguists, who had adopted the view that semantics, not syntax, should be at the core of the generative process. These generative semanticists steadily gathered momentum, until an almost inevitable rift opened up between Chomsky and his dissenters, several of whom were former colleagues or students.

Matters seemed to come to a head in 1969 when the various theorists attended a conference at the University of Texas on 'The Goals of Linguistic Theory'. War was waged through the presentation of various papers during which the linguists fired their shots at each other, generative grammarians against generative semanticists. And, according to some accounts, enmity was not confined to theoretical issues, but became personal. The 'linguistics wars', as they have come to be known, dragged on for several years: academic publications and university lecture theatres provided the battlefields. A truce was never really declared. Chomsky came out of the war scarred but ready to fight another day, while the wounded supporters of generative semantics began to look for new ways of promoting the centrality of meaning in linguistic theory.

One of the most interesting developments in semantics at that time is illustrated by the career of the American scholar, Barbara Partee, whose first area of study was mathematics. After graduating in 1961, she went to study at MIT with Chomsky and other generative grammarians in an environment where 'syntax was the center of the universe', as she describes it in her career retrospective (Partee, 2005, p. 4). Just as the linguistics wars were getting underway, she finished her work at MIT and moved west (in 1965) to work at UCLA. It was here she met the influential mathematician and philosopher, Richard Montague. Montague's belief was that there was no fundamental difference between a natural language and an artificial one, and it was therefore possible to create a semantic theory of natural language using the formulations and symbols of mathematical logic. This would enable meaning to be modelled as accurately and rigorously as Chomsky was attempting to model syntax, and for syntax and semantics to be treated as connected aspects of language. With this purpose in mind, Montague developed additional layers of logical analysis to account for examples which transformational grammar could not easily explain, such as the difference between *Mary wants to win* and *everyone wants to win* ('Mary' wants Mary to win, but 'everyone' does not want everyone to win) to use Partee's example (ibid., pp. 14–15). Sadly and shockingly, Montague was murdered in 1971, but his legacy of formal semantics (sometimes known as **Montague semantics**), developed after his death by Partee and others, remains an important one.

Another new area to emerge was **cognitive linguistics**, and one of its founders was George Lakoff, a veteran of the linguistics wars. (We looked at some of his work on word meanings earlier in this chapter.) Cognitive linguistics is a human-centred approach to language, and its aim is to explore the relationship between language and our perceptions of the world we inhabit. Meaning is central to this approach, and the autonomy of syntax is completely rejected as a theoretical position. Another principle is that our knowledge of language develops from using and experiencing it. In this respect, cognitive linguistics has a link with another field which developed in the 1970s, namely **functional linguistics**, which places language use at the heart of its theory. This brings us to another important consideration in the construction of meaning, the fact that meaning is often determined by the purpose for which it is used in a particular communicative context. In their paper on semantic theory, Katz and Fodor went as far as to say that the settings in which language was used should not be taken into account when constructing a theory of meaning, and no serious attention was paid to purpose and context in generative theories. Over in Europe, however, a movement which gave prominence to these aspects for understanding meaning had already started to take shape ...

The linguistic turn

Of all the thinkers who appear in this book, one of the most fascinating is the Vienna-born (1889) philosopher Ludwig Wittgenstein. He grew up in a wealthy, well-connected family but his life was dogged by depression and three of his brothers tragically committed suicide. He was proclaimed a genius by his fellow philosopher Bertrand Russell, but his published contribution to scholarship was relatively slight and he constantly struggled with the fear that he would not be understood. In between academic work, he took jobs that gave him the shelter of obscurity – a gardener, a hospital porter, a teacher in a remote village school. Nevertheless, he ended his career as a professor at the University of Cambridge. He died in Cambridge in 1951.

Wittgenstein's contribution to linguistics springs from his concern about the role of language in philosophical thinking. His ideas started to emerge in his somewhat enigmatic 1921 work *Logisch-Philosophische Abhandlung.* (The English translation was published the following year under the Latin title *Tractatus Logico-Philosophicus.*) In the *Tractatus* Wittgenstein observes that philosophers create philosophical problems for themselves because they don't understand how ordinary language works: to him, they seemed overly concerned with declarative sentences that made statements about the world which could be shown to be true or false, while they overlooked sentences which took other forms (such as questions) or whose meanings were not straightforward (that were ironic, for example) or verifiable. 'Most questions and propositions of the philosophers result from the fact that we do not understand the logic of our language', he wrote (Wittgenstein, 1922, 4.003).

Wittgenstein's ideas about language are developed far more in his posthumous *Philosophical Investigations.* Published originally in German in 1953, it is a collection of notes and fragments, with his ideas sometimes presented in dialogue form. Its primary theme is an idea from the *Tractatus* about how philosophers use (or misuse) language. Their search for independent meanings and definitions is fruitless, because meaning is only revealed through use. He demonstrates this concept that 'meaning is use' through a discussion of the process by which children learn the meanings of words – not simply by having designated objects named for them, but by participating in 'language-games' (Wittgenstein, 1953, Part I, §7), the various language-based activities of everyday life, such as playing with certain toys or buying something in a shop. Wittgenstein also points out that our understanding of meaning is typically based on a network of uses, not on a single example. So, for instance, the word 'game' can apply to a variety of uses and examples. Experience teaches us what the meaning of 'game' encompasses: we cannot rely on a simple definition. So the different uses of 'game' (such as *ball game, game of chess, Olympic games*) will overlap – Wittgenstein talks about **family resemblances** (ibid., §67) – but not necessarily contain a common feature.

Wittgenstein's ideas about language and meaning, and their relevance to the musings of philosophers, are credited with bringing about what is known as the **linguistic turn**. Wittgenstein effectively directed philosophers to pay more attention to language itself as the vehicle of philosophical thought. Understand language, and many philosophical problems would be solved. We can see the germ of this approach in the work of Gottlob Frege, with his notion of sense and reference that we considered earlier. Wittgenstein's influence on thinking about semantics has been significant, particularly for psycholinguists exploring how the mind processes meaning, and the notion of meaning being inextricably linked to language in use has proved a powerful one. In fact, even as Wittgenstein's ideas were taking hold in Cambridge, a parallel move towards language in use was developing not so far away among philosophers in Oxford.

Ordinary language philosophy

In 1955 the Oxford philosopher John L Austin gave a series of lectures at America's Harvard University in which he expounded some of the ideas he had been working on for a while. These ideas related to his belief that, if philosophers really wanted to understand meaning, then everyday language should be the focus of their attention. Not only this, but the meanings of everyday usage provided a means of understanding human experience of the world. With reference to the 'truth-conditional' approach to meaning much loved by philosophers, he remarked at the beginning of his first lecture:

> It was for too long the assumption of philosophers that the business of a 'statement' can only be to 'describe' some state of affairs, or to 'state some fact', which it must do either truly or falsely. (Austin, 1962, p. 1)

As a powerful counterexample to the type of statements which philosophers traditionally dealt with, Austin presented a type of utterance which is completely embedded in the context in which it occurs. He called these utterances **performatives**. These, he points out, cannot be claimed to be true or false, because they do not describe or report something. Instead, they carry out an action in the real world. Austin offers a range of examples, but here is a more recent one from when Queen Elizabeth II opened the 2012 Olympic Games:

> 'I declare open the games of London celebrating the 30th Olympiad of the modern era.'

This utterance is not a statement which can be shown to be true or false. Instead, the act of saying the verb *declare open* in the first person and in the present tense brings about the actual opening of the Olympic games. Performatives are not used just on special occasions but in everyday life too: *I promise, We apologise for …, We wish you a merry Christmas, I'm warning you* are some examples.

Austin's work on performatives (which, although interesting, make up only a tiny proportion of our total utterances) soon led him to a broader framework for looking at how everything we say is tied to the context in which we say it. In his theory of **speech acts,** Austin identified three aspects which come into play in spoken interaction: the process of uttering something meaningful is a **locutionary** act. Any function or intention behind the utterance (performative or otherwise) gives it its **illocutionary force**, while its effect on the audience is **perlocutionary**. So even a simple everyday utterance such as *It's cold in here* could have the illocutionary force of asking the hearer to close the window and the perlocutionary effect of getting them to do so. With this new focus on language use in the real world, it is not surprising that Austin and his colleagues came to be known as philosophers of 'ordinary language'.

Cooperation and relevance

One of Austin's students at Oxford in the 1930s was Paul Grice (H P Grice), who was to go on to become another influential figure in ordinary language philosophy, eventually taking his expertise from Oxford to the USA, where he spent the last 20 years of his life. He was less convinced about the weaknesses of philosophical language, but he certainly saw the value of studying ordinary language in order to gain insights into meaning and how it works. Grice, however, felt that an important element in the construction of meaning had been given insufficient attention, namely the role of the hearer in interpreting a speaker's intended message. In philosophical terms, it was assumed that sentences (or propositions) had absolute, literal meanings but this was clearly not true in everyday conversation, where there was a potential distinction to be made between what someone said and what they intended to happen as a result of their utterance (as Austin had demonstrated). But how exactly did the hearer know how to interpret the utterance? Consider this exchange between teenage brothers, both cycling fanatics:

> Ben: Are you coming out training?
> Dan: The Tour de France is about to start.
> Ben: Cool. Let's go out this evening instead.

Ben has clearly understood Dan's response to his question even though he hasn't received a direct answer, but on face value, the literal meaning of Dan's response has no semantic relationship with Ben's original question. To explain this apparent mismatch, Grice proposed a **cooperative principle** (Grice, 1967/1989, p. 26) based on assumptions (or maxims) about the way speakers behave in linguistic interactions – for example, that they will make relevant contributions and say enough to convey their intended meaning. This can be demonstrated by fleshing out the exchange to suggest what is understood (in addition to the knowledge the brothers share about the Tour de France, a major annual cycling event) but not actually said in each of the turns:

> Ben: Are you coming out training *right now on our bikes*?
> Dan: The Tour de France is about to start *right now and it is live on television. You know that we both like to watch it and if we go out training on our bikes right now we will miss the live coverage.*
> Ben: Cool. *I'm happy to watch The Tour de France right now.* Let's go out *training on our bikes* this evening instead.

The example illustrates how much of our spoken interaction is underspecified: we habitually say far less than we could because we rely on others to fill in the gaps. (Imagine how tedious conversation would be if we always had to state what we regard as obvious.) This economy is possible because of what Grice termed **conversational implicature** – the way we imply meaning on the assumption that our listeners will be aware of this, and able to infer what remains unsaid.

Grice's theory of conversational cooperation and implicature has proved an influential one. First and foremost, it sets out to explain something fundamental about the way human beings construct and infer meaning in their everyday interactions. Furthermore, Grice suggested that this behaviour was not the result of social conventions (such as saying *please* and *thank you*) but was psychologically motivated and could be observed in non-linguistic situations, such as two people silently doing a jigsaw together. We also need to remember that Grice was a philosopher, very aware of the debate taking place among philosophers about the meaning and use of natural language within their discipline. Grice's theory allows a distinction to be made between the use of natural language as a context-free logical/philosophical tool and its use by ordinary speakers in everyday contexts.

Grice first presented the ideas we have just been considering in 1967 when, like John Austin 12 years before him, he was invited to give the annual William James Lectures at Harvard. More recently, his ideas have been given a new slant by researchers Dan Sperber and Deirdre Wilson (a former student of Grice) in their **relevance theory**. This sees language in use as a contrast to a **code model** of language in which the total meaning is transparent and fully specified by the actual utterance with nothing needing to be inferred. (Examples of fully transparent statements might include *human babies spend a lot of time sleeping* or *the earth orbits the sun*.) Instead, the context of utterance, the intentions of the participants and the knowledge they share all play a part in interpreting utterance meaning. In Sperber and Wilson's theory, a conversational participant is regarded as wanting to make relevant contributions wherever possible while assuming the same to be true of all other participants. Once relevant meaning has been detected, then a participant will stop trying to process the meaning of what they hear. Relevance theory is based on two principles of relevance, identified by its creators as: a First (or Cognitive) Principle that 'human cognition tends to be geared to the maximisation of relevance', and a Second (or Communicative) Principle that 'every act of ostensive communication communicates a presumption of its own optimal relevance' (Sperber and Wilson, 1995, pp. 260–1). Again we can see how a theory of meaning involves some consideration of mental processes, and particularly of aspects of human behaviour and understanding which are not primarily linguistic.

The birth of pragmatics

In looking at the ideas of Austin and Grice, and then the more recent work of Sperber and Wilson, we have effectively witnessed the birth of what is now known as **pragmatics**. The precise scope and definition of this field of study is not entirely agreed upon, but in simple terms pragmatics is the study of meaning in context, and aims to account for those aspects of meaning which are not conveyed by linguistic content alone. The idea of a pragmatic study of language had certainly been gathering momentum in Europe as early as the 1930s, but it was Austin and his successors who demonstrated how context could be incorporated into a theoretical framework. Although the study of pragmatics has come a long way since then, the relationship of semantics to pragmatics is not entirely agreed upon. Are the two fields distinct, overlapping, or is pragmatics a sub-branch of semantics? The fact that linguists cannot agree on the answer to this question is, more than anything, a question about the nature of meaning itself.

Approaches to discourse

As pragmatics has expanded and been fully absorbed into linguistic research, several aspects of language in use have become part of its core focus. These include implicature and the speech acts we have already discussed as well as aspects such as **deixis**, which is concerned with the interpretation of time, place and person references. A request such as *Can you help me move this heavy box to the opposite corner of the room later today?* is highly dependent on the context of utterance to determine the meaning of *you*, *me*, *this*, *opposite* and *later today*. The linguist Stephen Levinson makes a nice observation about examples like these when he comments:

> The facts of deixis should act as a constant reminder to theoretical linguists of the simple but immensely important fact that natural languages are primarily designed, so to speak, for use in face-to-face interaction, and thus there are limits to the extent to which they can be analysed without taking this into account. (Levinson, 1983, p. 54)

Of course, the study of meaning is not confined to single, isolated sentences or utterances. The way in which longer stretches of text – discourse – are constructed has also become an important area of research in the field of pragmatics. Scholars have always been interested in analysing certain types of discourse – speeches, poetry, historical accounts and so on – and discussing how they should be interpreted. What has been significant in the last 40 years or so is the way in which everyday conversation – assisted by advances in recording equipment – has been elevated to previously unimaginable heights as a worthwhile area of investigation. Considerable work has been done on the analysis of data from all kinds of interactional situations in order to establish how exactly participants piece together stretches of organised, meaningful talk. Many interesting patterns and strategies have been revealed, for example how talk is managed when there are several participants, or how we bring conversations to an end. It seems fitting that the manner in which we weave these complex social interactions should at last be given the attention that this primary manifestation of language surely deserves.

Hand-in-hand with studying the contexts in which language is 'performed' has developed a concern to identify the attitudes and values conveyed in discourse. These are often connected with issues of power and inequality, as well as social and cultural beliefs. This approach – **critical discourse analysis** – aims to uncover those aspects of meaning which are less overt, in order to reveal the ideological position from which the discourse is composed (or interpreted) and explain how language has been used to embed this ideology. The goal of critical discourse analysis then is 'to show how society and discourse shape each other' as the British linguist Norman Fairclough put it in his introduction to a work on the related subject of critical language awareness (Fairclough, 1992/2013, p. 9). In theory, almost any instance of language in use is underpinned by social or cultural values, but Fairclough was particularly interested in how power relationships are revealed through the grammatical and semantic selections people make. His seminal (1989) work on *Language and Power* includes examples from public information leaflets, teacher/student interactions, advertising and news reporting. Significantly, Fairclough devotes an entire chapter to 'the discourse of Thatcherism', in which he critiques an interview given on BBC radio in 1985 by the then-Prime Minister, Margaret Thatcher, examining her language use from both a socio-political perspective as well as that of a female prime minister (the first in Great Britain) in a male-dominated institution.

The study of discourse, then, has presented a wealth of new ways for linguists to study meaning. These in turn have revealed more of the complexity of meaning, pervading as it does every level of language structure and at the same time gaining additional dimensions from the contexts of language use and from the users themselves. If this is apparent for any one language, then how much more is this thrown into relief in the process of transferring meaning from one language to another. In the next section, we will take one final, brief excursion into the past to see how scholars have regarded the intricate art of translation.

'The curse of the confusion of tongues'

'The curse of the confusion of tongues' is how the eminent seventeenth-century scholar John Wilkins described a problem that was occupying the minds of many of his contemporaries. As we saw in Chapter 4, there was a general belief at this time that the many languages of the world were the result of God's displeasure with the human race in seeking to build a tower – the Tower of Babel – which reached to heaven. To show his displeasure with the human race whose 'one language' had enabled such a collaboration, he caused linguistic confusion among them and dispersed the over-ambitious population to different parts of the earth. The consequence of this supposed dispersal was becoming even more apparent in Wilkins' time due to the amount of contact people were having with speakers of languages other than their own. More extensive travel and commerce, along with the decline in Latin as a *lingua franca*, meant that the need to learn and understand foreign languages had increased significantly.

One response to this situation was the production of bilingual dictionaries, of which a considerable number were being published at this time, in addition to the wealth of monolingual dictionaries which were appearing by then across Europe. Scholars had become well aware though of the problems translation presented, something that had been made apparent through the many classical texts which had been translated during the Renaissance of the previous two centuries. John Locke remarked in his 1690 *Essay* how anyone with a 'moderate skill in different languages' would be aware of how many of the words in one language 'have not any that answer them in another' (Locke, 1690, III.v.8). He goes on:

> if we look a little more nearly into this matter, and exactly compare different languages, we shall find that, though they have words which in translations and dictionaries are supposed to answer one another, yet there is scarce one often amongst the names of complex ideas … that stands for the same precise idea. (ibid.)

Concerns like these had, earlier in the century, prompted various scholars to circumvent natural language altogether by designing artificial languages. John Wilkins – a theologian and natural scientist who held prominent positions at both Oxford and Cambridge Universities, and within the Church of England – was one of these. Such constructed languages were hugely popular around this time and have in fact remained so both for philosophical and more practical purposes. Wilkins' universal language was not intended primarily for philosophers (although he did have them in mind), but as a solution to the increasing problem of cross-lingual communication. He begins by dividing the universe into 40 categories, then subdividing these according to types (the 'genera and species' approach which Locke had disparaged, as we saw earlier in this chapter). Each category is assigned a symbol (or character), which can be modified to represent its subcategories. Furthermore, because Wilkins intended his universal language to be spoken, he assigns a sound to each symbol. So the sound for 'flame' – 'deba' – is generated from 'deb' – 'a fire' – which itself is generated from 'de' meaning 'an element' (one of the original 40 categories) (Wilkins, 1668, p. 415).

Wilkins published his universal language in 1668 as *An Essay towards a Real Character, and a Philosophical Language*. Publication was delayed because his manuscript, while in the possession of his printers in London, was partly destroyed during the Great Fire of 1666 and Wilkins had to rewrite the lost material. History does not relate whether Wilkins viewed this destruction as a sign of divine displeasure at his attempt to reverse the confusion of tongues. In any case, his language was not destined for success although it remains a fascinating example of a constructed language.

Since the seventeenth century, many more artificial languages have been constructed, either for use by philosophers, logicians or mathematicians (computer programming languages are obvious examples) or in the hope of facilitating international communication. Esperanto, introduced in 1887, is probably the best known example, and has been remarkably successful. Meanwhile, linguists have continued to tackle the problems presented by translation of one language into another, the problems that Locke identified over 300 years ago. In the last 50 years or so, this has given rise to another fascinating subfield (or perhaps close cousin) of linguistics – **translation studies**. Within this field, linguists grapple with the challenges of translation, particularly within the context of written texts, which often prove a very different undertaking from the real-time translation of spontaneous speech. There is now a general acceptance that precise equivalence is rarely possible, and often not even desirable. Instead, consideration needs to be given to factors such as the purpose of the text, how cultural differences might affect the translation (in terms of, say, humour or the use of metaphor) and also what ethical issues might arise, whether in the representation of ideas or people, or in terms of the translator's responsibilities towards the original author of the piece. Clearly, what might be termed the *re*construction of meaning demands considerable skills on the part of translators. Whether the 'confusion of tongues' should still be regarded as a curse for humanity is an interesting question for all of us.

Suggestions for further reading and research

On aspects of semantics and semantic theory

Cruse, Alan (2011) *Meaning in Language: An Introduction to Semantics and Pragmatics*, 3rd edn (Oxford: Oxford University Press)

A highly readable introduction, with plenty of examples and exercises.

Evans, Vyvyan and Melanie C Green (2006) *Cognitive Linguistics: An Introduction* (Edinburgh: Edinburgh University Press)

A comprehensive introduction to this field, with a substantial section of the book devoted to cognitive semantics.

Harris, Randy Allen (1993) *The Linguistics Wars* (New York: Oxford University Press)

An account of the 'battles' that took place in the 1960s and 1970s between Chomsky and those who wanted to see semantics given a more prominent position in grammatical theory.

Jackendoff, Ray (2002) *Foundations of Language: Brain, Meaning, Grammar, Evolution* (Oxford: Oxford University Press)

A detailed consideration of research in the closing decades of the twentieth century, this important work also offers a theory of semantics that draws on philosophical, psychological and social perspectives.

Lakoff, George and Mark Johnson (1980) *Metaphors We Live By* (Chicago: Chicago University Press)

An important and influential work exploring how metaphors pervade language, shaping our thinking and behaviour.

Nerlich, Brigitte (1992) *Semantic Theories in Europe, 1830–1930* (Amsterdam: John Benjamins)

A book aimed at revealing how semantics, far from being neglected in this period, was the subject of some interesting and forward-looking ideas.

Ogden, Charles and Ivor A Richards (1923) *The Meaning of Meaning* (New York: Harcourt, Brace & World)

The authors present a theory of signs which remained influential for some decades after its publication. The edition also contains as an appendix the highly regarded paper 'The problem of meaning in primitive languages' by the Polish-born anthropologist Bronislaw Malinowski.

Zimmerman, Thomas Ede and Wolfgang Sternefeld (2013) *Introduction to Semantics: An Essential Guide to the Composition of Meaning* (Berlin: Walter de Gruyter)

An introduction to contemporary work in the field, full of interesting examples to help the reader understand what is a challenging but nevertheless fascinating subject.

On pragmatics

Chapman, Siobhan (2011) *Pragmatics* (Basingstoke: Palgrave Macmillan)

An excellent introduction to pragmatics, part of the Palgrave Modern Linguistics series.

Horn, Laurence and Gregory Ward (eds) (2003) *Handbook of Pragmatics* (Oxford: Blackwell)

A collection of essays on all the key areas of research in pragmatics.

Searle, John R (1969) *Speech Acts: An Essay in the Philosophy of Language* (Cambridge: Cambridge University Press

Written by one of the second generation of ordinary language philosophers, this important publication builds on Austin's theory of speech acts.

Strawson, Peter (1964) 'Intention and convention in speech acts', in *The Philosophical Review*, vol. 73, pp. 439–60

A discussion by a fellow Oxford philosopher on J L Austin's notions of the illocutionary act and illocutionary force, available at www.jstor.org/stable/2183301 (accessed October 2015).

On philosophical approaches to linguistics

Chapman, Siobhan (2000) *Philosophy for Linguists: An Introduction* (London: Routledge)

A very useful text for linguists who want to know more about philosophy given that 'there is so much philosophy in linguistics', as the author puts it.

Lycan, William G (2008) *Philosophy of Language: A Contemporary Introduction*, 2nd edn (Abingdon: Routledge)

An introduction to the philosophical questions that arise in the study of meaning, and the relationship between language and reality.

On the 'imperfections' of natural language

Eco, Umberto (1995) *The Search for the Perfect Language (Ricerca della lingua perfetta nella cultura europea)* translated by James Fentress (Oxford: Blackwell)

Originally published in Italian in 1993, this is a fascinating history of the way in which humans have dealt with the apparent imperfections of natural language, including a detailed chapter on John Wilkins.

Lewis, Rhodri (2012) *Language, Mind and Nature: Artificial Languages in England from Bacon to Locke* (Cambridge: Cambridge University Press)

A detailed study of the many attempts to create a perfect artificial language in the seventeenth century, and of the cultural context in which these projects took shape.

On the translation of natural languages

Holmes, James S (1972) 'The name and nature of translation studies', in James S Holmes *Translated!: Papers on Literary Translation and Translation Studies*, 2nd edn (Amsterdam: Rodopi, 1988)

This is the seminal paper which is regarded as the foundation for the field of translation studies.

Venuti, Lawrence (ed.) (2012) *The Translation Studies Reader*, 3rd edn (Abingdon, Routledge)

This fascinating collection of writings ranges from the fourth century to the twenty-first.

Useful websites

The International Association for Translation and Intercultural Studies
www.iatis.org/index.php (accessed October 2015)

This website will give you some idea of the extent and range of research activity in this field.

The International Pragmatics Association
http://Ipra.ua.ac.be (accessed October 2015)

Hosted by the University of Antwerp, this website is a useful source of information about research, publications and conferences on pragmatics.

semanticsarchive.net
www.semanticsarchive.net (accessed October 2015)

Supported by the University of California, this large collection of papers on semantics is well worth browsing.

8 The linguistic brain

Thinkers and researchers introduced in this chapter

Early physicians and anatomists:

Hippocrates (c. 460–c. 370 BCE)	Greek physician
Galen of Pergamon (130–c. 200)	Greek physician and philosopher
Andreas Vesalius (1514–64)	Brussels-born anatomist and physician

The founder of the field of phrenology:

Franz Joseph Gall (1758–1828)	German physician and physiologist

Researchers who have contributed to our understanding of the brain in general:

John Hughlings Jackson (1835–1911)	American neurologist
Santiago Ramón y Cajal (1852–1934)	Spanish neuroscientist
Hans Berger (1873–1941)	German neurologist
Juhn Wada (b. 1924)	Japanese–Canadian neurologist

Researchers who have identified parts or functions of the brain associated with language:

Marc Dax (1771–1837)	French neurologist and physician *(left hemisphere dominance)*
Gustave Dax (1815–93)	French physician (son of Marc Dax) *(left hemisphere dominance)*
Paul Broca (1824–80)	French physician and anatomist *(Broca's area)*
Richard Heschl (1824–81)	Austrian anatomist *(Heschl's gyrus)*
Carl Wernicke (1848–1905)	German physician and anatomist *(Wernicke's area)*
Korbinian Brodmann (1866–1918)	German anatomist and neurologist *(Brodmann areas)*
Norman Geschwind (1926–84)	American neurologist *(Geschwind's territory)*
Steven Hillyard (b. 1942)	American neuroscientist *(N400 wave)*
Marta Kutas (b. 1949)	American cognitive scientist and neuroscientist *(N400 wave)*

Researchers and thinkers interested in the relationship between language and thought:

Wilhelm von Humboldt (1767–1835)	German scholar and philosopher
Sigmund Exner (1846–1926)	Austrian physiologist
Edward Sapir (1884–1939)	American linguist and anthropologist
Benjamin Lee Whorf (1897–1941)	American linguist

The functions of the brain

We have already considered (in Chapter 3) the evolution of the organ which is responsible for the processing and production of language – namely, our brain. But the story of our growing understanding of the brain demands more attention, and this book would be incomplete without it. We are all aware of the brain's extraordinary capacity to control and regulate our bodies, and enable us to experience the world consciously, as we reason, imagine and feel our way through life. The complexity of the brain is daunting, and much remains unexplained. Nevertheless, we have come a very long way from the ancient Egyptians, for example, who believed that intelligence, and particularly the soul, were located in the heart, which appeared to be a very active organ in contrast to the seemingly inert brain. Herodotus (the ancient Greek historian of the fifth century BCE) confirms the Egyptians' view of the brain in his description of how they prepared bodies for burial. Prior to mummification, the heart and various other organs seen as crucial for life in the next world were carefully removed and stored in special burial jars, whereas the brain was messily hooked out of the skull via the nostrils and unceremoniously discarded!

The philosopher Aristotle (384–322 BCE) also shared the view that the brain's role was purely regulatory, its function being to keep the highly active heart from overheating. Other Greek scholars, however, were less dismissive of the brain. Hippocrates, a physician who successfully established medicine as an occupation in its own right, had made claims for the importance of the brain before Aristotle was even born. In his short work *On the Sacred Disease*, an account of what we now understand as epilepsy, he describes the brain as the source of emotion and of reason, and states his belief that 'the brain is the most powerful organ of the human body' and 'the interpreter of consciousness' (Hippocrates, 400 BCE/1923, p. 179). Further ideas followed from other thinkers, who began to speculate on which part of the brain contained a person's 'vital principle' and whether the folds in the surface of the brain had some connection with intelligence. Whether there was a specific relationship between the brain and language was not, as far as we know, a question that was raised.

The structure of the brain

In 1543, Andreas Vesalius, a professor of anatomy at the University of Padua in Italy, published his extraordinary *De humani corporis fabrica* (*On the fabric of the human body*), a comprehensive study in seven volumes, with an entire volume devoted to the brain. Most impressive were its 273 detailed illustrations revealing the architecture of the skeleton, muscles, circulatory system and organs. These drawings were the result of Vesalius's painstaking and innovative work in the dissection of human corpses. The knowledge contained within his book quickly superseded the long-standing teachings of the second-century Greek physician, Galen of Pergamon, whose own influential anatomical works had been based not on humans, but on animals – although astonishingly this fact had gone largely unnoticed for centuries. With his emphasis on dissection and close observation, Vesalius had revolutionised the study of human anatomy.

One of the many extraordinary illustrations of the brain looks down onto a head with the upper part of the skull removed (see Figure 8.1). The brain within is depicted with its characteristic folds and clearly shows the **ventricles** (or cavities) at the centre of the brain as well as its division into right and left **hemispheres** (like the two halves of a walnut). Through his meticulous dissections, Vesalius was also able to identify the difference between **grey matter** and **white matter**, which we now know to consist of different parts of the nerve cells – a discovery which had to wait until the very end of the nineteenth century and the ground-breaking microscopic investigations of the Spanish neuroscientist Santiago Ramón y Cajal. Only then did it become possible to see the structure of the minute **neurons** (the nerve cells) which make up much of the brain: a rounded cell body containing the **nucleus** and covered with many spiky, branching **dendrites**, and a long single thread – the **axon** – extending from it (see Figure 8.2). The function of the dendrites and axons is to transmit and receive electro-chemical signals to and from other cells. The axons cluster together as white matter, while the cell bodies make up the grey matter. This grey matter forms the **cerebral cortex**, the grooved outer layer of the brain, which was once believed to be merely a protective coating but is now understood to be where our conscious thoughts and feelings are located. And it is mainly here, in this complex network of billions of neurons, that language is generated and processed.

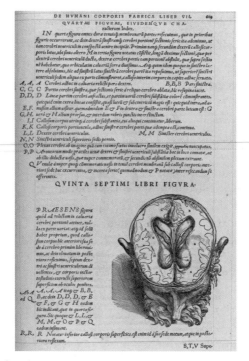

FIGURE 8.1   AN ILLUSTRATION OF THE HUMAN BRAIN FROM BOOK VII OF *DE HUMANI CORPORIS FABRICA* BY ANDREAS VESALIUS (1543)

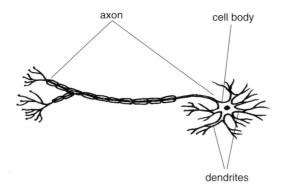

FIGURE 8.2   DIAGRAM OF A NEURON

The linguistic brain

Our brains have to do many things in order to operate linguistically. (First, of course, they have to acquire language – a process we will explore in the next chapter. Here, we will focus on language as a fully-fledged function of the brain.) For one thing, language requires a considerable amount of memory. We need to store words, and their associated sounds, meanings and uses. We also have to store the grammatical principles that enable us to construct acceptable sentences in the language we speak, as well as an understanding of the appropriate situations in which to use them. It is a sobering thought that the implicit linguistic knowledge we possess is equivalent to a set of very comprehensive reference books (a dictionary, a grammar and probably an encyclopaedia too) which we could never imagine learning by heart!

The production of any linguistic utterance has to begin with an intention to communicate and an idea of the message we wish to convey. This has to be formulated through an appropriate choice of words, organised in turn into a coherent and appropriate sentence or group of sentences. In the process of speaking our message, we need to exercise minute control over our nasal cavity, our mouth, our larynx and lungs in order to articulate these messages aloud, something we are able to do at the incredible speed of up to 25 speech segments a second. (Spoken aloud, the heading for this section contains 16 segments.) And of course we don't just produce language: we also hear it and interpret it, so these are two more jobs for the brain to do. In addition, we sometimes transmit language through a visual rather than an auditory mode, when the brain will need to process written language or sign language as well. Finally, we constantly monitor what we say and hear. If we make a production mistake of some kind (selecting the wrong word, for example), we usually realise it and instantly correct ourselves. In terms of comprehension, we may need to review our interpretations of the messages we hear if they are ambiguous or confusing. The linguistic functions performed by the brain are clearly very diverse. The storage and retrieval of grammatical information, for example, are very different processes from controlling the vocal tract to produce speech sounds. This raises the question of whether one specific area of the brain is dedicated to language, or whether different parts collaborate in this complex and varied process.

With so much for the brain to do, it is not surprising that different mechanical and technological inventions (such as an old-fashioned telephone switchboard) have been used as possible analogies for explaining how it works and how it deals with the amazingly complex phenomenon of language. The popular recent comparison with a computer has a certain appeal, not least because it captures something of the speed with which the brain works and the intricacy of its signalling network. But precisely how the brain converts the electrochemical signals which pass around the network of nerve cells into actual, meaningful language remains a mystery, as does the precise way in which the brain is organised to deal with language in its entirety. Having said that, scientists and linguists are slowly coming to understand something of these intricate processes, as we shall see.

Today, answering questions about the linguistic function of the brain is the aim of two related branches of science: **psycholinguistics** and **neurolinguistics**. Psycholinguistics, the slightly older of the two branches, established itself in the 1950s when linguists entered into a fierce debate with psychologists over how children acquire language (see Chapter 9). Inevitably, this also led to theorising about how language in general can reveal the workings of the human mind. Neurolinguistics developed from psycholinguistics under the influence of neurology, the study of the brain and the nervous system, and concentrates on looking at brain organisation and activity in relation to language. There is, inevitably, a significant amount of overlap between these branches and the difference between them is sometimes more a matter of emphasis and methodology. For psycholinguists, the mind is the focus of their attention, while neurolinguists are concerned with the brain as an organ. Psycholinguists frequently collect their data from verbal response experiments (such as how we process ambiguous sentences) or by looking at what can go wrong in everyday speech (slips of the tongue, for example), while neurolinguists examine the anatomical and physiological aspects of the brain, often using sophisticated equipment to do so. Of course, whether the mind and the brain are actually the same thing is open to debate, and not something researchers can agree upon. Nevertheless, the study of the brain illuminates our understanding of the mind, and the study of the mind prompts us to ask interesting questions about the brain.

Charting the brain for language

By the end of the eighteenth century, the first 'scientific' ideas started to emerge about how the brain, now universally accepted as the location of the mind, was organised. An idea proposed by the German physician Franz Joseph Gall quickly took hold in both Europe and America. Gall's proposal (as outlined in a series of works published from 1810) was that the brain was actually an amalgam of separate modules or organs, each one responsible for either a personal characteristic such as kindness or self-esteem, or a specific function such as taste, smell or language. This was the birth of **phrenology**, which became both popular and influential in the early decades

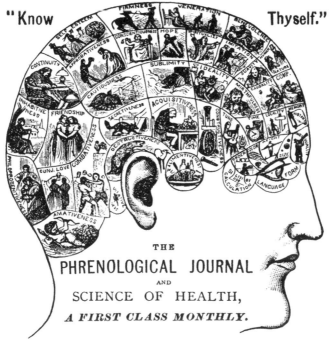

"Know   Thyself."

THE
PHRENOLOGICAL   JOURNAL
AND
SCIENCE   OF   HEALTH,
A FIRST CLASS MONTHLY.

Specially Devoted to the "SCIENCE OF MAN." Contains PHRENOLOGY
and PHYSIOGNOMY, with all the   SIGNS of CHARACTER, and how to read
them;" ETHNOLOGY, or the Natural History of Man in all his relations

FIGURE 8.3   A PHRENOLOGICAL CHART USED TO ADVERTISE *THE
PHRENOLOGICAL JOURNAL* (USA, MID-NINETEENTH CENTURY)

of the nineteenth century as phrenologists set out to map the areas of the
human brain and account for people's personal and behavioural differences
in doing so. The supposed locations of the various organs were deduced by
examining the skulls of individuals who demonstrated particular strength or
weakness in relation to a particular characteristic, looking for similar tell-tale
bulges (when the faculty was highly developed) or depressions (when it was
underdeveloped). The phrenologists produced extraordinary models and
drawings of the human head (see Figure 8.3), its surface divided into discrete
compartments, each one labelled with the particular attribute associated
with the corresponding area of the brain. (The language area was believed to
be just behind the eyes.) Although the phrenologists' methods of assigning
functions to different areas based on skull shapes, bumps and measurements
was dubious to say the least, there was a degree of truth, as it turned out, in
their belief that the brain is localised – in other words, that different areas
have specific roles.

Despite its popularity, not everyone was convinced by the claims of phrenology, and many preferred to believe that functions such as language were handled by the brain in its entirety. After all, other organs of the body – such as the lungs and kidneys – came in pairs, just like the brain's hemispheres, and there was no division of function in these organs. There was some discussion as to whether the front and back areas of the brain might have specific functions, or even some of the gyri (a **gyrus** is one of the folds in the corrugated surface of the cortex), but no conclusions were reached. It wasn't long, however, before some more scientifically sound research in the field of neurology (a very new science at this time) began to cast fresh light on how the brain might be localised. One of the first important discoveries, as far as language was concerned, was that the left hemisphere was more important than the right. This was initially proposed at a conference in Montpellier in 1836 by Marc Dax, a French neurologist and physician, who noticed how speech was particularly affected in patients who had suffered damage to the left side of the brain (Dax, 1836/1865). His son Gustave later narrowed language impairment down to a particular section of the left hemisphere. Although the work of Marc and Gustav Dax was, unfortunately, somewhat overlooked, it demonstrates the methodology that neurologists were employing in their research. Effectively, they were dependent on the study of patients whose brains were not functioning normally, usually due to injury or a clinical condition such as a stroke or tumour, as well as on the opportunity to examine the brain after the patient's death. The idea that the left side of the brain (in the vast majority of people) was dominant for language slowly became established, although some anatomists continued to dispute the view that the language faculty was localised at all.

The nineteenth century proved to be a very productive one for learning about the brain in general, and the linguistic aspects of the brain in particular. This accords with the growing excitement surrounding new ideas of evolution and human development which we explored in Chapter 3. Two neurologists stand out: the French physician Paul Broca and the German physician Carl Wernicke. A visitor to Paris can still see, if they care to call in at the *Musée Dupuytren*, the preserved brains of Broca's patients. These patients all suffered from **aphasia** – the loss of language, or some aspect of it. The first of these aphasic patients, a Monsieur Leborgne, who was referred to Broca just days before his death in 1861, exhibited only a partial loss. He understood what was said to him but had been unable to speak for over 20 years, except to utter 'tan, tan', which gave rise to his nickname. When 'Tan' died in 1861, Broca carried out an autopsy and discovered the precise location of the damage to the left side of his brain (the area already identified by Gustave Dax). Broca published a paper on his findings that same year (Broca, 1861), and then

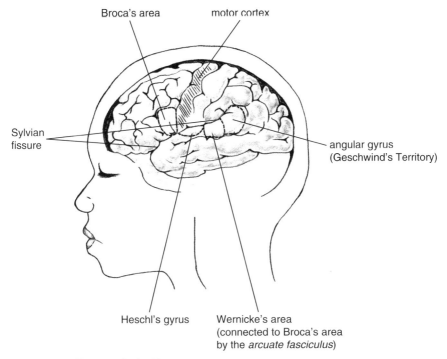

Broca's area   motor cortex

Sylvian
fissure

angular gyrus
(Geschwind's Territory)

Heschl's gyrus   Wernicke's area
(connected to Broca's area
by the *arcuate fasciculus*)

FIGURE 8.4 THE LANGUAGE AREAS OF THE HUMAN BRAIN

backed up his claims with a study of other patients with similar symptoms, all of whom were found to have damage in the same area of the cortex. This area became known as **Broca's area** and the type of language dysfunction experienced by Tan as **Broca's aphasia**. (You can see Broca's area in Figure 8.4, along with the other areas mentioned in this and the following section.)

The identification of an area localised for language quickly became known among other physicians and paved the way for further discoveries. Over in Germany, Broca's paper was read by Carl Wernicke, who also worked with patients suffering aphasia as a result of brain damage. Wernicke noticed that some of his patients had suffered damage in a different area of the left hemisphere and their difficulty was in understanding language rather than producing it (Wernicke, 1874). They could speak fairly fluently but their utterances made no real sense because the patients could not understand what they themselves were saying. The area he pinpointed as responsible for language comprehension became **Wernicke's area** and its associated difficulties, **Wernicke's aphasia**. Wernicke also went on to discover the way in which his area and Broca's were connected by nerve fibres, a kind of nerve cable named the **arcuate fasciculus**, from the Latin for a curved (*arcuatus*) little bundle.

Broca and Wernicke were the first to chart the brain's linguistic territory, although some of their colleagues were sceptical about their claims for specific language areas, citing counterexamples against such exclusivity. There was certainly a belief that other parts of the brain would be found to have linguistic functions too. Some years after Wernicke's discovery, an Austrian professor of anatomy, Richard Heschl, identified another language-related area and added his name to the topography of the brain (Heschl, 1878). **Heschl's gyrus** lies on the left hemisphere along the **Sylvian fissure**, the horizontal groove which separates the upper and lower sections of the cortex. The area below the fissure is particularly important for processing sound: Heschl's gyrus seems to be the area where speech sounds are filtered out from other noises being received by the ear.

The study of the brain continued to gather pace as the nineteenth century drew to a close and the nerve cell structures invisible to the naked eye were seen for the first time under a microscope. Early in the new century, the German anatomist Korbinian Brodmann developed a technique for mapping the areas of the cortex by staining sliced sections of the brain (Brodmann, 1909). The differences in shading proved to be due to the variations in the arrangement and layering of the nerve cells, architectural variations which suggested different functional purposes. Broca's and Wernicke's areas seemed to correlate with the areas Brodmann identified, and more recent analysis has supported the correlation between cell architecture and brain function.

The work of the early neurologists, based largely on the study of severely aphasic patients and the opportunity to perform autopsies on them when they died, led to significant developments in the understanding of the brain's linguistic capabilities. In the second half of the twentieth century, the study of the linguistic brain took another leap forward as the technology became available for working with subjects whose language faculty was not impaired. This was desirable not least because it was realised there was no absolute certainty of a direct association between a damaged area of the brain and the characteristics of a patient's impaired speech. At last there was an opportunity to observe the proposed language areas, previously mapped out on the damaged brains of deceased patients, activated and interacting in the brains of living – and fluent – speakers.

Technological breakthroughs

In a lecture of 1913, the famous Russian physiologist Ivan Pavlov spoke wistfully of being able to see through the skull of a living person to observe how an area of brain activity might be revealed by an animated glow on the surface of the cortex: 'we should see, playing over the cerebral surface, a bright spot with fantastic, waving borders constantly fluctuating in size and form, surrounded by a darkness more or less deep, covering the rest of the hemisphere' (Pavlov, 1913/1928, p. 222). Pavlov's death in 1936 meant he never lived to see his vision come true. By the 1950s, however, huge progress was being made in the techniques available for studying the brains of living subjects. Although it was not disputed that one side of the brain was dominant for language, there was no absolute certainty that this would be the left side of the brain, a fact which had been known since the nineteenth century. One of the most accurate tests for dominance was devised in the late 1940s by the Japanese neurologist Juhn Wada, hence its name of the **Wada test**. Patients requiring brain operations (particularly those with severe epilepsy) could be tested prior to surgery to ensure that important mental faculties would not be disrupted as a result of the operation. In this procedure the two hemispheres are injected one at a time with sodium amytal, a drug which effectively anaesthetises the injected half. The dominant hemisphere can then be deduced from whether or not the patient's language is impaired during the period before the drug wears off. As it turns out, the vast majority of people (about 95%) have left-hemisphere dominance, but both right-hemisphere dominance and even an absence of dominance occur.

As we have just seen, knowledge about brain damage and the opportunity to perform autopsies enabled neurologists like Broca and Wernicke to begin mapping the areas of the left hemisphere involved with language. In the 1970s the first **CT** (computer tomography) scans enabled X-rays to be taken which showed cross-sections through the brain. A decade later the technology had been dramatically improved: the introduction of **MRI** (magnetic resonance imaging) scans showed these cross-sections in extraordinary detail on a computer screen, and a refinement to this technology, fMRI (where f stands for 'functional'), meant that changes in brain activity could be tracked as they happened. This was a significant breakthrough for learning about how the linguistic brain actually works. Conscious patients could be asked to perform specific tasks while the scan was taking place, and areas of increased blood flow delivering additional energy-giving oxygen to the brain would light up on the screen. More recently, a new type of scanning – diffusion tensor MRI, which shows how water molecules spread through tissue – has enabled neurologists to look more closely at nerve connections. In the 1960s, an American researcher, Norman Geschwind, proposed that an area of the cortex adjacent to Wernicke's area, the **angular gyrus**, was also important in processing language. In 2005, diffusion tensor imaging revealed that there were indeed neural connections between Broca and Wernicke's areas and the angular gyrus, which has now been shown to play a role in connecting the images of written words (processed initially at the back of the cortex) with their meanings. In recognition of Geschwind's prediction about the role of the angular gyrus, it is now sometimes referred to as **Geschwind's territory**.

Gradually, then, the human brain is being charted more and more accurately for language, with the names of the relevant areas reflecting something of the history of neurological research. Although there are clearly areas of the brain dedicated primarily to language, other cerebral regions are also involved. As we have seen, the cortex is made up of two hemispheres. These are connected by a long band of nerve axons called the **corpus callosum** (from the Latin for a 'thick-skinned body'). Each hemisphere is divided into four regions, or **lobes**, as illustrated in Figure 8.5, so the overall pattern of the lobes is symmetrical. Each lobe has its own specific functions, and, as we have seen, specialised language functions are normally found in the left hemisphere. The **temporal lobe** is particularly important for auditory information: both Heschl's and Wernicke's areas are located in the temporal lobe. The **frontal lobe** is where most of our thinking (and some of our memory storage) takes place, and this is where Broca's area, which processes language output, is located. The section of the frontal lobe which is important for movement, the **motor cortex**, is on the rear edge of this lobe. Broca's area nudges up against the motor cortex at the section that controls the tongue and lips, crucial for the articulation of speech sounds. The **occipital lobe**, at the back of the brain, handles vision, and is important for reading and writing, although other brain areas also contribute to this process. The angular gyrus is positioned at the junction of the **parietal lobe** (which deals with sensory information) and the

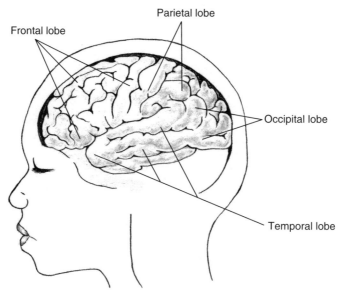

FIGURE 8.5   THE LOBES OF THE HUMAN BRAIN (SHOWN ON THE LEFT HEMISPHERE)

temporal and occipital lobes. This appears to be relevant to its work as an interface between different language areas and functions.

So far, most of our attention has been concentrated on the left hemisphere, the side of the brain which, for the majority of people, is dominant for language. However, the non-dominant right hemisphere also has been found to have a role to play. At an interactional level, it is the right hemisphere (which deals more with visual and spatial information) that enables us to recognise who we are speaking to. It also helps us recognise the symbols used in written language. Interestingly, though, brain scans show slightly different patterns of activity for readers and writers depending on the writing system they use – whether, for example, it is alphabetic (using letters) or logographic (using a single picture or symbol to represent an entire word). If sign language is used instead of speech, the right hemisphere has a role to play in interpretation of the gestures. It also comes into play on an emotional level, helping us to judge the tone of someone's speech and to determine an appropriate response. The implications of rhythm and stress in our speech are also calculated on the right, and figurative language seems to be interpreted here too, especially if it has a spatial or visual dimension, such as 'I wandered lonely as a cloud'.

Neurolinguists are at an exciting stage in their exploration of the brain. The work of the last 200 years has shown how there are certainly specific areas associated with language production and processing, but these do not work alone. With the advent of MRI scans, our knowledge has taken a dramatic leap forward and computer imaging has thrown light on language as an activity in which various parts of the brain cooperate. Language production, for example, although managed largely by Broca's area, can also activate Wernicke's area – which seems to be involved in matching thoughts and concepts with words – as well as other parts of the cortex. Language is a multi-faceted phenomenon, and this is reflected in the fact that the brain areas adapted for language do not function in isolation, but are networked to many other areas. This has led neurolinguists to focus their attention more recently on circuits or pathways for language rather than areas. Although one hemisphere is dominant for language, the other also has a crucial role to play, and interestingly it has been shown that damage to apparently non-linguistic areas of the brain can cause language processing problems. Although we now know considerably more than the early neurologists, there is a great deal still to learn about the brain's language capability. As the American neurologist John Hughlings Jackson, an earlier doubter of the existence of a separate language faculty, famously observed, locating an area associated with language (or speech, as he termed it) and locating language itself are undoubtedly 'two different things' (Jackson, 1874/1915, p. 80).

Closing in on language

In a discipline as non-pictorial as linguistics typically is, representations of the brain make for a welcome and varied gallery of images. The meticulous illustrations of Vesalius give way to the curious busts and charts of the phrenologists. Modern textbooks and websites about the human brain abound with images and diagrams (like Figure 8.4) showing the parts of the cortex associated with language, a mode of depiction dating back to the nineteenth century. To these can be added the full-colour images produced by MRI and other scanning techniques where areas active during linguistic events are illuminated much as Pavlov imagined. Scanned images reflect considerable scientific progress in understanding how our brains are organised for language. We can now identify exactly which parts of the brain come into play during, for example, the recital of a list of words from memory or the reading aloud of a written stimulus. But exactly how close have we got to connecting physiological events with linguistic minutiae? Furthermore, do we know anything about the way in which the electro-chemical signals passing among the networks of neurons in our brains are converted into language? How does a process of which we have no physi-cal awareness (unlike the beating of our heart) transmute into linguistic consciousness?

Partial answers to these questions are gradually starting to emerge. A technique which has been instrumental in this is **EEG** (electroencephalog-raphy), which was first pioneered in Germany in the 1920s by Hans Berger, a colleague of Korbinian Brodmann. By placing electrodes on the scalp and connecting them to a simple meter, Berger was able to detect electrical pulses generated by the neurons – in other words, **brainwaves**. Nowadays, of course, the brainwaves can be displayed and analysed on a computer screen. Although EEG is used primarily for medical and clinical purposes, it has pro-vided neurolinguists with the means to make detailed links between brain-wave patterns and specific language features. For instance, the N400 wave, discovered by Marta Kutas and Steven Hillyard (Kutas and Hillyard, 1980), has been the subject of a large number of experiments focussed on processing meaning. (The N400 wave usually peaks around 400 milliseconds after the brain receives the stimulus, which gives you some idea of the sophistication of the equipment needed to detect it.) Researchers have seen how the ampli-tude (the height of the wave) is increased when unexpected words occur in certain positions. So, for example, the final word in a request such as 'pass the salt and <u>pepper</u>' would not stimulate as much variation in amplitude as 'pass the salt and <u>sugar</u>'. As we might predict, anything unexpected would indeed place a greater demand on the brain's processing abilities, but it is now possible to detect and view the brainwaves at work – an extraordinary development, unimaginable a hundred years ago.

The findings of research such as that involving the N400 wave are helping linguists to slowly close in on the brain's linguistic activities. But there is still a long way to go. There is, for instance, a great deal more to learn about memory and its relationship to language. A patient suffering from Broca's aphasia will certainly struggle to find the words to construct linguistic messages, but the actual storage of vocabulary seems to be handled by several areas of the brain, including the (left) **hippocampus**, a structure on the inside of each temporal lobe shaped rather like a seahorse. Ingenious experiments using MRI data have revealed something of the brain's classification system when it comes to vocabulary, where the brain seems to be able to store words like a dictionary and like a thesaurus simultaneously. Understanding how the brain stores and processes grammatical information, however, is probably the holy grail of neurolinguistics. Experiments with EEG have shown brainwaves reacting to specific grammatical features, such as structural violations, but where grammar – with its guiding principles for generating the hundreds of sentences we utter on a daily basis – resides in the brain is likely to remain a mystery for the foreseeable future.

Language in the mind

We saw earlier that there is disagreement among neurolinguists and psycholinguists as to whether the mind and the brain are one and the same thing, or whether the mind is something greater than the sum of the brain activity which constitutes its existence. It might seem that the research undertaken by neurolinguists which involves connecting brain activity with language is gradually making the work of psycholinguists redundant. This is not, however, the case. Psycholinguists have a great deal to contribute to our understanding of how the mind (and therefore the brain) processes language, and the proposals they formulate provide theories that can be tested by their neurolinguistic counterparts. Interestingly, they often rely on language abnormalities to deduce what the mind might be doing, but these are not restricted to the kind of major impairments shown by the aphasic patients of their nineteenth-century predecessors. A considerable amount of attention has now been given to the tiny blips in fluency that we all make at some time or another. These include those annoying moments when a word is 'on the tip of your tongue' or those times when you come out with a word which is not precisely the one you wanted to say. These speech mistakes were thought by early psychoanalysts such as Sigmund Freud to reveal subconscious emotional states, but psycholinguists see them as revealing far more about how the mind stores and processes language.

Psycholinguists are very interested in what they term the **psychological reality** of language. As we saw in Chapter 6, a distinction is often made between our 'deep' level of linguistic knowledge, and the actual 'surface' utterances that we produce. In describing language, linguists have to rely on what people actually say as their starting point for discovering what might lie beneath. What psycholinguists want to know is whether a description of language which is physically real (because it is spoken and heard) matches the 'psychologically real' language in our minds. Here are two very simple examples courtesy of the author's mother, who unintentionally referred to a monastery she saw on holiday as a 'monarchy' and the velodrome at London's Olympic Park as the 'palindrome'. These production errors, apart from causing a certain amount of amusement among the family, suggest something of the way we store words in our memory as they obviously share some similar sound combinations. The palindrome/velodrome example is particularly telling. If we split these words into syllables, further similarities are revealed:

pa – lin – drome
ve – lo – drome

In both instances, the first syllable has a simple consonant + vowel structure, while the second syllable begins with the same sound. Not only this, but in both of these trisyllabic words, the main stress comes on the first syllable, while the second is the least stressed of the three. In addition, both words are nouns. The potential interchangeability of the words therefore exists on three levels: the phonological level (where sound, syllable and stress patterns are repeated), the morphological level (where the '-drome' element remains constant but combines with different initial elements), and the grammatical level (since both words are nouns). These are arguments for a subconscious awareness of the structure and function of words. As neurology advances, it is becoming possible to test claims about the psychological reality of language against brain activity. Slips of the tongue have been the meat and drink of psycholinguists who for many decades now have been trying to understand not the linguistic brain, but the linguistic mind. Now, however, the two are starting to come together.

Modelling is another strategy psycholinguists use to investigate not just how the mind stores linguistic information (as seen in the examples above) but how it deals with both the production and comprehension of speech. The advantage of modelling is that it enables researchers to start at the beginning of the process and try to determine how it might progress step by step. As a method for exploring linguistic processes, modelling goes back to the last two decades of the nineteenth century, when neurologists like Carl Wernicke devised all kinds of diagrams in their attempts to understand how language worked in the brain. The intention behind many of these diagrams was to explain the cause of different types of aphasia: if pathways for normal language processing could be mapped out, then interruptions at different points along the route (caused by localised damage to the brain) would result in a particular language impairment. The popularity of diagram-making provoked some interesting discussions about the possible relationship between the brain's neurological make-up and the sequence of events involved in the processing of language.

Not all nineteenth-century modelling relied on diagrammatic representation, however. An example of this is the Austrian physiologist Sigmund Exner's theory of word perception, in which he proposed that words are recognised by anticipation rather than retrospection (Exner, 1894). His ideas were to resurface in the 1980s as part of the **PDP** (parallel distributed processing) model, which aimed to explain how the brain processes speech, particularly bearing in mind that this is often done in less than 'ideal' circumstances – against a noisy background, for example. The PDP approach to word recognition is based on the notion that several possibilities are activated in the brain as soon as we hear the start of a word. As more phonological information is accrued, the incorrect possibilities are eliminated. So if, for instance, someone told you they were 'off to play c___', the moment your brain registered the 'c' (/k/) sound, several options would be activated, such as 'cards', 'cricket', 'croquet' and 'Chris'. 'Cards' would be eliminated if the 'c' became 'cr', 'croquet' if it became 'cri-' and so on. So information about speech segments is constantly interacting with information from the mental word store or lexicon. At the same time, our knowledge about the speaker and his or her habitual activities may also play a role in our decision-making about the word we are hearing. Of course, all this happens in a matter of milliseconds and in recent decades the use of computer technology for modelling has been able to show more precisely how this process could happen in real time. These are exciting developments. Nevertheless, in comparison with what we now know about other organs of the body thanks to technological advancements, the brain still retains many of its secrets.

Language and thought

We move in this final section to one of the central activities of the human brain (or mind), namely thought. Thought is involved in many of the mental processes which we carry out on a daily basis: making decisions, planning the future, forming judgements, understanding the world around us, solving problems and so on. Language is clearly important in these pursuits, and we often find ourselves thinking out loud as we carry them out. Alternatively, we silently formulate our thoughts through language, and our 'inner voice' is activated in the brain instead. In the course of a day spent on our own and without speaking to another human being, we would still make use of language for a range of purposes.

Does this mean that we cannot think without language, as the seventeenth-century French philosopher Descartes believed? He believed thought – or reason – was an endowment unique to human beings, and that language made thought possible. For many centuries, opinion has been divided on the relationship between thought and language. It is a question that also has a bearing on the emergence of language in the human species. Rousseau identified the conundrum in his *Discourse on Inequality* of 1755: '… if men needed speech in order to learn to think, they needed still more to know how to think in order to discover the art of speech' (Rousseau, 1755/1984, p. 93). Nowadays it's generally accepted, first, that thought is not unique to humans and that some animals (birds included) have the capacity to think, as shown by certain types of behaviour. (Crows, for instance, have been observed to 'problem-solve' by working out how to use sticks and stones to reach inaccessible food.) Also, pre-linguistic infants show an ability to think, so language is not a prerequisite for human thought. Furthermore, adult humans do not always use language in their thinking, since spatial or visual awareness can guide a thought process, such as when we follow a route on a map. However, language seems to be intimately bound up with more complex thinking. Saussure, for example, saw language as a means of organising thought: 'Thought, chaotic by nature, is made precise by this process of segmentation' (Saussure, 1916/1983, p. 110). He viewed language as a kind of systematic interface between thought and the sounds that enable us to express our thinking out loud.

One view of the relationship between language and thought that has been particularly influential springs from the considerable interest in linguistic diversity that developed towards the end of the eighteenth century. (We explored this in Chapter 4.) This was the belief that every language reflected a different view of the world (effectively, the world-view of the nation that spoke the language). This in turn meant that the language you spoke coloured your view of the world, and the way you understood and interpreted your experience of it. Among the scholars who held this belief was the German philosopher Wilhelm von Humboldt. You can see an impressive statue of him if you visit Berlin, where he sits in splendour outside the university he established there in 1810. Between 1801 and 1808, Humboldt worked as a diplomat at the Vatican where he was given the opportunity to examine records of Native American languages prepared by Jesuit missionaries. His personal interest in linguistic diversity was fostered by these records and also by his study of a wide range of other languages, including Basque, Aztec, Sanskrit, Chinese and various South Pacific languages, including the ancient Javanese language of Kawi. For Humboldt, language was the means by which our thoughts are constructed: 'Nothing within a human being is so deep … that it may not pass over into language and be recognizable there', he wrote in the introduction to his study of the ancient Javanese language, Kawi (Humboldt, 1836/1999, p. 81). He went on to describe the mutual influences of language and national or cultural identity: 'Every language receives a specific originality through that of the nation, and has on the latter a uniformly determining reverse effect' (ibid., p. 152). It is in these introductory observations that we can identify the roots of two linguistic concepts. The first of these is **linguistic relativity**, the belief that every language encapsulates the world-view of the community that speaks it, and that every language does this in a distinct way. The second concept is **linguistic determinism**, the view that the language we are brought up to speak predisposes us to see the world in a particular way, determined not just by the lexicon of the language, but its grammar too. Not only our thoughts but the world itself is chaotic, and language enables us to impose order on it. The belief that we live in an ordered world is, arguably, an illusion our language creates.

Humboldt's suggestion that language determines thought was taken up and revitalised nearly a hundred years later by two American anthropologists turned linguists, Edward Sapir and his pupil Benjamin Lee Whorf, both interested in the Native American languages which had intrigued Humboldt and others. Sapir started to think of language in terms of a 'prepared road or groove' which guides the way we think (Sapir, 1921, p. 14). Benjamin Whorf followed Sapir's lead and applied determinism particularly to his study of the Hopi language, a member of the Uto-Aztecan family, spoken in Arizona. In a 1937 article on Hopi he identifies, among many other differences between Hopi and English, a set of verb markings that bear no comparison to anything found in English or any other Indo-European language. Although there must have been some logical connection between these markings and the meanings of the verbal groups to which they apply, Whorf admits he was almost at a loss at first to explain the connecting principle, observing 'there must be to the Hopi speaker a dimly felt relation of similarity between the verb usages in each group … but one so nearly at or below the threshold of conscious thinking that it cannot be put into words by the user and eludes translation' (Whorf, 1937/1956, pp. 104–5). In fact, he went on to comment in an article the following year: 'It was to me almost as enlightening to see English from the entirely new angle necessitated in order to translate it into Hopi as it was to discover the meanings of the Hopi forms themselves' (Whorf, 1938/1956, pp. 112–13).

The relationship between language and thought has continued to be of interest to linguists working in the field of both psychology and cognitive science. Whorf's writings suggest a powerful influence of our native language over our thinking and our perception of the world around us, but he also seemed to be aware that acquiring new languages gave a speaker alternative perspectives on the world around them, something most learners of a foreign language have experienced. Linguists nowadays are reluctant to accept the extreme determinism which the **Sapir-Whorf hypothesis** (as the views of the two linguists came to be known after their deaths) seems to propose, but the interdependency between much of our thinking and language is generally well accepted.

As far as the human brain is concerned, there is still a great deal to discover then about this complex relationship. There remains also the perplexing phenomenon of consciousness, which has so far defied scientific definition or explanation. Consciousness was once thought to be a metaphysical phenomenon, unique to human beings. Now, however, it's accepted that other creatures have degrees of consciousness. The question of the part language plays in raising human consciousness and thought to a higher level is therefore a central one. And, in turn, this question is an indication of the importance for neurolinguists and psycholinguists of continuing to fathom, with the indispensible assistance of science and technology, the extraordinary workings of the linguistic brain.

Suggestions for further reading and research

On the brain in general, and on the brain's language capability

Carter, Rita (2010) *Mapping the Mind* (London: Phoenix)

A highly accessible general introduction to the human mind and brain, which also contains some interesting material on language.

Finger, Stanley (2000) *Minds Behind the Brain* (New York: Oxford University Press)

A fascinating account of the thinkers and researchers who have contributed to our understanding of the human brain over the centuries, including several of those mentioned in this chapter.

Ingram, John C L (2007) *Neurolinguistics: An Introduction to Spoken Language Processing and its Disorders* (Cambridge: Cambridge University Press)

A comprehensive introduction to the field of research that examines the various aspects of language in relation to the neurological make-up of the brain.

Obler, Loraine K and Kris Gjerlow (1999) *Language and the Brain* (Cambridge: Cambridge University Press)

With a particular focus on brain disorders, this title in the Cambridge Approaches to Linguistics series is an interesting survey of how language is embodied in the brain.

On psycholinguistics

Dabrowska, Ewa (2004) *Language, Mind and Brain: Some Psychological and Neurological Constraints on Theories of Grammar* (Edinburgh: Edinburgh University Press)

A detailed exploration of how the human mind processes language, with a strong focus on aspects of lexis and grammar.

Field, John (2003) *Psycholinguistics: A Resource Book for Students* (Abingdon: Routledge)

Part of an excellent series of resource books, this one covers all the key concepts and topics of psycholinguistics, and provides plenty of data examples as well as related extracts.

Levelt, Willem J M (2013) *A History of Psycholinguistics* (Oxford: Oxford University Press)

A detailed and scholarly account, covering the period from 1770 to the 1950s. It contains material relevant to both this and the following chapter.

Scovel, Thomas (1998) *Psycholinguistics* (Oxford: Oxford University Press)

A short but clear introduction to this branch of linguistics, covering the four key areas of acquisition, dissolution, production and comprehension.

On the relationship between language and thought

Everett, Daniel (2009) *Don't Sleep, There are Snakes* (London: Profile Books)

An American linguist's experience of living in the Amazonian jungle and attempting to learn the language of the Pirahã people who live there. A personal take on the question of linguistic determinism and the relationship between language, thought and culture.

Gumperz, John J and Stephen C Levinson (1996) *Rethinking Linguistic Relativity* (Cambridge: Cambridge University Press)

A re-examination of the connection between language and our perceptions and experiences of the world around us.

Whorf, Benjamin Lee (1956) *Language, Thought, and Reality: Selected Writings of Benjamin Lee Whorf,* 2nd edn, edited by John B Carroll, Stephen Levinson and Penny Lee (Cambridge, MA: MIT Press, 2012)

This selection includes the 1939 memorial article Whorf wrote for Edward Sapir, 'The Relation of Habitual Thought and Behavior to Language', often considered to encapsulate their central idea.

Useful websites

Brodmann areas
Available at http://en.wikipedia.org/wiki/Brodmann_area (accessed October 2015)

Clickable maps enable you to explore the brain area by area.

Problem-solving crow
www.youtube.com/watch?v=AVaITA7eBZE (accessed October 2015)

This clip provides an interesting example of an animal's ability to reason.

The Whole Brain Atlas
www.med.harvard.edu/aanlib/ (accessed October 2015)

A site designed for medical students which contains a wide selection of images from human brain scans.

9 Language acquisition

Jerry Fodor (b. 1935)   American philosopher and cognitive
                                   scientist
Catherine Snow (b. 1945)   American psycholinguist

Special mention must be made of the three neglected children discussed in this chapter:

Victor the 'wild child' (Victor of Aveyron), found in Saint Sernin-sur-Rance,
    Aveyron, France in 1800, aged around 12
Genie, found in California in 1970, age 13
Danielle (Dani), found in Florida in 2005, age 6

The forbidden experiment

In the ancient and picturesque southern French village of Saint Sernin-sur-Rance, there stands a statue of *Victor, l'Enfant Sauvage* – Victor, the wild child – who lived there over 200 years ago. Nothing is known about his parentage or why he came to be found, at the age of about 12, surviving alone in the nearby woods. There had been several sightings of Victor as well as an unsuccessful attempt to look after him before he was 'captured' in the village very early one January morning in 1800 while searching for food. He was virtually naked, scarred, undernourished – and he had no ability to speak or to understand language. Arrangements were made to take him to Paris, where he spent several months being studied at the National Institute for the Deaf before one of the physicians there, Jean Marc Itard, decided to adopt the boy.

Victor was clearly not deaf. He showed sensitivity to many natural sounds but initially no response at all to human language. Itard was convinced that Victor could learn to speak, and that, like any child, he possessed 'in an eminent degree, the susceptibility of learning every thing', including 'an innate propensity to imitation' (Itard, 1801/1802, p. 90) which Itard believed was the key to him learning language. He set about the task of teaching Victor both language and 'civilised' behaviour and wrote a detailed account of his educational efforts. Itard attributed Victor's inability to make speech-like sounds to his many years spent living without human company, but believed that this skill would develop in time. After all, he noted, it was usually about 18 months before babies began to utter their first words, so it would be unrealistic to expect anything more in this unusual instance.

Progress was indeed slow. Eventually, the boy started to respond to speech whenever he heard the exclamation 'oh', although he was unable to produce its simple vowel sound himself. Encouraged by this development, it was at this moment that Itard decided to call the boy 'Victor' since the name's final vowel is (in French) similar to 'oh' as well as to the French *eau*, meaning 'water'. However, even when offering water to the thirsty Victor, Itard was unable to elicit this sound from his pupil. He turned his attention instead to milk – *lait* in French – and was delighted when Victor suddenly attempted one day to reproduce this word. For Victor, however, the utterance seemed to be used not to ask for milk but to express his private delight at having it. Itard was disappointed by what he saw as a lack of communication between himself and his pupil. By 1802, when Itard published his first account of Victor's progress, Victor had managed to articulate a handful of vowel sounds as well as the consonants /d/ (copied from his housekeeper's frequent exclamation *Oh Dieu!*), /l/ (from *lait*) and the palatalised form of /l/ which appears in the name *Julia* (that of the housekeeper's daughter, to whom Victor appeared to have taken a liking). Itard remained optimistic that, given time, Victor could learn much more.

Although Victor showed almost no inclination to communicate using language, he showed a remarkably expressive ability to use gestures. Itard's account contains many interesting examples – many of them rather moving too – of Victor's interactional signs, such as offering up his wooden bowl as a request for milk. Itard was very struck with the significance of these actions, especially since Victor had acquired them with 'no need of any preliminary lesson' (ibid., p. 105), and he came to regard them as a reflection of 'that primitive language of the human species, originally employed in the infancy of society' (ibid., p. 106). Victor did, then, develop a means of communicating with his fellow beings even though, by the time he died in 1828, his language ability was barely greater than in those childhood years when Itard had worked so hard to nurture it.

Victor was not the first 'wild child' to have been discovered after years of isolation from human society. Legends of such feral children go back to antiquity. When the Swedish biologist Carl Linnaeus compiled the tenth edition of his *Systema naturae* in 1758, he even included *Homo ferus* ('wild human') as a distinct species, based on about ten known examples of such children. Itard himself was aware of other stories of children deprived of a normal upbringing and hoped that Victor, living in a more enlightened age, would have a better chance in life than they had had. Sadly, though, discoveries of children brought up in situations of extreme deprivation are not a thing of the past. One of the most recent occurred in Florida in 2005 when a six-year-old girl, Danielle, was rescued from conditions so appalling that the police and welfare officers who found her could hardly believe what they saw. Within two years, Dani (as she became) had started school and intense speech therapy, and had been adopted into a family where she acquired some new siblings. Slowly, she started to lead a normal life, but her language has been slow to develop and, like Victor, Dani relies a great deal on gestures to communicate with those around her. Dani's story of deprivation is resonant of a similar – and more widely known – episode in the United States involving a 13-year old girl, who was found in 1970 and became known as Genie. She too had suffered severe isolation and physical neglect, and developed only a very limited language capacity during the years after her discovery when she was cared for (and studied) by a range of psychologists and scientists. Her sad story features in many textbooks on psycholinguistics and language acquisition.

Children like Victor, Dani and Genie have, understandably, been of intense interest to researchers into children's growth and development. Victor was discovered towards the end of the Enlightenment, a period when emphasis was placed on reason as a primary faculty in human beings, with language being regarded as the vehicle for expressing human reason and thought. Without language, could Victor become a civilised member of society? Furthermore, how important was education in enabling someone to achieve this status? Itard shared the influential view of his age that the mind was a blank sheet (or *tabula rasa*) ready to receive the imprint of human society. Without reason and language, human beings were no more than wild animals, the *Homo ferus* identified by Linnaeus. Today, views have shifted, but many questions remain in relation to children like these, particularly the many questions their stories raise about the nature of language acquisition itself. If children do not learn language in their early years, what governs the likelihood that they will be able to catch up later on (as some children have been able to do)? How is the development of language related to other aspects of the child's development and socialisation? How strong is the instinct to communicate and hence to acquire language, and what is the nature of that instinct?

The Forbidden Experiment is the title given to a 1980 study of Victor's story by Roger Shattuck. The stories of Victor and other children like him beg the question of how much the trauma of their early experiences and treatment prevented them from developing normally. In addition, were any of these children suffering from learning disabilities, a possible cause of rejection by their parents? (It has been proposed, for example, that Victor suffered from autism.) So whatever we can learn about the development of this thankfully tiny group of children may not apply to 'normal' children. However, psycholinguists would no doubt learn a considerable amount about language acquisition by conducting controlled deprivation experiments on growing infants.

Even though these children would be well cared for, this would, of course, be utterly unethical – a forbidden experiment. Instead, psycholinguists must do what they can with children who follow the expected trajectory of language development. One eminent theorist has even managed to dispense with the study of real children altogether, as we shall see later.

Studying language acquisition

The acquisition of language is an extraordinary phenomenon in terms of the apparent speed and ease with which the very young achieve it. And the actual language a child learns makes only a negligible difference, as does the acquisition of two languages simultaneously. Because language acquisition, for most children, happens so readily and so effortlessly, it is easy to overlook its social and cultural significance. Language, the means by which we achieve so much as a species, relies for its existence on transmission from generation to generation. This is a process we take very much for granted, but seeking to understand exactly how this transmission takes place serves only to highlight its importance.

In the previous chapter, we considered the remarkable ability of the human brain to process something as multifaceted as language. Everything a fully-fledged speaker can do linguistically, they have most typically learnt as a very young child, some of it possibly from before birth, as we will consider in a later section. A developing child has many things to learn in the process of acquiring language, not least how to actually interpret what she (or he) hears around her: she can hardly get started until she begins to pick out individual sounds from the speech to which she is exposed, just as Victor tuned in to the 'oh' sound he heard so frequently. From a production point of view, the child then needs to learn to articulate the sounds of the **target language** and gradually build them up into strings of sounds to form syllables and words. The articulation of these words then needs to be manipulated to add rhythm, stress, intonation and variations in voice quality and volume. In conjunction with these skills, words and their associated meanings have to be acquired in their tens and hundreds, and later in their thousands. The complex network of grammatical rules which enable the construction of well-formed sentences has to be put in place, and then the ability to connect those sentences into longer sequences must be added. On top of all this, there are pragmatic skills to acquire – skills which enable us to participate effectively in conversations, interpret the implicit meanings of our fellow speakers and adapt the way we use language according to the circumstances in which we find ourselves.

One of the challenges, then, in studying the acquisition of language is in dealing with the vast array of processes that are going on. Children do not learn language one strand at a time: instead, several learning processes are often happening simultaneously. A typical two-year-old, for instance, will be starting to put together very short sentences, still be mastering many aspects of pronunciation and expanding her vocabulary at a remarkable rate, as well as developing the uses to which she can put her linguistic talents. The systematic study of children's linguistic development requires the collection of suitable data and very young children are not the easiest of respondents to work with. Nevertheless there exists a vast corpus of data that has provided the foundations for this study as we will see in the next section.

The diary keepers

It is not unusual for proud parents to keep a linguistic record of their children's early years, recording first words and amusing remarks, for example. Records like these have a long tradition in the study of children's language. Parents and other carers are well placed to keep such records as they spend long periods of time with the children and are therefore likely to be present when relevant vocalisations occur. They can also observe the children in their home environment, where much language learning initially takes place. The role of the observer/recorder in collecting this kind of data is of course a crucial one for the study of language acquisition: very young children, having no awareness of themselves as language learners, are unable to cooperate in the data collection process, and yet it is only from them that data can be collected. After all, adults who have completed the process are totally unable to remember how they did it!

One of the first historically important diaries of a child's development was written at the end of the eighteenth century by the German philosopher Dietrich Tiedemann. This was prompted by the birth of his son, Friedrich, in 1781, and composed in the wake of the publication in 1762 of Rousseau's *Émile*, a substantial treatise on education which sparked a lively debate among his contemporaries about a child's upbringing. (Victor's mentor, Jean Marc Itard, would of course have been familiar with this work.) Tiedemann had become very interested in child development. In his diary entries, kept for the first three years of his son's life, language is considered within the context of the child's growing understanding of the world around him, but only receives a small amount of attention in comparison to other aspects of Friedrich's mental development. Tiedemann's range of observations led him to the conclusion that children possess knowledge and understanding prior to their acquisition of language, a theme to be found in many subsequent studies of early development. Tiedemann published his diary in 1787.

There was a flurry of diary-keeping activity around the time Tiedemann's study of Friedrich was published, probably fuelled by rumours of a prize for the diary which contributed the most to contemporary knowledge about children's growth and development. The next significant burst of diary-keeping was nearly a century later and this time one of the central figures was none other than Charles Darwin, now something of a celebrity following his publication in 1859 of *On the Origin of Species*. Interested, of course, in natural development of all kinds, Darwin had kept a record of the first two years in the life of his eldest child, William Erasmus Darwin, who was born in 1839. With its focus on gestures and expressions, it was written very much with a comparison between humans and animals in mind. In 1876, the French cultural critic and historian, Hippolyte Taine, had an article published in *Mind* magazine about his daughter's early linguistic progress, of which he too had kept a diary. Seeing this article a year later when it appeared in English, and responding to its evolutionary tone, Darwin was prompted to dust down his notes about William and write an article for *Mind* himself. The result was 'A biographical sketch of an infant' (Darwin, 1877). A considerable amount of this article is devoted to language: William's early sounds and intonation patterns, how he started to associate objects and actions with words and his inventiveness with vocabulary.

Also interesting in Darwin's article are his comments on aspects which became highly relevant to the later study of language acquisition. One of these is the striking difference between the natural ability of babies and animals: 'The facility with which associated ideas … were acquired, seemed to me by far the most strongly marked of all the distinctions between the mind of an infant and that of the cleverest full-grown dog that I have ever known', remarked Darwin (1877, p. 290). He also comments on the role of imitation in early language learning, and on the remarkable speed with which William acquired his vocabulary through imitation. The publication of Darwin's article gave a new impetus to the study of a child's linguistic development, so much so that by the end of the century language acquisition was becoming a field of study in its own right. Substantial works had already been published such as the physiologist William Preyer's 1881 work *Die Seele des Kindes*, which was quickly translated into English and published the following year as *The Mind of the Child*. This included a significant section on the language development of Preyer's son Axel, as well as a review of other diaries (and there were a lot of them!) of the nineteenth century.

By the start of the twentieth century, child language diarists had been at work across Europe (and therefore in many languages) and also in the United States, where articles were being published in the various new journals which were springing up as a result of the growing interest in children's general development. These included titles such as the *American Journal of Psychology*, *The Child Study Monthly* and the *Journal of Childhood and Adolescence*. In Europe, the first major work of the new century was the collaboration of Clara and William Stern, German psychologists who were living at the time in Poland, where William was a teacher at the University of Breslau. The Sterns had three children and, in what was now a well-established tradition among academics interested in child development, kept a very detailed diary of their early years. This provided the material for their 1907 publication *The Language of Children* (*Die Kindersprache*), which is the first work devoted wholly to language acquisition. Their methodology for data collection was also different from previous diarists in that they were often both present when the data was collected, William sitting at his desk pretending to work but actually jotting down the interactions between the children and Clara, with whom he shared a study. *The Language of Children* is the result of systematic analysis of all three children. Apart from the detailed consideration of the children's utterances in terms of German phonology, vocabulary and grammar, the work identifies stages of development across these aspects, an advantage derived from the study of more than one child. Although previous diarists had considered the stages of the first two to three years, particularly in relation to sounds and vocabulary, the Sterns also introduce observations about the development of syntax (an aspect which had to wait until 1973 for the American psycholinguist Roger Brown to fully outline these crucial steps). Not only this, but the Sterns also tackle in some detail what was to become the central consideration of the field of study: to what extent is the acquisition process due to native ability, and how much is due to external influences? The **nature/nurture** question was certainly not a new one, and had already been touched on in relation to language, but the Sterns address it as a central issue.

This question surfaces again in the work of the Danish linguist Otto Jespersen, who has already appeared several times in this book. His son Frans was the subject of some intensive diary keeping, and Jespersen had already written extensively on children's language (republishing this work – *Börnesprog* – in 1923 as a guide for parents). When Jespersen came to write his seminal work on language – *Language: its Nature, Development and Origin*, published in 1922 – he devoted a considerable portion of the book to children's acquisition of their first language. For this, he drew not only on the data he had collected from Frans but also from a wide range of data from both English and Danish-speaking children. What is interesting about Jespersen's study is that his view is not that of a psychologist, but of a linguist. He comments on the value of this in his preface:

> This study seems to me very fascinating indeed, and a linguist is sure to notice many things that would be passed by as uninteresting even by the closest observer among psychologists, but which may have some bearing on the life and development of language. (Jespersen, 1922, p. 8)

Jespersen's approach is certainly systematic and thorough, and he makes extensive use of the data he has collected, even reflecting on the appropriate methodology for gathering it. As well as considering the specifics of acquisition in relation to sounds, vocabulary and grammar, Jespersen, like the Sterns before him, also proposes identifiable stages of development: screaming (!) in the early months, followed by babbling (when speech-like sounds start to appear) and then the 'little language' of children which precedes fully developed 'common language' (ibid., p. 103).

The content of the many diaries which preceded Jespersen's 1922 work was not dissimilar to Jespersen's study, especially in their attention to phonological and lexical development. In essence, however, those diaries were largely descriptive, with only limited consideration of the driving forces behind acquisition, although the Sterns, for instance, considered how the different purposes for which a child can use language could influence their development. Jespersen tackles some of the theoretical issues head-on. Both he and several other observers before him comment on the child's own contribution to her or his learning. Jespersen, also struck by children's seemingly conscious processing of language, gives the example of Frans at the age of nearly three, drawing attention to his ability to articulate sound combinations such as /bl/, /fl/ and /kl/ at the beginning of words. 'It is certain', comments Jespersen, 'that … the little brain is working, and even consciously working, though at first it has not sufficient command of speech to say anything about it' (ibid., p. 111).

Continuing his theoretical speculations about what the child contributes to the learning process, Jespersen devotes a whole chapter (Chapter 8) to some of the 'fundamental problems' at the heart of understanding language acquisition. Central among these is the question of how the young child is able to learn its native language so very easily and with such obvious success. Jespersen considers the relationship between the child's mental ability and the role of parents and other caregivers: 'The real answer in my opinion … lies partly in the child itself, partly in the behaviour towards it of the people around it' (ibid., p. 141). However, it is the child's own capability he believes in most strongly. He quotes the work of the eminent psychologist Wilhelm Wundt who, in his 1900 book on language, commented that "the child's language is the result of the child's environment, the child being essentially a passive instrument in the matter", describing this as 'one of the most wrong-headed sentences I have ever read in the works of a great scientist' (ibid., p. 152). For one thing, Jespersen sees the child's liking for imitation – what he calls echoism – as an important means of learning, stating that it 'explains very much indeed' (ibid., p. 135). When discussing grammar, by far the most difficult aspect of language to acquire, Jespersen criticises those who say it comes by 'instinct' or 'comes quite of itself' as though it involved no mental effort by the child: 'so far is it from "coming of itself" that it demands extraordinary labour on the child's part' (ibid., p. 128). Within 20 years of his death in 1943, the precise nature of this 'labour' was to become the hottest topic in linguistics, as we shall see shortly.

Data collection continued to play an important role in the study of children's language throughout the twentieth century, with large amounts of data being gathered in a range of languages and new methods being introduced to ensure collections were systematic. Cross-sections of data from a large number of children, for example, started to take precedence over long-term studies of individuals, and increasingly they were not the children of the actual researchers. Also new was the introduction of statistical analysis of the data in order to establish developmental norms. The problem of accuracy was resolved as portable tape recorders became more widely available in the 1960s (although the first recordings of children's speech had been made as early as the 1930s). In terms of the researchers themselves, the profile was also changing, with more and more women working in the field: Dorothea McCarthy, for example, who worked at the Minnesota Child Welfare Institute in America from 1929–1953, did a great deal to make the study of children's language more 'scientific' through rigorous and systematic data collection.

Diary-keeping has to some extent fallen into disuse, although a recent media project in America has injected an extraordinary new lease of life into this traditional method. This is the Human Speechome Project based at the Massachusetts Institute of Technology (MIT). Using both video and audio equipment installed throughout his home, Professor Deb Roy recorded over 230,000 hours of material charting the first three years of the life of his son, born in 2005. (Figure 9.1 shows you a video still from one of these home recordings.) Sophisticated techniques for analysing and synthesising the recordings have made it possible to cast new light on the role of interaction in a child's language learning. Earlier researchers such as William and

FIGURE 9.1 A STILL FROM THE VIDEO RECORDINGS MADE AS PART OF THE HUMAN SPEECHOME PROJECT (2005–2008)

Clara Stern and Otto Jespersen certainly included 'conversations' with their children in their diaries, but would be utterly amazed to see the graphics generated by Professor Roy's team and the 'secrets' of language learning which these reveal. This is certainly a 'diary' with a difference.

Behaviourism

We return now to a book which we have already discussed in some detail in previous chapters, Leonard Bloomfield's 1933 work *Language*. Here, he presents human language as a type of behaviour, comparable to any non-verbal types. These all arise as responses to external stimuli. As an (often-quoted) illustration of this, Bloomfield (1933, p. 22ff) offers an account of Jack and Jill out for a walk when the hungry Jill spots an apple on a tree. If Jill had been alone, and able to reach the apple, she would have picked it for herself, just as a hungry animal would also attempt to obtain food. The sight of the food for both Jill and the animal (along with the feeling of hunger) is described by Bloomfield as a **stimulus**, while the attempt to obtain it is a **reaction** to the stimulus. However, because Jill was with Jack when she first spotted the apple, she was able to ask him to get it for her. In other words, she could use a **linguistic substitute reaction** as a response to the stimulus and in turn get a reaction from Jack, for whom her request is also a verbal stimulus. Language, then, is – put simply – a type of reaction to a stimulus, which can also in turn function as a stimulus itself.

The interplay between stimulus and reaction (or response) is at the heart of **behaviourism** (or behaviorism, to use the American spelling), an approach taken towards language (and behaviour in general) by many psychologists and linguists in the 1930s–1950s. This branch of psychology emerged in the early twentieth century partly following some observations about animal conditioning (involving the famous salivating dog!) made by the Russian physiologist Ivan Pavlov in 1904 at his Nobel Prize award ceremony in Stockholm. The term 'behaviorist' was first used in a 1913 article by the American psychologist John B Watson entitled 'Psychology as the behaviorist views it'. In his view, language was a conditioned habit in which words form the interface between a person and their environment – effectively how Bloomfield presents it in his discussion of Jack and Jill. For behaviourists, language was something external, observable, measurable. They did not see it as within their remit to try to investigate internal, mental processes. Instead, they focussed on the context in which behaviour occurs as the only admissible data (and therefore the only scientific way) to explain that behaviour. By drawing a comparison between Jill's response to food and that of an animal, Bloomfield was reflecting the belief that language does not represent a significant difference between human and animal behaviour. It is simply an additional, albeit far more complex, form which reactions to stimuli can take.

Bloomfield's account of children's language acquisition (which follows his discussion of Jill and the apple) continues in this vein. He devotes just a handful of pages to the topic, possibly indicative of the relatively simple process he believes it to be, despite his comment that the acquisition of language is 'doubtless the greatest intellectual feat any of us is ever required to perform' (Bloomfield, 1933, p. 29). Using the example of a child learning the word 'doll', Bloomfield identifies five seemingly straightforward steps involving the interplay between the visual stimulus of the actual doll and the accompanying verbal stimulus of the sound of 'doll', which lead the child to form habits relating to the use of the word in an increasing number of contexts (ibid., pp. 29–31). These habit-forming patterns occur again and again, and in relation to more and more words and word combinations, until eventually a child arrives at the point of having successfully acquired their target language (or what Jespersen called 'common language'). Language, says Bloomfield, is essentially 'a matter of training and habit' (ibid., p. 34).

This view of language was to surface again in 1957 with the publication of *Verbal Behavior* by B F Skinner, the first major publication on the subject of language acquisition in the modern era. Skinner was an American psychologist based at Harvard University whose work with laboratory animals over a period of more than 20 years convinced him that a child's acquisition of language could indeed be explained as the habit-forming process described by Bloomfield. Like other behaviourists, Skinner saw language as a subdivision of human behaviour in general, but as a unique behaviour in the animal world. With that uniqueness comes a special challenge in accounting for the child's linguistic development. However, Skinner was undaunted: 'It would be foolish to underestimate the difficulty of this subject matter', he writes, 'but recent advances in the analysis of behavior permit us to approach it with a certain optimism' (Skinner, 1957, p. 3). He also defends the fact that 'much of the experimental work responsible for this advance has been carried out on other species', believing that 'the methods can be extended to human behaviour without serious modification' (ibid.).

Despite his reliance on experiments with pigeons and rats as the basis for his ideas, *Verbal Behavior* is a detailed account of the response forms which human language can take and the processes by which it is apparently acquired even though, as Skinner attests, 'little use is made of specific experimental results' on humans (ibid., p. 11). Skinner's interest in children's language is due to the fact that the process of **operant conditioning** – the establishing of habits through reinforcement – 'is most conspicuous when verbal behavior is first acquired' (ibid., p. 29). A child's acquisition of language is likened to a laboratory pigeon being trained to walk around its cage in a figure of eight. At first, any marginally appropriate movement is reinforced by means of some edible reward. Later, only those movements which contribute to the formation of the precise shape are reinforced. So a child 'acquires verbal behavior when relatively unpatterned vocalizations, selectively reinforced, gradually assume forms which produce appropriate consequences in a given verbal community' (ibid., p. 31). The notions of conditioning and reinforcement are central to Skinner's explanation. Although Skinner deals with all aspects of language, including grammar, at no point does he hypothesise about what hidden mental processes might enable the child to become a proficient, grammatical speaker. Skinner's concentration on the observable, circumstantial aspects of language learning effectively rendered a theory about acquisition unnecessary – or so he believed. The certainty of this position would not go unchallenged for long.

Chomsky's revolutionary idea

In the same year as B F Skinner published his book on *Verbal Behavior*, Noam Chomsky brought out his first book following the completion of his PhD thesis. This was the influential and groundbreaking *Syntactic Structures* which we last discussed in Chapter 6. The working principle of *Syntactic Structures* was that however much 'real' data you collected, it would be impossible to represent, and therefore describe, all the grammatical sentences in a language. Instead, the goal of the linguist should be to construct a grammar capable of generating any grammatical sentence. Furthermore, the grammar which is the linguist's aim should not be language-specific, but contain elements which would be applicable, in theory, to any natural language. Chomsky's approach to language was, in complete contrast to that of the behaviourists, concerned with linguistic knowledge in the mind. It was abstract, theoretical and mentalist, everything behaviourism rejected. We can imagine then the mood in which Chomsky read Skinner's book and why he was moved, almost immediately, to write a substantial review of it.

This review – running to over 14,000 words – was published in 1959 in the journal *Language* and its influence on the study of language acquisition can still be detected today. It is worth considering therefore some of the specific points Chomsky made and which relate to his views on how language acquisition should be studied. First, Chomsky recognises the significance of Skinner's work as a major attempt to give an account of language acquisition from a behaviourist point of view. It is not, in fact, Skinner's achievement that Chomsky criticises, but the premise on which it is based, hence the 'magnitude of the failure' of Skinner's work – 'an indication of how little is really known about this remarkably complex phenomenon' (Chomsky, 1959/2008, p. 3). For Chomsky, an understanding of a complex organism like a human being requires both external and internal factors to be examined. He doesn't deny the value of looking at external stimuli, but the child's own abilities are far from negligible:

> As far as acquisition of language is concerned, it seems clear that reinforcement, casual observation, and natural inquisitiveness (coupled with a strong tendency to imitate) are important factors, as is the remarkable capacity of the child to

generalize, hypothesize, and 'process information' in a variety of very special and apparently highly complex ways which we cannot yet describe or begin to understand … (ibid., p. 16)

Skinner, he believes, has placed too much emphasis on external factors to the detriment of considering internal, mental ones. What is more, Chomsky makes it clear that it is a mistake to make deductions about human children based on laboratory experiments with other organisms: 'the insights that have been achieved in the laboratories … can be applied to complex human behavior only in the most gross and superficial way', he remarks (ibid., p. 3).

Grammar, as we saw above, was the central focus of Chomsky's linguistic interests, and it is at the core of his demolition of Skinner's account of language acquisition. He demonstrates the inadequacy of Skinner's view of a sentence as 'a set of key responses (nouns, verbs, adjectives) on a skeletal frame' to which compositional elements such as word order or relational aspects (like *through* or *with*) are added as a secondary response (ibid., p. 26). The two sentences *Struggling artists can be a nuisance* and *Marking papers can be a nuisance* have, Chomsky points out, the same frame but not the same structure, as the following substitutions reveal:

Struggling artists <u>can be</u> a nuisance   Struggling artists <u>are</u> a nuisance
Marking papers <u>can be</u> a nuisance   Marking papers <u>is</u> a nuisance

Skinner's claim that sentences are constructed through acquired habits would not account for the deeper structures needed to generate and interpret examples like these, nor for the developing child's remarkable ability to distinguish grammatical from non-grammatical structures. Furthermore, Chomsky considered Skinner had seriously underestimated the child's own role in language learning – something that had been observed and commented on by all manner of diary keepers over a long period of time – and his 'refusal to study the contribution of the child … permits only a superficial account of language acquisition' (ibid., p. 30). Chomsky admits that it isn't easy to accept how much a child seems able to do in relation to the construction of grammar, but any theory of acquisition must account for this ability, as well as the speed with which a child appears able to establish the grammatical principles of the target language.

What, then, of innateness? In his review of Skinner, Chomsky seems only to hint at the innate abilities of the child for learning language. He does, however, make clear his belief that grammar should take centre-stage in any hypothesis since 'a direct attempt to account for the actual behavior of speaker, listener, and learner, not based on a prior understanding of the structure of grammars, will achieve very limited success' (ibid., p. 29). Another remark which foreshadows the proposals he would make within a few years puts the focus on innate capacity: 'The fact that all normal children acquire essentially comparable grammars of great complexity with remarkable rapidity suggests that human beings are somehow specially designed to do this ...' (ibid.). By the mid-1960s, Chomsky had crystallised his thoughts on this question. He proposed, first, that we are born with some kind of hard-wiring for language in the form of a **language acquisition device**, and then superseded this suggestion with the claim for a genetically pre-programmed universal grammar (or UG), a set of structural principles shared by all human languages which enabled the child, once exposed to a language, to deduce, acquire and apply its grammatical rules. Concentrating, from that point onwards, on theorising about the nature of universal grammar, Chomsky effectively abandoned the study of actual children, leaving it to other researchers, much as Skinner had done in the shelter of his animal laboratory.

Nevertheless, Chomsky's claims were to have far-reaching effects, and the debate about our innate knowledge of language is still very much alive. Chomsky's review of *Verbal Behavior* is credited as one of the driving events for the cognitive revolution, when the study of the mind was reinstated as an appropriate means of explaining human behaviour. We saw in the previous chapter how the majority of present-day linguists, psychologists and neurolinguists believe in the brain's innate capacity for language (and genetics and neuroscience are providing evidence for this) but not necessarily of the specific character Chomsky claimed for it. However, there are some who claim there is still a place for universal grammar within the theoretical study of language acquisition. One of the liveliest supporters of Chomsky's position has been the Hawaiian-based linguist Derek Bickerton, whose field of research is in the pidgin and creole languages we considered briefly in Chapter 4. He proposed that the observable formation of these hybrid languages reveals universal grammar at work. (And some evolutionary linguists have even gone so far as to suggest it replicates the origin of language itself, as does children's language acquisition in general.) Since creoles develop when children start to learn pidgin languages as their native tongue, the children must be applying their innate grammatical framework in constructing fully-fledged languages from these less developed pidgins. However, the theory only convinces if the resulting creoles are essentially similar to each other in grammatical terms, which more recent scrutiny reveals is not the case. Chomsky's legacy with regard to language acquisition is more likely to be the research and debate his claim prompted rather than a lasting belief in universal grammar, although this remains to be seen.

The developing brain, the developing mind

We saw in the previous chapter how our understanding of the human brain has deepened over the last 200 years or so. Neuroscience is now taking this understanding of the brain's language capacity to new levels, and is revealing a great deal about the child's linguistic development. Even the gradual growth of the brain in the womb has been revealed. Amazingly, a new-born baby already has its full complement of neurons (about 86 billion!) and, although the neurons are not yet fully developed, the brain is ready to start building the millions of connections that will, in time, allow the baby to become conscious of itself, to understand the world, to remember, to think and to acquire language.

One feature of the young brain is its extraordinary **plasticity**. We know that the brain is lateralised, but at birth the two hemispheres of the brain have an equal potential to become the primary hemisphere for language. In practice, however, it is normally the left side which gradually becomes dominant for both language and right-handedness, a fact which still requires full explanation. Young children who suffer damage to (or even loss of) the left hemisphere are still able to develop or even reacquire language, unlike adults, who lack this adaptability. (Think of the patients of Broca and Wernicke.) The stories of the feral children we considered in the opening section, however, beg the question of why, with youthful plasticity on their side, was it not possible for children like Victor or Genie to acquire language like other children? Clearly, possibilities such as learning difficulties and severe deprivation have to be taken into consideration, but an alternative proposal is that there is a **critical period**, beyond which the brain loses its plasticity and normal language acquisition becomes impossible. This idea was put forward in the middle of the twentieth century, first by the neurologists Wilder Penfield and Lamar Roberts in 1959, and then by the German-born neurologist and linguist, Eric Lenneberg, who pursued his career in the United States. It is his name which is usually connected with the **critical period hypothesis**.

Like Chomsky, Lenneberg rejected behaviour as a cross-species phenomenon. For him, behaviour – including language – was biologically-determined and species-specific. Biological determination could be age-related, such as in the way some young birds 'imprint' onto a parent bird, opting for any suitable replacement if the real parent is absent during the critical period for imprinting. In his 1967 study, *Biological Foundations of Language*, Lenneberg carefully examines the biological maturation of the brain, and finds a correlation between this and the optimum 'critical' period for the acquisition of language between the ages of 2 and 12 years. The end of the critical period is marked by the 'termination of a state of organizational plasticity linked with lateralization of function' (Lenneberg, 1967, p. 176). Beyond this, automatic acquisition of a language becomes impossible, which explains why older learners of foreign languages almost never achieve the degree of fluency found in native speakers. When 12-year-old Genie was discovered and taken into care in 1970, it inevitably led to speculation that her case might provide proof of Lenneberg's hypothesis. It appeared that Genie was using her right hemisphere to process language, which suggested that typical lateralisation had not taken place, but evidence for her having passed a critical period was not conclusive, as it was impossible to tell how her early traumatic deprivation had affected her language learning abilities.

Interestingly, Lenneberg sets the start of the critical period at the age of two years, when the first signs of grammar have normally appeared in the form of two-word utterances (such as 'want juice' or 'there doll'). Children are now generally regarded as having made significant linguistic advances before this. The maturation of Wernicke's area – associated with comprehension – seems to come after about 12 months, which correlates with the ability of one-year-olds to understand a range of simple words. Broca's area matures a little later, perhaps explaining why early production always lags behind comprehension, although most children exhibit considerable success before the age of two. Some aspects of a baby's readiness for language have even been shown to be present at birth: for example, an ability to distinguish between very similar speech sounds such as /p/ and /b/.

One thing that is certain about language acquisition is that all healthy infants will succeed at it, assuming they are properly cared for and are exposed to at least one natural language. Furthermore, the predictable course of the process is a further argument in favour of language development being biologically determined – or genetically determined, as we would probably say now. We saw how some of the early diary keepers and data collectors were able to identify stages of development when comparing children of similar ages, and linguists now usually work within a framework of developmental stages. In English, for example, it is possible to predict not just when children will start to construct negative sentences, but also the steps they will go through (such as 'milk no', 'I no want milk') before arriving at the target structure ('I don't want milk'). One early-twentieth-century psychologist who was interested in the stages of children's general development and its relationship to the acquisition of language was the Swiss psychologist Jean Piaget, based at the University of Geneva. He set out his ideas in his 1923 work, *The Language and Thought of the Child*. His developmental stages had a bearing on the understanding of language acquisition because, for him, the stages of language acquisition could not precede the development of certain associated cognitive skills.

Piaget viewed language as following on from the development of the mind and understanding. This implies thought can occur in very young, pre-linguistic children. This brings us back to the innateness question. If we are not programmed specifically to learn language (or grammar) in the way Chomsky suggested, are we pre-programmed to think in a particular way? After all, surely thought is required as a prerequisite for learning language? This is the more recent view of the American philosopher Jerry Fodor, who proposed (1975) a **language of thought** hypothesis to explain children's ability to learn language without the benefit of language itself. Admittedly, this language of thought would need to be a complex system if it is capable of acting as a foundation for the acquisition of language, and many linguists have found this view no more convincing than the universal grammar proposal. However, both ideas point to the same conclusion: that the child's ability to learn language so effortlessly, an ability that is not reflected in the later learning of a second language, will take some explaining.

The child's world

However we learn language, the fact remains that we are all dependent, as babies and young children, on someone providing us with the model of a language to learn. Cultural transmission is crucial to the continuing life of any human language. Whatever our innate biological or genetic capacity to acquire language may turn out to be, the actual acquisition of it takes place in the real world, with the transmission being conducted, so to speak, by real everyday speakers. Surprisingly, the implications of this have only been fully appreciated in the last 50 years or so.

Chomsky's claims about a universal grammar certainly prompted a great deal of theorising about the nature of this putative faculty – something which could be done without much reference to children's actual speech, only to the target languages they were learning. It wasn't long, however, before other researchers saw the danger of ignoring the actual context in which a child's language develops and asserted the need to look more closely at the various uses to which language could be put by children in the earliest stages of development in order to explain their motivation to learn. One such researcher was the British linguist Michael Halliday (another diary keeper!), who spent much of his career at the University of Sydney. The study of his son Nigel (published in 1975) enabled Halliday to identify the first functions of a child's language. For example, as he approached his first birthday, one of the earliest uses Nigel made of language was the **instrumental** function, in which he sought to get what he wanted with his initial attempts to articulate words like 'powder' and 'clock'. Halliday claimed it is the satisfying of needs, the desire to interact with others and the urge to express a sense of self which drive the child's early language development. Following this, the child starts to develop language abilities that enable him or her to learn more about the environment in which they are growing up. Halliday's functional approach to language seemed to many of his colleagues a more convincing way to explain a child's instinct to learn, and a new divide seemed to open up in acquisition research, this time between the mentalists and the functionalists.

When Chomsky first proposed his concept of universal grammar, he claimed it was a solution to what he described as 'the logical problem of language acquisition'. This problem was that the child grew up able to generate sentences and structures that she had never been exposed to. Not only this, but, in Chomsky's view, much of the normal everyday language to which a child was exposed was a deficient model to learn from – we all sometimes muddle our words, or mumble, or abandon an utterance mid-sentence. The proficiency a child achieves therefore needs explaining in the light of the 'poverty of the stimulus' (a complete contrast to Skinner, who saw the stimulus as sufficient for the task) and therefore the child must have some innate capacity to help her on her way.

In the 1970s, an alternative suggestion was put forward about what type of help the child receives on her journey to full language competence. This was the proposal of the American psycholinguist Catherine Snow who turned the focus on the child's caregiver and observed the ways in which mothers adapted their speech according to the child's level of linguistic development. Her research (undertaken for her PhD) drew on extensive data from tape-recorded exchanges between 36 children, their mothers, and a small group of women who were not mothers. In a 1972 report of her findings, Snow begins by stating the importance of considering the quality of the linguistic input children receive: 'The speech young children hear is their only source of information about the language they are to learn' (Snow, 1972, p. 549). This sounds, of course, like stating the obvious. But, as Snow points out, 'despite its unquestioned importance … very little is actually known about the kind of language which is addressed to children'. This is why 'it must be taken into account in any attempt to explain the process of language acquisition' (ibid.). Snow's research looked at a range of features used by the mothers, including sentence complexity, use of third person pronouns (children take a while to acquire all personal pronouns) and different types of repetition. Significantly, the mothers thought it was their children's language which was being studied, not their own, so this guaranteed natural data. The findings certainly bore out a pattern of differences in relation to the ages of the children studied. Snow concludes that, although the mothers were primarily concerned to interact with their children, this fulfilled the additional, unwitting purpose of providing the children 'with tractable, relatively consistent, and relevant linguistic information from which to formulate the rules of grammar' (ibid., p. 564). Snow's work in what has come to be termed **child directed speech** has extended to the whole range of caregivers who come into contact with children and this field is now a significant part of the research into language acquisition.

Acquisition, impairment and loss

Apart from some early philosophical musings about children's language, the study of language acquisition effectively began with the data collections of the first diary keepers. These observational and descriptive activities soon gave way to more theoretical approaches, the most radical being Chomsky's claim for an innate universal grammar. In many respects, the current research in the field of language acquisition reflects both the significance of Chomsky's claim and the considerable backlash it prompted. Currently, theories about acquisition abound, often with fairly subtle differences between them, but all positioned somewhere between the extremes of nativism and behaviourism. These positions reflect the different ways in which it is possible to view language, and the long-running argument as to whether it is right to place grammar at the core of the acquisition process, thereby demoting all other factors.

Despite the rejection of Skinner's 1957 portrayal of language as a conditioned habit, aspects of behaviourism have resurfaced in a range of current theories. Most of these, however, incorporate the child's own abilities into the process to some degree, so that an interplay between nature and nurture is used to account for the child's success in becoming a fluent speaker. Other approaches include a development of functionalist ideas by exploring the benefits which language can bring to the child, an emphasis on the relationship between the child and her caregiver, and a more considered exploration of the child's environment. While it seems as if no stone is being left unturned in unearthing possible underlying factors, a full and definitive account of the acquisition process still seems some way off. This situation parallels the search for an answer to one of the other big questions of linguistics: how did language emerge in the human race in the first place?

Research into native language acquisition has blossomed not just in relation to the typical paths which most children take, but in relation to less typical ones too. Many children grow up being bilingual, and a great deal of research centres on the acquisition of two (or more) languages simultaneously, as well as on second language learning as a process undertaken by speakers fluent in their native language. Sadly, many developing children experience difficulties in acquiring language, the majority of which are now viewed as genetically determined. Two hundred years ago, children like these would have been dismissed by many (as Victor was) as hopeless idiots. Nowadays, considerable effort is being made to understand how they can best be helped to overcome their impairments, and how the formation and functions of their brains differ from that of typical language learners. The effect of deafness on language acquisition is now more fully understood, and extensive study of sign language has revealed its remarkable properties.

The study of acquisition is a constant reminder that language, whatever the innate capacities of the brain to acquire it, remains a cultural, symbolic system which needs to be passed on from generation to generation. With the giving and receiving of language comes the potential for its loss. We saw in Chapter 4 how languages in their entirety can 'die' from one cause or another. Language loss can also affect the individual speaker in a number of ways. A recent area of growing research concerns the attritional effect a second language can have on a first one, particularly in the case of migrants, for whom the adoption of a new language can cause the gradual loss of aspects of their native tongue, and with that the loss of identity. Neuroscience is slowly casting more light on the complex and not entirely predictable relationship between brain damage (or deterioration, as suffered by those with Alzheimer's disease) and language loss. And no one would dispute the distress caused by the loss of language to both the sufferers and those people who feel they can no longer interact with them. But to read the stories of the children we encountered at the start of this chapter shows how the failure of any human mind to acquire language in the first place, whatever that process may eventually be shown to involve, results in an absence it is hard for most of us to fully appreciate.

Suggestions for further reading and research

On first language acquisition

Aitchison, Jean (2011) *The Articulate Mammal: An Introduction to Psycholinguistics*, 5th edn (Abingdon: Routledge)

First published in 1976, this classic introduction has been updated to take account of recent developments in the field.

Clark, Eve V (2009) *First Language Acquisition*, 2nd edn (Cambridge: Cambridge University Press)

An accessible and comprehensive survey of acquisition, which also explores theoretical approaches.

Evans, Vyvyan (2014) *The Language Myth: Why Language is Not an Instinct* (Cambridge: Cambridge University Press)

Evans argues the case against universal grammar – a response to Steven Pinker's book, listed below.

Pinker, Steven (1994) *The Language Instinct* (New York: Morrow & Co)

Enjoyable and interesting, if at times challenging to read, Pinker's book has caused controversy in relation to his support for Chomsky's theory of universal grammar.

Stilwell Peccei, Jean (2006) *Child Language: A Resource Book for Students* (Abingdon: Routledge)

A very useful book, covering key concepts and providing guidance on analysing data. It also contains key readings in the field.

On bilingualism and on second language acquisition

Ellis, Rod (1997) *Second Language Acquisition* (Oxford: Oxford University Press)

An accessible and well-regarded text, covering both the practical and theoretical issues surrounding the learning of second languages.

Romaine, Suzanne (1995) *Bilingualism*, 2nd edn (Oxford: Blackwell)

An authoritative introduction to all aspects of growing up with two languages.

Saville-Troike, Muriel (2012) *Introducing Second Language Acquisition*, 2nd edn (Cambridge: Cambridge University Press)

Covering all the key aspects of this topic, the non-technical and practical approach makes this a very useful text for anyone approaching it for the first time.

On child language acquisition in relation to evolution

Bickerton, Derek (1992) *Language and Species* (Chicago: University of Chicago Press)

Essentially a book about the origin of language, but acquisition is considered as one of the ways of casting light on this process.

Slobin, Dan I (2004) 'From ontogenesis to phylogenesis: what can child language tell us about language evolution?', in Sue Taylor Parker, Jonas Langer and Constance Milbrath (eds) *Biology and Knowledge Revisited: From Neurogenesis to Psychogenesis* (New York: Psychology Press, 2014)

Slobin's article reviews the evidence for various proposals about what we can learn about language evolution from the way a child acquires language.

Useful websites

Human Speechome Project
www.media.mit.edu/cogmac/projects/hsp.html (accessed October 2015)

Information about Professor Deb Roy's ambitious project to record his son's linguistic development for several hours every day for the first three years of his life.

Deb Roy '*The birth of a word*'
www.ted.com/talks/deb_roy_the_birth_of_a_word#t-1163909 (accessed October 2015)

This talk given in March 2011 at a TED conference (Technology, Entertainment and Design) includes a 40-second audio clip of Roy's son's acquisition of 'water' over a period of six months.

The diaries of Clara and William Stern
www.mpi.nl/resources/data/stern-diaries (accessed October 2015)

Access to the electronic version of the Stern diaries through the website of the Max Planck Institute for Psycholinguistics.

10 The continuing story

Thinkers and researchers introduced (or reintroduced) in this final chapter

Daniel Jones (1881–1967)   British phonetician
Alan Turing (1912–54)   British mathematician
Jan Svartvik (b. 1931)   Swedish linguist
David Crystal (b. 1941)   British linguist
Anthony (Tony) Monaco (b. 1959)   American geneticist and neuroscientist
Simon Fisher (b. 1970)   British geneticist and neuroscientist

---

Branches of linguistics covered in this chapter

applied linguistics
clinical linguistics
computational linguistics
corpus linguistics
evolutionary linguistics
forensic linguistics
neurolinguistics
preventive linguistics
theoretical linguistics

Branches of linguistics covered previously in this book

areal linguistics
cognitive linguistics
comparative linguistics
descriptivism / descriptive linguistics
desk linguistics
field linguistics
functional linguistics
general linguistics
historical linguistics
pragmatics
psycholinguistics
sociolinguistics
structuralism / structural linguistics
theoretical linguistics
translation studies

The expanding field of linguistics

This is an exciting time for linguistics. The year 2016 marks a hundred years since the publication of Saussure's *Course in General Linguistics*, which signposts the beginning of the modern era of language study. As the stories of the preceding chapters have revealed, this last century has seen linguistics transformed from a relatively unknown and modest pursuit into an established discipline involving thousands of researchers in a vast array of projects, making up an intricate network of interwoven branches, many of which overlap with or even function as part of other disciplines. Contemporary linguistics may not seem a particularly unified pursuit – and it is probably impossible to provide a definitive and comprehensive overview – but the seeming disorder is largely a reflection of the fact that linguists are busy investigating language in all its guises as they seek to understand more and more about their fascinating object of study.

In this final chapter, we will be considering what the future might hold for linguistics. Of course, it is naïve to think that this is entirely predictable. Many of the thinkers we have met in previous chapters could no more have foreseen the ideas that would supersede their own than we can do now. However, it is possible to anticipate the kind of work linguists will continue to undertake, and to say with certainty that science and technology will play a crucial role in much of their research. Later in this chapter, we will also consider whether the 'big questions' of linguistics will remain unanswered, but for now we will begin by taking a look at some of the specific ways in which linguistic expertise is proving to be of real value to people and communities throughout the world.

Making the world a better place

There is little to suggest that early scholars of language considered how their linguistic knowledge could be put to practical use, other than in the teaching of foreign languages. This occupation has its own interesting and well-documented history (too extensive for inclusion here) charting how, over the centuries, there has been a significant shift in focus from enabling learners to read and write in the target language (often for scholarly purposes alone) to the promotion of spoken fluency and the ability to use the newly acquired language in a range of interactional contexts. The growing interest in the early part of the twentieth century in teaching strategies led to the publication in 1948 of *Language Learning: A Journal of Applied Linguistics*, the first formal recognition of the notion of ***applied* linguistics**, a name suggestive of its likely benefit to the world we live in as well as of its status as a broad contrast to more theoretical approaches to language.

Nowadays, the scope of applied linguistics extends well beyond an interest in foreign and second language learning to encompass a range of other real-life applications. In particular, workers and researchers within this field are concerned with the issues that surround communities according to the languages they speak – issues such as the status of minority languages, communication in the multilingual communities of many large cities, levels of literacy and educational provision. Linguistic matters often become urgent. In recent years, millions of refugees from the war in Syria have found their way to countries of asylum where the speedy acquisition of a new language will be vital to their future. Worldwide, then, there is a vast amount of important and valuable work for applied linguists to undertake. Importantly, applied linguistics has retained its core interest in the best methods for language learning and teaching, and the benefits of this hardly need spelling out, particularly in an era when effective global communication seems more critical than ever before. These methods are still the subject of lively debate but have become more informed by our greater understanding of cultural variation, as well as by psycholinguistic insights into how language is acquired, stored and processed in the mind.

The diversity of the world's languages is something linguists regard as a great treasure, although it is sadly often undervalued in an age of increasing dominance by a handful of so-called global languages. Widely spoken in various parts of the world as a native language or a foreign language and commonly used for a range of international purposes, global languages include English, Spanish, Chinese and Arabic. As mentioned just now, the advantages of millions of people learning and sharing the same language are not difficult to identify, and if people can learn new languages while retaining their first languages as part of their personal and cultural identity then this is undoubtedly a positive.

But the picture is not always so rosy. We saw at the start of Chapter 4 that many of the world's 7,000 or so languages are in danger of extinction. Some calculations suggest that there may once have been 12,000 or more languages spoken concurrently in the world. As for the future, the most doom-laden (but maybe realistic) linguistic prophets foresee a time when only one language is spoken worldwide – and English is a likely candidate. Despite the ease with which we can now access resources for foreign language learning, and despite the fact that a considerable proportion of the world's population is bilingual, an apocalyptic shift towards fewer and fewer world languages is undoubtedly underway. Sadly, whole language communities can be lost as a result of natural disasters – earthquakes, floods, disease – but there are many other reasons why languages are becoming extinct at an alarming rate, and the spread of global languages is one of them. Sadly, the displacement of populations due to war, poverty and famine constitute other reasons.

Since the 1990s, the increasing concern among linguists for endangered languages has prompted a number of initiatives not only to try to record them, but also to attempt revitalisation wherever possible. Writing in 2000, the British linguist David Crystal made the case for language preservation with great force: '… we are at a critical point in human linguistic history', he wrote, 'and most people don't know' (Crystal, 2000, p. ix). Languages need preserving as much as the environment, and Crystal has proposed a field of **preventive linguistics** concerned exclusively with the need to protect languages from extinction. By all accounts, this is not easy work: speakers themselves are often resistant to what they perceive as outside interference, and endangered languages are often spoken in politically sensitive contexts. This is why, wherever possible, native speakers are being trained to record their own languages, so that a cultural 'outsider' is no longer needed. But anything linguists can do in the future to save dying languages – not just for the benefit of linguists and human knowledge, but first and foremost for the sake of the people and communities who speak them – will surely make the world a better place, as Crystal's impassioned plea persuades us.

Moving into a different sphere of linguistic usefulness, we saw in Chapter 5 how, in the 1960s, the Swedish linguist Jan Svartvik was able to demonstrate that the murder 'confession' of Londoner Timothy Evans had been partly fabricated by the police officers who interviewed him. This was the first time that a linguist had made a contribution to the cause of justice (although other cases quickly followed) and it is generally regarded as the first event of what was to become **forensic linguistics**. Writing about his involvement in the official inquiry into Evans's conviction, Svartvik commented on how 'it has provided the linguist with one of those rare opportunities of making a contribution that might be directly useful to society' (Svartvik, 1968, Preface). Forty years later, in 2008, the first ever Centre for Forensic Linguistics was opened at Aston University in Birmingham, testimony to the importance which this field has now attained. Forensic linguists now play a significant part in assisting the police and the judiciary with their work: as well as helping to establish the authorship of incriminating material and the authenticity of documents such as suicide notes, they can identify anonymous callers through voice analysis, address problems of translation during interviews and determine the precise meaning of arcane legal clauses. These are just some of the many applications of forensic linguistics, one of the discipline's newest branches, in which linguists take on the roles of both detective and expert witness.

Linguists are also making a major contribution in the field of speech and language pathology, helping people with various language disabilities. This is the territory of **clinical linguistics**, which has its origins in the work of nineteenth-century physicians like Paul Broca and Carl Wernicke whom we met in Chapter 7. The main practitioners in this field are speech and language therapists, whose primary concern is with the assessment and treatment of individuals with language impairments, either in production or comprehension and whether the problems are phonological, grammatical or pragmatic. Clinical linguists aim to look at the bigger picture by studying the increasing collection of case studies in order to learn more about the conditions from which people suffer. The analysis of data is also of assistance in deciding what might be regarded as typical or atypical linguistic behaviour or development – not an easy benchmark to establish when speakers are naturally idiosyncratic. As well as contributing to clinical and educational therapy for those with language difficulties, clinical linguists are using the data they gather to learn more about language itself. Their work, then, inevitably overlaps with other branches of linguistics, particularly neurolinguistics (with its focus on the brain as an organ) and psycholinguistics (focussed on the workings of the mind). The practitioners themselves would no doubt agree with Jan Svartvik that it is good to be able to make a useful contribution to society, although such opportunities are no longer rare, but seem increasingly plentiful.

What technology has done for linguistics

There is no doubt that in the last century or so technology has transformed linguistics, much as it has so many other fields of research as well as our everyday lives. The first successful collaborations between linguist and machine were in the early decades of sound recording. In 1917, for instance, the British phonetician Daniel Jones was enabled by the recording company His Master's Voice (later HMV) to produce a gramophone record of himself demonstrating the set of **cardinal vowel** sounds he had established as a framework for phonetic classification, a performance which now sounds quaint and even mildly comical, but which proved extremely useful to phoneticians for many decades. As recording equipment became more portable, dialectologists quickly began to use sound recording as a means of collecting data from regional dialect speakers, as we have seen previously. By the 1980s, the advent of digital recording methods was bringing about a further transformation as storage became more efficient and sound quality improved. The ability to record speech for the purposes of linguistic analysis is now something we very much take for granted and has guaranteed that in future spoken language will always get the attention it merits as our primary mode of communication.

As the twentieth century progressed, technology started to provide the means not just to record language, but to interpret it too. Many people know the story of Alan Turing and his work during World War II to crack the code used by German military commanders to send messages to their forces. These messages were encrypted letter by letter using a sophisticated 'Enigma' machine and were almost impossible to decipher due to the complexity of the encoding process and the fact that the Germans changed the initial settings for the machine every 24 hours. Millions and millions of configurations were possible: it was beyond the ability of human mathematicians to decode the messages, but, as it turned out, not beyond their ability to design and build a machine to do the decryptions for them. The work done by Turing and his Polish predecessors who had worked on German encryption in the 1930s was the first time that computing power had been used to decipher linguistic content. After World War II, when much of the Northern Hemisphere was in the grip of the Cold War, the US Air Force began to use machine translation to interpret decoded messages they intercepted from the Russians, although the outcomes were far from accurate.

Over half a century later, the dream of a machine that can do our translating for us lives on beyond the political world, and accurate, idiomatic machine translation has become one of the goals of **computational linguistics**. If you are used to using translation tools such as Google Translate or BabelFish you will be aware of how much has already been achieved but also how much remains to be done. The word-for-word strategy first used by the Americans in the 1960s was always going to be a hit-and-miss affair due to the differences that exist between any two languages, differences that occur at all structural levels, and of course in semantics. We saw in Chapters 6 and 7 what has been understood in the last 50 years or so about how language works. The many grammatical theories that have emerged in the wake of generative grammar have provided researchers with various possible bases for encoding languages digitally to achieve a translation that is both grammatically acceptable and stylistically convincing. Hardest of all is to deal with the semantic and pragmatic subtleties which are the most elusive aspects of language to map systematically. Nevertheless, we can expect in future to rely more and more on machine translation – not that one would ever wish, for all kinds of reasons, to do away with the human touch of living, breathing translators.

Computational linguistics also plays a significant role within the field of artificial intelligence, where considerable development work is taking place to enable computers to perform **natural language processing** at a complex level. In other words, they will be able to 'understand' human language and to provide the kind of interactional response that might be expected from a human participant. They may even be able to pass what has become known as the Turing test (after Alan Turing) where machine and human intelligence become indistinguishable. We are already becoming used to talking to a computer on the telephone when relatively simple operations are involved, and voice activation and recognition are becoming part of other aspects of our everyday lives. Researchers have now built robots that are disarmingly similar to us in terms of simple behaviour and movement, and are in possession of simple linguistic abilities. It is only a matter of time before they become more versatile language users. Advances in the field of voice synthesis mean that they will probably even sound like us.

Apart from furthering the cause of machine translation and contributing to a science-fiction-like human/android future, computational linguistics interacts with a number of other fields in which linguists build computer-based models to test their theories about language. In psycholinguistics, for example, researchers are combining neurological research with computational models in order to understand more about how the brain processes sentences. They also create models to generate predictions about how language acquisition takes place: if a prediction proves correct by mirroring what actually happens, then the premise on which it is based is probably correct too. A similar strategy has been used to help researchers in the fields of historical and evolutionary linguistics learn about the process of language change: accurate modelling will result in accurate predictions about future change, and reversing the process could enable researchers to make valid deductions about linguistic prehistory.

Many of the exciting activities outlined above are possible only because of the considerable sophistication and processing power with which computers now provide us. This has also resulted in a growing body of online **corpora**, collections of spoken and written language data consisting of thousands of examples of language in use and amounting to millions of words. **Corpus linguistics** has its roots in the 1960s when linguists at Brown University in the United States transferred a vast amount of written material onto magnetic computer tape and provided guidance for how it might be analysed. Since then, there has been a proliferation of corpora (many of them now offering audio-visual data as well as written). The British National Corpus, for example, describes itself on its website as a '100 million word collection of samples of written and spoken language from a wide range of sources, designed to represent a wide cross-section of British English, both spoken and written, from the late twentieth century' (University of Oxford, 2015). Of course, in theory, anyone could compile a collection of linguistic texts and use it to examine patterns of language use. The beauty of online data-bases, however, is that no matter how large the corpus, specially designed software means that detailed, extensive linguistic analysis can be performed quickly and accurately. Consequently, linguists have used corpora to learn about aspects such as word frequency over time, collocational trends (show-ing which words typically appear together), regional variation, the use of metalanguage, and contexts in which particular grammatical or stylistic features are most likely to occur.

Corpora, then, are enabling linguists to make huge advances in their study of language in use, drawing their evidence from substantial quantities of data. Online databases are also bringing about significant changes in the form and use of dictionaries. The steady shift from the printed to the online dictionary is set to continue. Dictionaries are being linked to electronic data collections so that changes and innovations in language use can be instantly incorporated into the definitions. Long regarded by many as authoritative works compiled by an elite group of lexicographers, dictionaries are now becoming dynamic and consequently more democratic. Online diction-ary Wordnik, for instance, sees its users as part of a community helping to generate its content by contributing their own examples and experiences of language in use (something which is also becoming part of online translation tools). Wordnik also draws on examples of current usage from other sources (such as Twitter) and enables you to compare definitions from a range of other dictionaries. It is a telling example of where dictionaries are going in the future, and a vindication of all the linguists who have promoted language users as the ultimate determiners of meaning. Even that most venerable and authoritative institution the Oxford English Dictionary now invites public contributions to help the editors find out more about the origin and development of words: 'The website enables the public to post evidence in direct response to *OED* editors online, fostering a collective effort to record the English language and find the true roots of our vocabulary' (Oxford University Press, 2013).

The ability to exploit databases in order to learn more about the languages of the world is also proving fruitful, especially when data from two differ-ent fields of research can be merged. We saw in Chapter 4 how philologists speculated about possible reasons for language change and for languages to develop some of the phonetic features they do. More recently, findings by a team at the Max Planck Institute for Evolutionary Anthropology in Leipzig have established a connection between climate and tonal languages (in which phonetically similar words are distinguished only by different intonation patterns). Using climate data, they were able to show that tonal languages are more common in geographical regions where humidity levels are high, and were even able to demonstrate the effect of moisture in the atmosphere on the vocal cords of the larynx. This is an example not just of what can be done with large amounts of data, but also of the benefits of interdisciplinary approaches, where linguistic and non-linguistic data are integrated. This is increasingly the way many areas of linguistics have developed, as we have already seen, and this trend is likely to continue in the future.

The big unanswered questions of linguistics

The stories that have been told in this book, though often seemingly unconnected, have hopefully provided you with a sense of how much has been debated, researched and understood about language in the last 2,500 years, and particularly in the last two centuries. In the last 50 years or so, technological advances have made a substantial contribution to our linguistic knowledge. But of course there is still a great deal linguists would like to know. For some researchers, such as comparative linguists or sociolinguistics, the fact that language is constantly changing means there will always be plenty to record and research. They can expect to be kept busy indefinitely, accumulating more and more knowledge about language in its social and cultural contexts. For other linguists, the research in their particular field is driven and united by the search for answers to big, overarching questions about language in its 'purest' sense. In the next three sections, we will take a look at the state of current research into these questions and consider whether there is any prospect of getting answers to any of them in the near future, if at all.

The future of evolutionary linguistics

In March 2015, scientists made an exciting announcement about a section of fossilised human jawbone (with teeth!) that had been excavated in the Afar area of Ethiopia two months earlier. Dated at 2.8 million years old, the fossil had been identified as belonging to the earliest member of the *Homo* genus found so far, and a probable missing link between our ancestor *Homo habilis* and 'Lucy', an even older member of the hominid family who also originated from that area. Only a few months later, news broke of an equally exciting – and much more substantial – find in an almost inaccessible cave in South Africa of a remarkable *15* partial skeletons all belonging to a previously unknown human species – *Homo naledi* – that could have lived three million years ago, but shares some significant features with modern humans, such as the shape of our hands and our small teeth. In the future, we can certainly expect more and more fossilised fragments like this to come to light. Currently, excavations to look for human fossils are taking place not only in South Africa and in East Africa, where humans originated, but also in Mozambique, and further afield in countries like India, Indonesia and China. With dating and other analytical techniques becoming more and more sophisticated, these fossils will doubtless help to fill some of the current gaps in the jigsaw of human evolution. It would be surprising if, in turn, these new discoveries did not also tell us a little more about how we came to be a linguistic species.

Realistically, however, it is highly unlikely that we will ever have an answer to the big question of exactly how human language came into existence, as the discussion at the end of Chapter 3 implied. But the 'jawbone' episode alone is an example of how, by degrees, we can expect to improve upon our current knowledge, perhaps quite substantially. As the evolutionary biologist Tecumseh Fitch points out, language 'is not a monolithic whole, and from a biological perspective may be better seen as a "bag of tricks" pieced together via a process of evolutionary tinkering' (Fitch, 2010, p. 5). The composite, multifaceted nature of language means that a multidisciplinary approach is essential if progress is to be made in discovering its origin. Linguists will need to seek ways to integrate their perspectives with those of researchers from other fields and, warns Fitch, not elevate any one aspect of language to an assumed or unwarranted position of centrality.

Apart from archaeology, there are various fields of research that are likely to uncover more about the 'bag of tricks' that is human language. Studies of the communicative abilities of other species (not just our close relatives), research into human migration, and anthropological findings about communities of early humans and how they lived are all likely to add to the mix. Linguists themselves will contribute further insights from the study of language change and grammaticalisation, the formation of pidgins and creoles, and language acquisition, as well as from their increasing knowledge about the many languages of the world. The use of sophisticated computer modelling to replicate how certain linguistic developments might have occurred can also be expected to provide some significant results. What we are likely to learn about the human brain, however, perhaps provides the most exciting prospect for our understanding of language evolution, as we will see in the next section.

The future of brain exploration and neurolinguistics

The discovery at Cambridge University in 1953 of the structure of DNA – the molecule that carries our genetic information – was a significant scientific breakthrough and led to the complete sequencing by 2003 of a human genome, the extraordinarily complex knitting pattern of genetic material that determines our physiological make-up. A further genetic breakthrough which caused great excitement among linguists came about in the late 1990s, this time at Oxford University, where the neuroscientists Simon Fisher and Tony Monaco identified a gene now known to play a part in preparing the growing brain for language. Similar to the early neurologists we met in Chapter 8, the team at Oxford were working with patients suffering from severe language impairments. What was unusual about these patients is that they were all related: 15 family members across three generations exhibited the same difficulties in articulating speech, selecting words and processing certain types of complex sentences. Genetic comparisons between the unaffected and affected family members revealed (in the latter) a single mutation in the structure of a gene the scientists labelled **FOXP2**. (There are over 40 'FOX' type genes, all responsible for the production of a particular group of the proteins needed to build body tissue.)

When the news of this discovery broke, some media commentators were quick to label FOXP2 'the language gene'. It was exciting to think that a genetic basis for language had been discovered, but of course this representation was somewhat misleading, suggesting as it did that one gene alone was responsible for our entire human linguistic ability. FOXP2 is clearly important in language: its biological function seems to be to prompt the development of various areas of the brain, including Broca's area. But the discovery of FOXP2 is really only the start of a long journey to discover exactly how the human genome is encoded for language, and what it means to claim, as most psycholinguists do, that our capacity for language is something we are born with.

Already, further progress is being made and a handful of other genes have been identified that seem, in mutated forms, to be linked to difficulties in the acquisition of language. Soon, it is hoped, researchers will begin to identify the full range of genes that prepare our brains for language, and we will start to understand the precise nature of this 'biological endowment', as Chomsky called it. Progress in this field should provide answers to more of the big questions about language and the brain, particularly relating to acquisition and the notion of a critical period for language, and possibly even throw light on Chomsky's proposal that we all share an innate universal grammar. However, many other discoveries will be made, thanks to the work of research institutes such as the Max Planck Institute for Psycholinguistics and the Donders Institute for Brain, Cognition and Behaviour, both located in Nijmegen in the Netherlands. A quick browse of their websites is enough to give you a good impression of the kind of work that is being done in the field of genetics and human communication.

Over in Switzerland, another exciting project relating to the human brain has been underway for about a decade now. This is the Blue Brain Project based at the École polytechnique fédérale in Lausanne. Here, researchers are attempting to build a computer simulation of the human brain neuron by neuron (the brain has about 86 billion of these) in order to model precisely how these smallest of components interact to generate brainwaves. In the next decade or so, it is hoped, this virtual brain will begin to shed light on precisely how the brain functions through the transmission of signals from cell to cell, and perhaps reveal what goes wrong in a diseased brain. The mystery of consciousness could be unfolded, and with it something of the mystery of how exactly language works.

The future of theoretical linguistics

In Chapters 6 and 7 we saw how Noam Chomsky sparked a revolution in linguistic theory in the 1950s and 1960s. Since then, there have been reactions and counter-reactions to his ideas, and linguists have formulated many different theoretical approaches in order to produce generative grammars based on specific languages as well as explore the possibility of the existence of a universal grammar for natural language. While Chomsky believes syntax to be preeminent, other theorists have placed more emphasis on phonology or semantics (indeed, the American linguist Ray Jackendoff believes that 'meaning is the "holy grail" not only of linguistics, but also of philosophy, psychology and neuroscience' (Jackendoff, 2002, p. 267)), or on the lexicon and the different roles that words play in sentences. The role of transformations has been ascribed varying degrees of importance. The functions of sentences have also been considered as a driving element in grammar. For several decades this seemed to be a productive time but how many theories could linguists devise? The proliferation of ideas and possibilities at first seemed to be leading somewhere, and then appeared to have stalled.

There was something in this situation reminiscent of the many speculations in the eighteenth and early nineteenth centuries about the origin of language, which philosophers seemed to enjoy but ultimately were getting them nowhere. If you remember from Chapter 3, this resulted in the Linguistic Society of Paris imposing a ban on papers on the subject. In another age, it might not be unreasonable for a similar ban to be placed on papers theorising about the structural core of language. After all, how much theorising could be done with no possibility of proof? Science and technology, however, are providing a means to overcome the apparent impasse. Theoretical linguists are increasingly working with researchers in fields such as neurolinguistics to discover more about the core aspects of language, and their own research has become increasingly empirical, either drawing on large databases (and fieldwork too) to validate their ideas or using the kinds of modelling and simulation that we have explored in previous sections. There is even a belief that if the artificial intelligence of a computer could eventually enable it to use, understand and translate language as a human can (in other words, to pass the Turing test), then effectively the internal workings of the human language faculty will have been understood.

The continuing story of linguistics

The continuing *story* of linguistics is actually, like its history, destined to be a collection of stories as varied as the ones that have already been told, and thinkers and researchers from a range of disciplines will continue to appear in its chapters (while animals will continue to play an unwitting part in revealing exactly what it means to claim that human language is unique). Events will be played out in a variety of settings, as linguists across the planet document and study the rich diversity of the world's languages and the uses to which speakers put them. Other linguists will be at work in the many gleaming palaces that have been built to human language – research establishments such as the institutes of the Max Planck Society or the Massachusetts Institute of Technology where Chomsky rose to linguistic stardom – and, although it took a long time for universities to open departments dedicated specifically to linguistics, aspiring linguists will be able choose from courses offered throughout the world as places to learn their craft. There is no doubt that the future is bright for the study of human language, and from time to time the chronicles of linguistics will be illuminated by a discovery that takes us a step closer to answering one of the discipline's big questions. The stories of linguistics are certainly far from over.

The final words of this chapter, however, must be devoted not to the future of linguistics, but to its past. This book is first and foremost about the history of linguistics, a subject that is still establishing itself as an important component within the discipline as a whole. It currently has fewer specialists than many other areas, and not all universities offer modules in the subject. There are a good number of textbooks on the history of linguistics – some of them making up a series of weighty and detailed studies – as well as several academic journals, but there are relatively few introductory books to choose from. In a sense, though, this is immaterial because the technological advances which have so transformed linguistic research and will be an indispensable part of its future have provided the means for students of linguistics to explore its past as easily as opening a door into an unlocked room. There are many websites to browse where you can glimpse the future of linguistics, but so many of the important documents that make up the history of language study can now also be accessed at the press of a computer key. Hopefully, this book will have inspired you to look at some of them and feel, as you do so, that you are experiencing part of a long and intriguing story as it unfolds.

Suggestions for further reading and research

On branches of linguistics covered in this chapter

Coulthard, Malcolm (2007) *An Introduction to Forensic Linguistics: Language in Evidence* (London: Routledge)

The author is an expert on forensic linguistics and the first professor of forensic linguistics in the world.

Crowley, Terry (2007) *Field Linguistics: A Beginner's Guide* (Oxford: Oxford University Press)

A comprehensive guide to the practical work carried out by field linguists, with a particular focus on what David Crystal terms 'preventive linguistics' – the protection of endangered languages.

Howatt, A P R and Richard Smith (2014) 'The history of teaching English as a foreign language, from a British and European perspective', in *Language and History*, vol. 57, no. 1, pp. 75–95

An overview of the development of English teaching to foreign learners over the last 250 years.

Kennedy, Graeme (1998) *An Introduction to Corpus Linguistics* (London: Addison Wesley Longman)

A comprehensive introduction, which also includes some history of the development of the field.

Mitkov, Ruslan (ed.) (2003) *The Oxford Handbook of Computational Linguistics* (Oxford: Oxford University Press)

A wide-ranging collection of articles, including a large section on some of the applications of computational linguistics.

Useful websites

Blue Brain Project
http://bluebrain.epfl.ch/page-52063.html (accessed October 2015)

Site of the extraordinary long-term project to build a simulation of the human brain.

British National Corpus
http://www.natcorp.ox.ac.uk (accessed October 2015)

Only subscribers can use the full range of functions and examples, but non-subscribers can use a simpler search facility to explore 50 examples at a time. The home page gives guidance on advanced search functions offered by other universities.

Center for Advanced Study in Theoretical Linguistics (CASTL)
https://castl.uit.no (accessed October 2015)

Based at the University of Tromsø in Norway, the work done at this establishment gives you an idea of the current healthy state of theoretical linguistics!

Centre for Forensic Linguistics (at Aston University)
www.forensiclinguistics.net (accessed October 2015)

The centre was opened in 2008 and its website provides lots of information on the kind of work and research that is done there.

Daniel Jones *The Cardinal Vowels*
Available at www.youtube.com/watch?v=6UIAe4p2I74 (accessed May 2015)

Jones's 1917 recording of the cardinal vowels produced by His Master's Voice.

Donders Institute for Brain, Cognition and Behaviour
www.ru.nl/donders/research/ (accessed October 2015)

Based in the Netherlands at Radboud University, Nijmegen, the institute's website includes information about their research into speech and language.

Massachusetts Institute of Technology (MIT) Department of Linguistics & Philosophy
http://web.mit.edu/linguistics/ (accessed October 2015)

Again, a wide range of research papers are available online.

Max Planck Institutes
www.mpg.de/en (accessed October 2015)

The homepage for all the Max Planck Institutes. Click on 'research' or search 'linguistics' to explore the wide range of articles relating to language.

Oxford English Dictionary
www.oed.com (accessed October 2015)

Full access to the dictionary is by subscription, but many libraries subscribe and offer free access to their members.

Smithsonian Human Origins Program
http://humanorigins.si.edu/research (accessed October 2015)

The website of the USA's National Museum of Natural History provides an excellent overview of the research being done into the origins of humankind.

University Centre for Computer Corpus Research on Language (at Lancaster University)
http://ucrel.lancs.ac.uk (accessed October 2015)

The work of this research group illustrates the many uses that can be made of electronic linguistic corpora.

WordNet
http://wordnet.princeton.edu (accessed October 2015)

An interesting database of English words designed to be used for computational linguistics, including machine translation.

Wordnik online dictionary
www.wordnik.com/about (accessed October 2015)

Still being developed, but a fascinating glimpse of where dictionaries are going in the future.

Phonetic symbols

These are the IPA symbols needed for the transcription of English.

		Vowels		
Consonants		**Monophthongs**		**Diphthongs**
/b/	<u>b</u>ead	/æ/	b<u>a</u>t	/aɪ/	b<u>uy</u>
/d/	<u>d</u>eed	/ɑ/	b<u>ar</u>d	/aʊ/	b<u>ough</u>
/dʒ/	<u>j</u>et	/e/	b<u>e</u>t	/eɪ/	b<u>ay</u>
/f/	<u>f</u>eed	/ɜ/	b<u>ir</u>d	/ɛə/	b<u>ear</u>
/g/	<u>g</u>et	/ə/	<u>a</u>bout	/əʊ/	b<u>eau</u>
/h/	<u>h</u>eed	/i/	b<u>ea</u>d	/ɪə/	b<u>eer</u>
/j/	<u>y</u>et	/ɪ/	b<u>i</u>t	/ɔɪ/	b<u>oy</u>
/k/	<u>k</u>eep	/ɒ/	b<u>o</u>mb	/ʊə/	t<u>our</u>
/l/	<u>l</u>et	/ɔ/	b<u>oar</u>d		
/m/	<u>m</u>et	/u/	f<u>oo</u>d		
/n/	<u>n</u>et	/ʊ/	b<u>oo</u>k		
/ŋ/	ri<u>ng</u>	/ʌ/	b<u>u</u>t		
/p/	<u>p</u>et				
/r/	<u>r</u>eed				
/s/	<u>s</u>eed				
/ʃ/	<u>sh</u>ape				
/t/	<u>t</u>ape				
/tʃ/	<u>ch</u>eat				
/θ/	<u>th</u>in				
/ð/	<u>th</u>en				
/v/	<u>v</u>et				
/w/	<u>w</u>in				
/ʒ/	mea<u>s</u>ure				
/z/	<u>z</u>one				

The symbol : is used (as in Chapter 1) to denote that a vowel has been lengthened.

Glossary

(All entries are nouns, unless stated otherwise.)

A

adaptation   In evolution, a change which occurs in a species to improve its chances of survival by adjusting to its environmental conditions.

adjective   A word which typically occurs both attributively (*a sad story*) and predicatively (*the story is sad*), and in comparative and superlative forms (*sadder, saddest*). Traditionally, adjectives are defined as having a describing function.

adverb   A word that can qualify other words, or whole sentences. Adverbs perform a variety of functions: some indicate manner (e.g. *silently*), place (*away/abroad*), time (*tonight*) or degree (*usually*) while others provide comment on a statement (*obviously*) or link sentences to each other (*however*).

affective meaning   An alternative term for **connotation**.

agglutinative language   In **linguistic typology**, a language such as Swahili in which words typically consist of more than one **morpheme**, and there is extensive use of prefixes and suffixes as in, for example, *fairness can minimise inequality*. (See also **inflecting language** and **isolating language**.)

angular gyrus   An area of the **cerebral cortex** adjacent to Wernicke's area which plays a role in the processing of language. It was discovered in the 1960s by American neurologist Norman Geschwind and is sometimes known as **Geschwind's territory**.

antonym   A word which is opposite in meaning to another word with which it can be paired. For example, *rich* and *poor*.

aphasia   A clinical condition involving the loss of some aspect of a person's language capacity.

applied linguistics   A branch of linguistics, sometimes used to refer to any field which is not theoretical, or which has real-life applications, but more often to the educational field of language learning and teaching, particularly in relation to bilingualism and second language acquisition.

arbitrariness   The lack of any direct or 'natural' connection between the sound of a word or linguistic sign and the concept it represents. The connection is purely a matter of convention. (Arbitrariness is one of Charles Hockett's **design-features** of communication.)

arcuate fasciculus   A bundle of nerve fibres in the brain which connects **Wernicke's area** and **Broca's area**.

areal linguistics   The branch of linguistics concerned with studying linguistic features that spread geographically from language to language.

article   A blanket term for the determiners *a*, *an* and *the*.

auditory-vocal channel   The means (using the ear and the voice) by which humans and many other species receive and convey messages. (One of Charles Hockett's **design-features** of communication.)

axon   A long thread that extends from the cell body of a **neuron** and enables the cell to transmit signals to other cells.

B

behaviourism (*American* **behaviorism**)   A branch of psychology which sees behaviour primarily as a series of observable conditioned responses to external stimuli. It flourished in the 1930s–1950s. The term 'behaviorist' was first used by American psychologist John B Watson in 1913.

brainwave   The electrical pulses generated in the brain by its nerve cells, or **neurons**.

Broca's aphasia   A language dysfunction, first identified by the French physician Paul Broca, in which sufferers have difficulty with speech production and fluency. (See also **Broca's area**.)

Broca's area   The area of (the left hemisphere of) the brain, identified by the French physician Paul Broca, which is heavily involved in speech planning and production.

C

cardinal vowel   A member of a set of reference vowels used to establish a framework for vowel classification. The cardinal vowels were first introduced by the British phonetician Daniel Jones in 1917.

cerebral cortex   The grooved outer layer of the brain, made up of grey matter, where our conscious thoughts and feelings are located and where language is mainly processed.

child directed speech (CDS)   Any speech used to interact with a child when the speaker has adapted their language to accommodate the child's linguistic immaturity. The concept of CDS was first associated with the work of American psychologist Catherine Snow in the 1970s.

clinical linguistics   A branch of linguistics, originating in the work of nineteenth-century physicians and neurologists, concerned with the assessment and treatment of language impairments as well as with studying and identifying the various conditions of loss and impairment from which people suffer.

code model   A view of language that sees meaning as essentially a matter of a message being encoded by the speaker and then decoded by the hearer, with no reference to contextual considerations.

cognate   A word that resembles a word from another language in form and meaning because they share a common linguistic ancestor.

cognitive linguistics   A branch of linguistics concerned primarily with how language reflects our understanding and perception of the world around us.

cognitive meaning   An alternative term for **denotation**.

combinability   A feature possessed by the meaningful elements of an evolutionary **protolanguage**, which have the potential to combine to form new messages. The concept was proposed by the British linguist Derek Bickerton in 2009.

common noun   A noun other than a **proper noun**.

communicative competence   A term coined by the American sociolinguist Dell Hymes to refer to a speaker's ability to use language appropriately in any particular context.

comparative linguistics   The branch of modern linguistics which deals with the relationships, similarities and differences between languages. It is often linked with historical linguistics, which deals with linguistic change over time.

competence   American linguist Noam Chomsky's term for a speaker's innate linguistic knowledge, enabling them to process and understand their native language(s). (See also **performance**.)

componential analysis   An analytical approach used in both semantics and phonology in which a linguistic element can be described in terms of presence or absence of component features. For example, 'woman' can be analysed as +human, +adult, -male, +female. (See also **semantic component**.)

computational linguistics   The branch of linguistics in which computers are used to model language so researchers can learn more about aspects such as how grammars work, how language might have evolved and how language is acquired. It also includes machine translation.

conjugation   A set of verb forms consisting of all persons singular and plural in a specified tense.

conjunction   A connective word with either coordinating (e.g. *and*, *but*) or subordinating (e.g. *although*, *because*) properties.

connotation   In semantics, the association(s) of a particular word, as opposed to what it actually refers to or denotes. (See also **denotation**.)

constituent   Any element that makes up a complex linguistic form. For example, *blackberry* is a complex form, divisible into the constituents *black* and *berry*. (See also **immediate constituent**, **ultimate constituent**.)

conversational implicature   A term introduced by British philosopher Paul Grice (1967) for the way we imply meaning (rather than state it explicitly) on the understanding that others will be able to infer the rest. (See also **cooperative principle**.)

cooperative principle   The idea proposed by British philosopher Paul Grice (1967) that participants in spoken interaction are normally cooperating in a conversation, even if what they say does not, on the surface, seem to be relevant or appropriate. (See also **conversational implicature**.)

corpus (*plural* **corpora**)   A collection of spoken or written language data (now usually electronic) used to study patterns in language structure or use.

corpus callosum   The Latin name (meaning 'thick-skinned body') for a long band of nerve **axons** which connects the two hemispheres of the brain.

corpus linguistics   A branch of linguistics in which researchers study language through large collections (**corpora**) of material. This data is usually stored electronically, and can be analysed with the help of specially designed software.

cortex   (See **cerebral cortex**.)

cranium   The bone casing which protects the brain.

creole   A former **pidgin** language which has become used as a native tongue.

critical discourse analysis   An approach to the study of discourse which aims to uncover less overt aspects of meaning and reveal the ideological position or cultural values embedded in the language of a text or texts.

critical period   The period of a child's development during which the innate capacity for learning language is fully operational, meaning language can be acquired effortlessly and fluently.

critical period hypothesis   The theory that there is a **critical period** for language acquisition. It was first proposed by neurologists Wilder Penfield and Lamar Roberts in 1959 and then developed by American linguist Eric Lenneberg in 1967.

CT scan   A computer tomography scan that takes and processes X-rays in order to show cross-sections of the brain or other parts of the body.

D

declension   A set of (usually) noun forms showing any inflectional endings which occur according to the noun's function within the sentence.

deep structure   The underlying abstract form of a sentence as opposed to its surface realisation. The concept is most typically associated with American linguist Noam Chomsky and his transformational generative grammar. (See also **surface structure**.)

deixis   The use of linguistic elements such as *today*, *this* and *you* whose references to time, place or person are dependent on context for their interpretation.

dendrite   A spiky branch extending from the cell body of a **neuron** which enables the cell to receive signals from other cells.

denotation   In semantics, the meaning or **referent** of a word (as opposed to any associations or **connotations** it may possess).

descriptivism/descriptive linguistics   A branch of American linguistics, active particularly in the 1920s and 1930s, with the main aim of recording the endangered indigenous languages of North America. Descriptivists believed that any account of language should be based only on what is observable, and that there was unlimited variety in natural languages. Leonard Bloomfield was their leading light.

design-feature   Any of the distinct characteristics (such as **arbitrariness** or **semanticity**) which can be found in a system of communication. Design-features were introduced by the American linguist Charles Hockett in 1960.

desk linguistics   A term, used in contrast to field linguistics, for introspective linguistic study based on the researcher's own intuitions about language. 'Armchair linguistics' is a more disparaging term.

determiner   A word which occurs only at the beginning of a noun phrase (as in *all the world*), and is distinct from adjectives, which can occur in other positions.

diachronic (*adjective*)   A diachronic approach to language involves the study of change and development over time. (See also **synchronic**.)

dialect   A language variety distinguished by its grammatical and lexical features. Dialects are usually thought of as regional, but social dialects also occur.

dialectology   The study of dialects.

diphthong   A vowel sound which is produced by gliding from one vowel position to another.

discourse   The largest unit of language construction, usually consisting of more than one sentence. **Text** is an alternative term.

discovery procedure   In descriptive/structural linguistics, an analytical strategy used to identify the forms and features which make up a language, and thereby construct a grammar of that language.

displacement   The ability of a linguistic message to refer to the past or the future, or to something that is not physically present. (One of Charles Hockett's **design-features** of communication.)

double articulation   An alternative term for **duality of patterning**.

duality of patterning   The linguistic phenomenon by which sounds possessing no specific meaning are combined to form meaningful utterances. (One of Charles Hockett's **design-features** of communication.)

E

E-language   Externalised language. E-language was Noam Chomsky's term for a speaker's or a community's actual language use, what he earlier referred to as the **performance** aspect of language. (See also **I-language**.)

EEG   Electroencephalography (EEG) is a means of detecting and measuring electric currents in the brain through electrodes placed on the scalp. The **brainwaves** are then viewed on a computer screen.

ethnography of communication   The term coined by American sociolinguist Dell Hymes for what he originally called **ethnography of speaking**.

ethnography of speaking   The term coined by American sociolinguist Dell Hymes (1962) for the systematic study of language use in relation to the social and cultural contexts in which it occurs.

etymology   The historical origin of a word or words, or the study of word origins.

evolutionary linguistics   The branch of linguistics concerned with the origin and development of human language as an evolutionary process.

exaptation   In evolution, any additional beneficial development which occurs as a result of a previous **adaptation** for survival.

F

family resemblance   A term introduced by the Austrian philosopher Ludwig Wittgenstein to refer to the partial similarities in the ways a particular word (e.g. 'game') can be used, although the instances will not necessarily contain a common feature.

field linguistics   A branch of linguistics primarily concerned with recording and analysing the world's languages, especially those that are endangered. 'Field linguist' can also refer to any linguist who goes out and about to collect data.

forensic linguistics   The branch of linguistics concerned with language matters relating to the law in relation to the work of the police and judiciary.

frontal lobe   The upper front region of a brain hemisphere, associated particularly with thought, behaviour and personality. **Broca's area** is located in the frontal lobe (usually of the left hemisphere).

functional linguistics   A branch of linguistics (or any approach to linguistic theory) which places language use and the communicative context at the heart of its theory. It is often associated with Australian linguist Michael Halliday.

G

general linguistics   The study of language, focussing largely on the internal structure of language, but also including aspects such as linguistic change and variation.

generative (*adjective*)   In theoretical linguistics, any account of language that identifies or formulates rules for producing well-formed linguistic units.

generative grammar   A theory of grammar formulated by Noam Chomsky in 1957, with the aim of identifying the set of rules needed to produce (or generate) any well-formed sentence in a language.

Geschwind's territory   The **angular gyrus** of the cerebral cortex, discovered in the 1960s by American neurologist Norman Geschwind.

grammar   1. The set of rules in a language which enable a speaker to construct any well-formed sentence in that language. Grammar is subdivided into syntax and inflections.
  2. A reference book that describes that set of rules systematically.
  3. A theory of how the constructional rules of (a) language operate, such as the theory of transformational grammar.
  4. An intellectual or academic discipline, as studied in classical and medieval times.

grammaticalisation   The process by which inflections and grammatical words develop from nouns, verbs and adjectives, thus making language more complex.

grey matter   The material formed in the brain by the amassed bodies of nerve cells which form the **cerebral cortex**.

gyrus (*plural* **gyri**)   A fold in the corrugated surface of the **cerebral cortex**.

H

hedge   A word or expression (e.g. *kind of*, *I guess*) which conveys an element of uncertainty or an unwillingness to be more definite.

hemisphere   One of the two halves (right and left) into which the brain is divided. In humans, the left hemisphere is usually the dominant one for language.

Heschl's gyrus   A fold in the brain's left hemisphere which lies along the **Sylvian fissure** and is particularly important for processing linguistic sounds. It was identified by Austrian anatomist Richard Heschl in 1878. (See also **gyrus**.)

hippocampus   A structure within the brain's **temporal lobes** shaped rather like a sea horse. The left hippocampus is involved in the storage of vocabulary.

historical linguistics   The branch of modern linguistics which deals with language change over time. It owes much to its predecessor, the discipline of **philology**. (See also **comparative linguistics**.)

hominid   Any member of the hominid (Hominidae) family, which is made up of the *Homo* genus (to which modern humans belong) and the older *Australopithecus* genus.

hominin   Any extinct member of the **hominid** family, of which modern humans are the only surviving species.

hyoid bone   A tiny horseshoe-shaped bone which in humans sits in the neck below the lower jaw to anchor the tongue and is attached by ligaments to the larynx below.

hypernym   In semantics, an overarching category for a group of related words. (For example, *vegetable* is the hypernym for *carrot*, *potato*, *pea* and so on.) (See also **hyponym**.)

hyponym   In semantics, a member of a lexical set or category. (For example, *carrot* is a hyponym of *vegetable*.) (See also **hypernym**.)

I

I-language   Internalised language: Noam Chomsky's term for the mental language system, placing emphasis on language as a cognitive phenomenon. It replaces his earlier term, **competence**. (See also **E-language**.)

idiolect   The distinctive speech or language use of any individual.

illocutionary force   In J L Austin's speech act theory of 1955, the illocutionary force of a speech act is the intention behind the utterance, such as getting the hearer to perform a particular action. (See also **locutionary**, **perlocutionary**.)

immediate constituent   In descriptive/structural linguistics, a constituent resulting from the division of a complex form. For example, *poor John ran away* would be divided into [*poor John*] and [*ran away*]. (See also **constituent**, **ultimate constituent**.)

Indo-European   A language family made up of various languages spoken in Europe and parts of Asia (or its ancestral language). English belongs to this family. The term was coined in 1813 by the English philologist Thomas Young.

inflecting language   In **linguistic typology**, a language such as Russian which makes extensive use of grammatical endings, or **inflections**. (See also **agglutinative language**, **isolating language**.)

inflection   A grammatical word ending which indicates features such as number, possession, person and tense.

instrumental function   In the 1975 taxonomy of Australian linguist Michael Halliday, one of the functions of a child's early language. The instrumental function refers to the child's attempts to get what she or he wants.

interjection   An emotive or spontaneous word such as *ouch*, *wow* or, *gosh* that does not enter into syntactic structures.

International Phonetic Alphabet (IPA)   An alphabet designed by the International Phonetic Association. It is used for transcribing speech and contains a symbol for every known distinct speech sound.

isogloss   A geographical boundary between two linguistic variants or the boundary of an area of specific usage.

isolate (*or* language isolate)   A language such as Basque which has no known living or extinct relatives.

isolating language   In **linguistic typology**, a language such as Vietnamese in which words are typically morphologically indivisible. (See also **agglutinative language**, **inflecting language**.)

L

language acquisition device (LAD)   An innate mental component, proposed by Noam Chomsky in the 1960s, which enables the developing child to acquire the complexities of language, especially of grammar. (See also **universal grammar**.)

language of thought   The hypothesis formulated by American philosopher Jerry Fodor (1975) proposing an innate mental 'language' which enables us to think and, in turn, acquire language.

langue (*la langue*)   Ferdinand de Saussure's term for any system of linguistic signs internalised in the minds of its speakers. (See also *parole*.)

larynx   In anatomy, the voice box, the upper section of the windpipe which contains the vocal cords.

lexical semantics   The branch of semantics which focuses on word meanings.

lexis   An alternative term for vocabulary, or the words of a language.

linguistic area   A geographical region where specific linguistic features are found in neighbouring but not necessarily related languages.

linguistic determinism   The view that the language we are brought up to speak predisposes us to see the world in a particular way.

linguistic relativity   The belief that every language encapsulates the world view of the community that speaks it, and that every language therefore presents the world in a different way.

linguistic substitute reaction   In **behaviourism**, a **reaction** to a **stimulus** which takes the form of language as opposed to some other kind of behaviour. It was proposed by Leonard Bloomfield in his 1933 work *Language*.

linguistic turn   In philosophy, the shift towards paying more attention to ordinary language and how it is used, in order to understand language better as the vehicle of philosophical thought. The move in this direction is usually credited to Austrian philosopher Ludwig Wittgenstein.

linguistic typology   A method of classifying languages according to their structural features, irrespective of whether or not they are related. German philologist August von Schlegel is usually credited with devising this approach in the nineteenth century. (See also **agglutinative**, **inflecting** and **isolating**.)

lobe   One of the regions of a brain hemisphere – **frontal**, **occipital**, **parietal** or **temporal** – each with its own specific functions.

locutionary (*adjective*)   In J L Austin's speech act theory of 1955, the process of uttering something meaningful is a locutionary act. (See also **illocutionary force** and **perlocutionary**.)

M

metalanguage   Language which is used to talk about or describe language, or to comment on language use.

minimalist program   The project of Noam Chomsky, with the aim of discovering the most efficient, economical design possible for the mind's **universal grammar**.

modists (*modistae*)   A group of **speculative grammarians** who expressed the relationship between language and the world in terms of modes. A natural truth had a 'mode of being', a person possessed a 'mode of understanding', and a word provided a 'mode of signifying'.

monogenesis   The theory that all human languages have developed from a common ancestor.

Montague semantics   A branch of semantics based on formal mathematical logic devised by the American mathematician and philosopher Richard Montague.

morpheme   A minimal unit of word meaning and construction. For example, *late* consists of one morpheme only, while *fairness* consists of the morphemes *fair* and *-ness*.

morphology   The formation of words or the study of the formation of words.

motor cortex   The section of the **frontal lobe** of a brain hemisphere that is concerned with movement. The motor cortex is located at the rear edge of the frontal lobe and, in the hemisphere dominant for language, is adjacent to **Broca's area**.

MRI scan   A high resolution scan of the brain (or other parts of the body) produced using magnetic resonance imaging (involving the use of magnetic fields and radio waves). Functional MRI (fMRI) tracks oxygen flow in the brain to identify activated areas. Diffusion tensor MRI tracks water molecules as they spread through tissue, enabling neurologists to look more closely at nerve connections.

N

narrowing   In semantics, a process of meaning change in which the field of meaning becomes more restricted. For example, *meat* has been narrowed from its original meaning of 'food in general'.

natural language processing   In computational linguistics, the use of computers to interpret and produce human language, as opposed to any artificial computational language.

nature/nurture   In language acquisition, the distinction between our innate ability to learn language (nature) and the external influences (nurture) which help us to acquire it. There is considerable debate about the role and relative importance of each aspect.

Neogrammarians   (See **Young Grammarians**.)

neurolinguistics   The branch of linguistics concerned with the neurological aspects of how the brain processes language, including the study of language impairment and loss.

neuron   A nerve cell, of which there are on average 86 billion in the human brain.

noun   A word characterised, among other things, by its ability to function as a sentence subject or object (as in *cats* like *cream*), and by the property of being able to be preceded by *the* (*the cats liked the cream*). Traditionally, a noun is described as a naming word, but this is not a watertight definition.

O

occipital lobe   The upper back region of a brain hemisphere. It is associated with vision and, in the dominant hemisphere, involved with reading and writing.

operant conditioning   In **behaviourism**, the process by which behaviour is established through positive or negative reinforcement. It is particularly associated with the work of B F Skinner.

ordinary language philosophy   A term used for the ideas of philosophers like J L Austin who placed emphasis on everyday language as an important area of philosophical study.

P

palatalised (*adjective*)   A speech sound is palatalised when it is articulated with the tongue spread against the hard palate. For example, the /l/ at the end of *nail* is palatalised.

parietal lobe   The lower back region of a brain hemisphere which deals with sen
sory information and coordination of movement.

parole (*la parole*)   Ferdinand de Saussure's term for the social, interactive aspect
of a speaker's language, in contrast to the internalised knowledge represented by
(la) langue.

part of speech   A traditional term for a **word class**.

participle   A verb form that has no marking for tense. In English, participles end
in *–ing* or *–ed* (or the latter's irregular equivalent) as in, for example, *she is winning*
or *he will have decided*.

PDP (parallel distributed processing)   In psycholinguistics, a model which aims
to explain how the brain processes language through a series of selections from
various interconnected possibilities.

performance   Noam Chomsky's term for language as it is used, in contrast to
internal linguistic knowledge or **competence**.

performative   An utterance which carries out an action, such as *I declare* or *we apologise*. The concept was introduced by the British philosopher J L Austin (1955).

perlocutionary (*adjective*)   In British philosopher J L Austin's **speech act** theory
of 1955, the perlocutionary effect of an utterance is the outcome it brings about,
such as getting the hearer to do something. (See also **illocutionary force**,
locutionary.)

philology   The historical and comparative study of languages and their relationships, focussing particularly on language change. The discipline thrived particularly in the nineteenth century.

phoneme   A distinct speech sound in its representative, abstract form. The concept was introduced at the end of the nineteenth century by Polish linguist Jan
Baudouin de Courtenay.

phonetics   The study of the production and reception of speech sounds.

phonology   The sound system of a language or the study of that system.

phrase structure rule   A rule which indicates the linguistic elements that can combine to form larger syntactic structures. For example VP > Verb + NP shows that a
verb phrase can be made up of a verb and a noun phrase, as in *(the man) hit the ball*.

phrenology   An approach to the study of the human brain, popular in the
nineteenth century, based on the belief that the brain was divided into discrete
modules, each one responsible for a different human characteristic or function.

pidgin   A hybrid language originally formed for a specific purpose (such as trade)
through contact between speakers of two dissimilar languages. A pidgin has no
native speakers.

plasticity   A feature of the developing brain of a baby or young child whereby the
brain is able to overcome damage by reassigning affected functions to other parts
of the brain.

polygenesis   The theory that human languages share no common ancestor, having
developed from more than one source language. In modern linguistics, polygenesis is particularly associated with American linguist Johanna Nichols.

polysemous (*adjective*)   Of a word, having more than one meaning. (The associated noun is 'polysemy'.)

pragmatics   The branch of linguistics dealing with meaning in the context of
language use and aiming to account for those aspects of meaning not conveyed
by linguistic content alone. Some linguists regard pragmatics as a sub-branch of
semantics.

Prague Linguistic Circle   A group of eastern European linguists founded in Prague in 1926. Their interests included phonetics and phonology, with a particular focus on distinctive features.

predicate   In a sentence, the verb element and any obligatory elements that follow it. For example *is a wise man* in *Socrates is a wise man*. **Subject** and predicate are the traditional divisions of a sentence, used by linguists and logicians alike.

pre-language   An alternative term for the emergent **protolanguage** of the first speakers, prior to human language becoming fully developed.

preposition   A word such as *by, with, from*, usually used to express the relationship between two elements, especially two noun phrases, as in, for example, *the house by the sea*.

preventive linguistics   A branch of linguistics proposed by British linguist David Crystal (2000) to refer to the work of those linguists concerned with the preservation and protection of endangered languages.

productivity   The creative aspect of human language, where there is no limit to the number or type of messages that speakers can convey. (One of Charles Hockett's **design-features** of communication.)

projection problem   The question for a linguistic theorist of how a speaker can produce and understand an infinite number of messages when they have only experienced a finite number of examples.

pronoun   A word which can occur in the same position as a noun or noun phrase, such as *she* in *she asked for help*. (Compare *the injured girl asked for help*.) For several reasons, the traditional definition of a pronouns as 'standing for' a noun is not entirely accurate.

proper noun   A noun which names someone or something unique, such as *Socrates* or *Rome*. (See also **common noun**.)

prosodics   The suprasegmental aspects of speech, namely pitch, intonation, stress, volume, tempo and voice quality.

Proto-Indo-European   The common ancestor of the Indo-European languages for which only indirect evidence remains, although attempts have been made to reconstruct it.

protolanguage   1. In evolutionary terms, the earliest, non-grammatical form of human language. (See also **pre-language**.)
2. In historical linguistics, a reconstructed ancestral language for which no original evidence remains.

Proto-World   The hypothetical original language from which all human languages are sometimes claimed to have sprung.

psycholinguistics   The branch of linguistics concerned with language and the mind, particularly in terms of acquiring, storing, understanding and using language. (See also **neurolinguistics**.)

psychological reality   In psycholinguistics, a theoretical linguistic description or model will have 'psychological reality' if it succeeds in mirroring the way language is actually stored or processed in the brain.

Q

quantitative (*adjective*)   A quantitative approach to linguistic data is one that makes use of statistical analysis. It is used particularly by sociolinguists to research language variation and change.

R

reaction   In **behaviourism**, the behaviour that occurs as the result of a response to a stimulus. (The term 'response' is also used for 'reaction'.) (See also **linguistic substitute reaction**.)

recursion   The way in which one linguistic element can be embedded within another, in theory without limit, as for example in *Julia believes (that) Terry believes (that) the earth is flat*. Recursion was proposed by Fitch, Hauser and Chomsky (2003) as the **design-feature** which distinguishes human communication from that of all other species.

reference   In semantics, whatever it is that a linguistic expression actually refers to, or the link between that thing and the linguistic element. So both *the Nile* and *earth's longest river* have the same reference. Reference was contrasted with **sense** by German philosopher Gottlob Frege in 1892.

referent   A general term for the thing (person, object, concept etc.) that a linguistic expression refers to.

relative pronoun   A pronoun used to introduce a relative clause and connect that clause to something previously mentioned, such as *who* and *which* in *God, who is invisible, created the world, which is visible*.

relevance theory   A theory proposed by French psychologist Dan Sperber and British linguist Deidre Wilson (1986) in which relevance is seen as the primary aim of conversational participants, and the driving force behind the interpretation of utterances.

rhotic (*adjective*)   A rhotic accent is one where /r/ is pronounced in certain positions in contrast to other accents of the same language. For example, only some English speakers pronounce /r/ in *car* and *card*.

S

Sapir-Whorf hypothesis   A term for the views of American anthropologists/ linguists Edward Sapir and Benjamin Lee Whorf who saw a person's native language as a powerful influence on their thinking and particularly on the way they perceived the world around them.

semantic component   One of a set of possible features which can be used to define and distinguish word meanings. For example, the components '±human', '±adult', '±male' and '±female' can be used to distinguish *girl, boy, child, woman, man*.

semantic field   A term coined by German linguist Jost Trier in 1921 to refer to word groups that are related by meaning, for example *forest, wood, tree*. The meanings of words within a semantic field are defined in relation to each other and are not necessarily the same in every language.

semantic prototype   A member of a set which typifies what the set represents and against which other set members can be judged. For instance, 'robin' is a semantic prototype for the set of birds. The idea was proposed by American linguist George Lakoff in 1973.

semanticity   The ability of a transmitted signal of communication to convey a consistent, intended meaning. (One of Charles Hockett's **design-features** of language.)

semantics   The meaning of linguistic elements, or the study of meaning.

semiotics   The study of signs and systems of signs. Language is one of these systems. Swiss linguist Ferdinand de Saussure was the first to propose that language should be studied within this field, or what he called 'semiology'.

sense   In semantics, the meaning associations of a word or phrase, as opposed to its **reference**. For example, *Nile* and *earth's longest river* have the same reference but difference senses. The distinction between sense and reference was made by German philosopher Gottlob Frege in 1892.

sense relation   In semantics, the relationship between two words in terms of their meanings. For example, through contrast, similarity or hierarchy. (See also **antonym, hypernym, hyponym, synonym.**)

shortening   In semantics, a process of meaning change by which the shortening of an existing word or phrase results in a new word. For example, *private soldier* becomes simply *private*.

sign   A meaningful element within a communication system. The notion of the sign is often associated with the Swiss linguist Ferdinand de Saussure. (See also **signified** and **signifier.**)

signified   In Swiss linguist Ferdinand de Saussure's definition of a linguistic **sign**, the mental concept to which the sign refers. His original French term is *signifié.*

signifier   In Swiss linguist Ferdinand de Saussure's definition of a linguistic **sign**, the sound image associated with the mental concept the sign represents. His original French term is *signifiant.*

social network   In sociolinguistics, an identifiable social group whose members are connected to one another through, for example, family, friendship or employment relationships. The concept was used by British sociolinguist Lesley Milroy in her 1970s Belfast study.

sociolect   The distinctive speech or language use shared by members of a social group, such as working class speakers or teenagers.

sociolinguistics   The branch of linguistics concerned with the study of language in the context of society, including aspects such as class, gender roles and cultural values. The study of linguistic change and variation is an important part of the field.

speculative grammar   A medieval approach to grammar in which grammar was seen as holding a mirror up to the universal truths of the physical world and the human mind. The first work of speculative grammar was written by Thomas of Erfurt in the early fourteenth century.

speech act   A term introduced by the British philosopher J L Austin for the acts we carry out in spoken interaction. (See also **locutionary, illocutionary force, perlocutionary.**)

speech event   Any specific type of speaking. For example, telling a joke, making a phone call, or paying a compliment.

stimulus   In **behaviourism**, any event or situation which brings about a **reaction**.

structuralism/structural linguistics   A theoretical approach which treats the elements of a system (linguistic or otherwise) as defined primarily in relation to each other. Swiss linguist Ferdinand de Saussure introduced a structuralist approach to language, seeing it as a system of interrelated **signs**.

stylometry   The study of an individual's distinct linguistic style, undertaken through (often statistical) analysis of their speech or writing. It developed at the end of the nineteenth century.

subject   The element of a sentence which (in a regular declarative sentence) precedes the verb and determines the form the verb takes. For example, *Socrates* in *Socrates is a wise man*. (See also **predicate**.)

substitution   In semantics, the way in which a word's meaning changes as external circumstances change. For example, *ship* comes to include any new type of ship.

surface structure   The outward spoken or written form of a sentence, as opposed to its underlying abstract form. Surface and **deep** structures play an important role in **transformational generative grammar**.

Sylvian fissure   In the brain, the horizontal groove that separates the upper and lower sections of the cortex. It is named after Franciscus Sylvius, the seventeenth century physician who discovered it.

synchronic (*adjective*)   Relating to a particular moment in time. A synchronic study of language is in contrast to a **diachronic**, or historical study.

synonym   A word which has the same meaning as another word in the same language. For example, *faith* and *trust*. However, because pairs like these are not always interchangeable, it is arguable that any true synonyms exist.

syntax   Word order, or the rules which govern word order. Syntax is one of the two aspects of **grammar**, the other being **inflections**.

T

target language   In language acquisition, the language a learner aims to acquire. The term can be used for both a native language and a foreign language.

temporal lobe   The lower frontal region of a brain hemisphere. **Wernicke's area** is located in the temporal lobe (usually of the left hemisphere).

text   An alternative term for **discourse**.

theoretical linguistics   The branch of linguistics concerned with providing an account of the internal nature and structure of language.

transfer   In semantics, a process of meaning change whereby a word comes to be used metaphorically, for example *bed* as a term for a flat part of a machine.

transformational generative grammar   The approach to grammar pioneered by American linguist Noam Chomsky (1957) in which the aim of a grammar is not just to reveal how well-formed sentences can be generated but also to indicate the relationship between structural types (such as active and passive sentences) where one type can be seen as resulting from the transformation of the other.

translation studies   The discipline (sometimes regarded as a branch of linguistics) concerned with the process of translation and all its attendant issues, both theoretical and practical.

trivium   A group of three associated subjects – grammar, rhetoric and dialectic (or logic) – originating in classical times, and taught as the foundation of learning in medieval universities.

U

ultimate constituent   In the descriptive/structural linguistics of the 1930s, a linguistic element which cannot be subdivided. So in *poor John ran away*, *poor*, *John* and *ran* are ultimate constituents, although *away* can be divided into *a-* and *way*. (See also **constituent** and **immediate constituent**.)

universal grammar (UG)   The innate linguistic knowledge of human beings which enables them to acquire language and then to produce and understand a limitless number of well-formed sentences in the specific language acquired. UG was the concept of American linguist Noam Chomsky, and superseded his idea of an innate **language acquisition device**.

V

ventricle   A cavity of the brain. Human brains have four in total.

verb   The most central word type, identified by its ability to make a contrast of present and past tense.

vernacular culture index   In sociolinguistics, a means of grading a speaker's commitment to non-mainstream values. The index was used by British sociolinguist Jenny Cheshire in her Reading 'playground' study.

vocal tract   Some connected parts of the human anatomy used in the production of speech, namely the oral and nasal cavities, and the upper section of the windpipe as far as the **larynx**.

W

Wada test   A test devised in the late 1940s by Japanese neurologist Juhn Wada which identified the dominant hemisphere for language in a patient about to undergo brain surgery.

Wernicke's aphasia   A language dysfunction associated with damage to **Wernicke's area**, in which sufferers experience problems with language comprehension.

Wernicke's area   The area (usually of the left hemisphere) of the brain, first identified by German physician Carl Wernicke, which is responsible for language comprehension.

white matter   The material formed in the brain by the mass of long threads (**axons**) that extend from the bodies of the brain cells.

widening   In semantics, a process of meaning change in which a word's meaning becomes broader. For example, the Old English *brid* ('bird') referred only to a baby bird, but the word gradually came to refer to any bird.

word class   A category of words (like nouns or verbs) whose members share grammatical properties. **Part of speech** is a more traditional term.

Y

Young Grammarians   The second wave of nineteenth century philologists (*'Jung Grammatiker'*) who believed, among other things, that there were no exceptions to sound rules. They are sometimes referred to as Neogrammarians.

Life dates of thinkers and researchers

(The information in brackets indicates the reason(s) why they are mentioned in this book.)

Aristotle   *Greek philosopher*   384–322 BCE
(nature of words; sound segments; metalanguage)
Arnauld, Antoine   *French grammarian/philosopher*   1612–94
(Port-Royal Grammar)
Austin, John L   *British philosopher*   1911–60
(performative utterances; speech act theory)

Bally, Charles   *French linguist*   1865–1947
(editor of Saussure's *Course in General Linguistics*)
Basso, Keith   *American anthropologist*   1940–2013
(silence among the Western Apache)
Baudouin de Courtenay, Jan   *Polish linguist*   1845–1929
(definition of the phoneme)
Beauzée, Nicolas   *French grammarian*   1717–89
(*Grammaire Générale*)
Berger, Hans   *German neurologist*   1873–1941
(pioneer of electroencephalography – EEG)
Bickerton, Derek   *British linguist*   b. 1926
(pidgins and creoles; evolutionary protolanguage)
Bloomfield, Leonard   *American linguist*   1887–1949
(descriptive/structural/behaviourist linguistics)
Boas, Franz   *German–American anthropologist*   1858–1942
(Native American culture and language)
Boxhorn, Marcus van   *Dutch scholar*   1612–53
(proposed Scythian as an ancestral language)
Bréal, Michel   *French philologist*   1832–1915
(regarded as founder of modern semantics)
Breton, Raymond   *French missionary*   1609–79
(vocabulary of the Carib language of the Antilles)

Broca, Paul   *French physician/anatomist*   1824–80
(Broca's area of the brain)
Brodmann, Korbinian   *German anatomist/neurologist*   1866–1918
(Brodmann areas of the brain)
Brown, Roger   *American psycholinguist*   1925–97
(stages of syntactic development)
Brugmann, Karl   *German philologist/Young Grammarian*   1849–1919
('Neogrammarian Manifesto')
Buffier, Claude   *French grammarian*   1661–1737
(equality of all languages)

Cheshire, Jenny   *British sociolinguist*   b. 1946
(Reading 'playground' study)
Chomsky, Noam   *American linguist*   b. 1928
(generative grammar; universal grammar etc.)
Coates, Jennifer   *British sociolinguist*   b. 1942
(language and gender)
Condillac, Étienne Bonnot de   *French philosopher*   1715–80
(the origin of language)
Crystal, David   *British linguist*   b. 1941
(language death)

Darwin, Charles   *British naturalist*   1809–82
(evolution by natural selection; child development)
Dax, Gustave   *French physician (son of Marc Dax)*   1815–93
(brain's left hemisphere dominant for language)
Dax, Marc   *French neurologist/physician*   1771–1837
(brain's left hemisphere dominant for language)
Descartes, René   *French philosopher*   1596–1650
(reason is unique to humans)
Dionysius Thrax   *grammarian/teacher of Greek*   c. 160–85 BCE
(*The Art of Grammar – Tekhne grammatike*)

Edmont, Edmond   *French dialectologist*   1849–1926
(*Atlas linguistique de la France*)
Epicurus   *Greek philosopher*   341–270 BCE
(origin of names)
Exner, Sigmund   *Austrian physiologist*   1846–1926
(theory of word perception)

Fairclough, Norman   *British linguist*   b. 1941
(critical discourse analysis)
Fisher, Simon   *British geneticist/neuroscientist*   b. 1970
(FOXP2 gene)
Fitch, Tecumseh   *American evolutionary biologist*   b. 1963
(recursion as a design-feature of language)
Fodor, Jerry   *American philosopher/cognitive scientist*   b. 1935
(language of thought hypothesis; semantic theory)

Frege, Gottlob   *German philosopher/mathematician*   1848–1925
(sense and reference)

Galen of Pergamon *Greek physician/philosopher*   130–c. 200
(influential works on anatomy)
Gall, Franz Joseph   *German physician/physiologist*   1758–1828
(founder of the field of phrenology)
Gardner, Beatrix   *American psychologist*   1933–95
(worked with chimpanzee Washoe (1965–2007))
Gardner, R Allen   *American psychologist*   b. 1930
(worked with chimpanzee Washoe (1965–2007))
Gauchat, Louis   *Swiss linguist*   1866–1942
(the dialect of the Swiss village of Charmey)
Geoffrey of Monmouth   *Welsh historian*   c. 1100–c. 1155
(wrote a history of the kings of Britain)
Geschwind, Norman   *American neurologist*   1926–84
(angular gyrus of the brain – Geschwind's territory)
Gessner, Conrad   *Swiss linguist/naturalist*   1516–65
(collected Lord's Prayer examples)
Gilliéron, Jules   *Swiss dialectologist*   1854–1926
(*Atlas linguistique de la France*)
Greenberg, Joseph   *American linguist/anthropologist*   1915–2001
(language universals)
Grice, Paul   *British philosopher*   1913–88
(cooperative principle; conversational implicature)
Grimm, Jacob   *German philologist*   1785–1863
(Grimm's Law)

Haeckel, Ernst   *German naturalist*   1834–1919
(friend of August Schleicher)
Halliday, Michael   *British-born Australian linguist*   b. 1925
(functional approach to language)
Hauser, Marc   *American evolutionary biologist*   b. 1959
(recursion as a design-feature of language)
Hensel, Gottfried   *German philologist*   1687–1765
(collected Lord's Prayer examples)
Herder, Johann Gottfried   *German philosopher*   1744–1803
(prize-winning essay on the origin of language)
Herodotus   *Greek historian*   c. 484–c. 425 BCE
(story of Psamtik I's language experiment)
Heschl, Richard   *Austrian anatomist*   1824–81
(Heschl's gyrus – a language area of the brain)
Hillyard, Steven   *American neuroscientist*   b. 1942
(N400 wave of the brain)
Hippocrates   *Greek physician*   c. 460–c. 370 BCE
(the human brain)
Hjelmslev, Louis   *Danish linguist/structuralist*   1899–1965
(semantic fields)

Hockett, Charles   *American linguist/anthropologist*   1916–2000
(design-features of language)
Humboldt, Wilhelm von   *German scholar/philosopher*   1767–1835
(relationship between language and thought)
Hymes, Dell   *American sociolinguist/anthropologist*   1927–2009
(ethnography of communication)

Itard, Jean Marc   *French physician*   1774–1838
(mentor of Victor of Aveyron – the 'wild child')

Jackendoff, Ray   *American linguist*   b. 1945
(semantics)
Jackson, John Hughlings   *American neurologist*   1835–1911
(nature of the brain's language faculty)
Jakobson, Roman   *Russian–American linguist*   1896–1982
(Prague Linguistic Circle; phonetics and phonology)
Jespersen, Otto   *Danish linguist*   1860–1943
(general linguistics; seminal text *Language* in 1922)
Jones, Daniel   *British phonetician*   1881–1967
(gramophone recording of cardinal vowels)
Jones, Sir William   *British philologist/orientalist*   1746–94
(common Indo-European language source)
Joos, Martin   *American linguist*   1907–78
(descriptive linguistics from 1925)

Katz, Jerrold   *American linguist*   1932–2002
(semantic theory)
Kellogg, Winthrop   *American psychologist*   1898–1972
(worked with chimpanzee Gua (1930–1933))
Kloeke, Gesinus   *Dutch dialectologist*   1887–1963
(the 'Dutch expansion')
Kutas, Marta   *American cognitive scientist/neuroscientist*   b. 1949
(N400 wave of the brain)

La Mettrie, Julien Offray de   *French philosopher/physician*   1709–51
(believed apes were capable of speech)
Labov, William   *American sociolinguist*   b. 1927
(Martha's Vineyard and New York City studies)
Lakoff, George   *American linguist*   b. 1941
(fuzziness in natural language; semantic prototypes)
Lakoff, Robin Tolmach   *American sociolinguist*   b. 1942
(*Language and Woman's Place*)
Lancelot, Claude   *French teacher/linguist/grammarian*   c. 1616–94
(Port-Royal Grammar)
Legman, Gershon   *American writer/critic*   1917–99
(language and sexual orientation)
Leibniz, Gottfried   *German philosopher*   1646–1716
(reason is unique to humans)

Lenneberg, Eric   *American linguist/neurologist*   1921–75
(critical period hypothesis)
Levinson, Stephen   *British psycholinguist*   b. 1947
(pragmatics)
Linnaeus, Carl   *Swedish naturalist*   1707–78
(*Systema naturae* – classification of species)
Locke, John   *English philosopher*   1632–1704
(*Essay Concerning Human Understanding*; semantics)
Lucretius   *Roman philosopher/poet*   c. 95–c. 55 BCE
(animal and human sounds; origin of names)
Lutoslawski, Wincenty   *Polish philosopher*   1863–1954
(stylometry)
Lyons, John   *British linguist*   b. 1932
(semantics)

McCarthy, Dorothea   *American psychologist*   1906–74
(methods for collecting children's language data)
Meillet, Antoine   *French linguist*   1866–1936
(grammaticalisation)
Milroy, Lesley   *British sociolinguist*   b. 1944
(Belfast networks)
Monaco, Anthony   *American geneticist/neuroscientist*   b. 1959
(FOXP2 gene)
Montague, Richard   *American mathematician/philosopher*   1930–71
(Montague semantics)
Morgan, Augustus de   *British mathematician*   1806–71
(average word length analysis)
Müller, Friedrich Max   *German philologist*   1823–1900
(disputed Darwin's views on evolution and language)

Nichols, Johanna   *American linguist*   b.1945
(linguistic diversity; polygenesis)

Osthoff, Hermann   *German philologist/Young Grammarian*   1847–1909
('Neogrammarian Manifesto')

Pāṇini   *Indian scholar*   c. 520–460 BCE
(grammar of Sanskrit)
Partee, Barbara   *American mathematician/linguist*   b. 1940
(formal semantics)
Pavlov, Ivan   *Russian physiologist*   1849–1936
(animal conditioning)
Piaget, Jean   *Swiss psychologist*   1896–1980
(children's cognitive development)
Plato   *Greek philosopher*   428–348 BCE
(*Cratylus* – the correctness of names)
Preyer, William   *English-born German physiologist*   1841–97
(*The Mind of the Child*)

Priscian (Priscianus Caesariensis)   *teacher of Latin*   active c. 500
(Latin grammar – *Grammatical Foundations*)

Ramón y Cajal, Santiago   *Spanish neuroscientist*   1852–1934
(nerve cell structure)

Rask, Rasmus   *Danish philologist*   1787–1832
(polyglot; pioneer in the field of philology)

Robins, Robert H   *British linguist*   1922–2000
(history of linguistics)

Rochefort, Charles de   *French cleric*   1605–83
(study of the people of the Antilles)

Rosch, Eleanor   *American psychologist*   b. 1938
(lexical set membership)

Rousseau, Jean-Jacques   *French philosopher*   1712–78
(the origin of language; a child's education)

Roy, Deb   *Canadian cognitive scientist*   b. 1969
(Human Speechome Project)

Ruhlen, Merritt   *American linguist*   b. 1944
(language family classification)

Sanctius (Francisco Sánchez de las Brozas)   *Spanish linguist*   1523–1600
(principles of Latin)

Sapir, Edward   *American linguist/anthropologist*   1884–1939
(Native American languages; linguistic relativity)

Saussure, Ferdinand de   *Swiss linguist*   1857–1913
(seminal *Course in General Linguistics* of 1916)

Savage-Rumbaugh, Sue   *American primatologist*   b. 1946
(worked with bonobo Kanzi (b. 1980))

Schlegel, August von   *German philologist*   1767–1845
(pioneer in the field of philology; linguistic typology)

Schlegel, Friedrich von   *German philologist*   1772–1829
(pioneer in the field of philology)

Schleicher, August   *German philologist/Darwin supporter*   1821–68
(Schleicher's fable; the *Stammbaum* model)

Schmeller, Johann   *German philologist*   1785–1852
(Bavarian dialects)

Schmidt, Johannes   *German philologist*   1843–1901
(wave theory)

Schuchardt, Hugo   *German philologist*   1842–1927
(wave theory)

Sechehaye, Albert   *Swiss linguist*   1870–1946
(editor of Saussure's *Course in General Linguistics*)

Skinner, Burrhus F   *American psychologist/behaviourist*   1904–90
(*Verbal Behavior*)

Snow, Catherine   *American psycholinguist*   b. 1945
(child directed speech)

Sperber, Dan   *French psychologist*   b. 1942
(relevance theory)

Stern, Clara   *German psychologist*   1877–1948
(*The Language of Children*)
Stern, Gustaf   *Swedish philologist*   1882–1948
(meaning change)
Stern, William   *German psychologist*   1871–1938
(*The Language of Children*)
Stiernhielm, Georg   *Swedish linguist*   1598–1672
(believed Gothic was the original language)
Süssmilch, Johann Peter   *German scholar/theologian*   1707–67
(language as a divine creation)
Svartvik, Jan   *Swedish linguist*   b. 1931
(analysis of the 'confession' of Timothy Evans)
Sweet, Henry   *British phonetician/philologist*   1845–1912
(*A Handbook of Phonetics*)

Taine, Hippolyte   *French cultural critic/historian*   1828–93
(diary of his daughter's language development)
Terrace, Herbert   *American cognitive psychologist*   b. 1936
(worked with chimpanzee Nim Chimpsky (1973–2000))
Thomas of Erfurt   *(?German) speculative grammarian*   active 1300–25
(modes of signifying)
Tiedemann, Dietrich   *German philosopher*   1748–1803
(diary of his son Friedrich)
Trier, Jost   *German linguist*   1894–1970
(semantic fields)
Trombetti, Alfredo   *Italian linguist*   1866–1929
(theory of monogenesis)
Trubetskoy, Nikolai   *Russian linguist*   1890–1938
(Prague Linguistic Circle; phonetics and phonology)
Trudgill, Peter   *British sociolinguist*   b. 1943
(social differentiation in Norwich)
Turing, Alan   *British mathematician*   1912–54
(machine-based code-breaking)

Varro, Marcus Terentius   *Roman scholar/writer*   116–27 BCE
(*De lingua latina*)
Verner, Karl   *Danish philologist/Young Grammarian*   1849–96
(Verner's Law)
Vesalius, Andreas   *Brussels-born anatomist/physician*   1514–64
(human dissection)

Wada, Juhn   *Japanese–Canadian neurologist*   b. 1924
(Wada test for brain hemisphere dominance)
Wallace, Alfred Russel   *British naturalist/evolutionist*   1823–1913
(theory of mouth-gestures)
Watson, John B   *American psychologist*   1878–1958
(founder of behaviourism)

Wegener, Philipp   *German dialectologist*   1848–1916
(the industrial Magdeburg region)
Wells, Rulon S   *American linguist/philosopher*   1918–2008
(immediate constituent analysis)
Wenker, Georg   *German dialectologist*   1852–1911
(language atlas based on questionnaires)
Wernicke, Carl   *German physician/anatomist*   1848–1905
(Wernicke's area of the brain)
Whitney, William Dwight   *American linguist*   1827–94
(language belongs to a community)
Whorf, Benjamin Lee   *American linguist*   1897–1941
(Native American languages; linguistic relativity)
Wilkins, John   *theologian/natural scientist*   1614–72
(devised a universal language)
Wilson, Deirdre   *British linguist/cognitive scientist*   b. 1941
(relevance theory)
Wittgenstein, Ludwig   *Austrian philosopher*   1889–1951
(meaning is use; the linguistic turn)
Wundt, Wilhelm   *German physician and psychologist*   1832–1920
(the child's role in language acquisition)

Young, Thomas   *British philologist/scientist*   1773–1829
(coined the term 'Indo-European')

Zadeh, Lofti   *Azerbaijani mathematician*   b. 1921
(fuzzy set theory)

References and sources

Foreign titles are given first in English.
Many of these titles are hard to get hold of, so URLs are provided if they are available to view online.
To access articles on JSTOR you will need a personal account, or access provided by a library or academic institution.

Aristotle (c. 350–330 BCE) *On Interpretation (De interpretatione / Peri hermeneias)*, translated by E M Edghill in W D Ross (ed.) *The Works of Aristotle*, Vol. 1 (Oxford: Clarendon Press, 1928)
Available at https://archive.org/details/worksofaristotle01arisuoft (accessed September 2015).

Aristotle (c. 350–330 BCE) *Poetics (Peri poietikes)*, translated by I Bywater in Jonathan Barnes (ed.) *The Complete Works of Aristotle (The Revised Oxford Translation)*, Vol. 2 (Princeton, NJ: Princeton University Press, 1984), pp. 2316–40
Available at https://books.google.co.uk/ (accessed November 2015).

Austin, John L (1962) *How to Do Things with Words* (Oxford: Clarendon Press)
Austin's collected William James Lectures given at Harvard in 1955.

Ballard, Kim (2013) *The Frameworks of English*, 3rd edn (Basingstoke: Palgrave Macmillan)

Basso, Keith H (1970) '"To give up on words": Silence in Western Apache culture', in *Southwestern Journal of Anthropology*, vol. 26, no. 3, pp. 213–30
Available at https://www.jstor.org/stable/3629378 (accessed September 2015).

Baudouin de Courtenay, Jan (1894) 'An attempt at a theory of phonetic alterna-tions' ('Próba teorji alternacyj fonetycznych'), in Edward Stankiewicz (ed./trans.) *A Baudouin de Courtenay Anthology: The Beginnings of Structural Linguistics* (Bloomington: Indiana University Press, 1972), pp. 144–212
This was published originally in the *Transactions of the Philological Section (Rozprawy Wydział filogiczny)* of the Cracow Academy of Sciences, vol. 20, 1894, pp. 219–364.

Beauzée, Nicolas (1767) *General Grammar (Grammaire générale)* (Paris: J Barbou)
Available in the original French at https://books.google.co.uk/books?id=kXIRAAAA IAAJ&source=gbs_navlinks_s (accessed September 2015).

Bickerton, Derek (1990) *Language and Species* (Chicago: Chicago University Press)

Bickerton, Derek (2009) *Adam's Tongue* (New York: Hill & Wang)

Bloomfield, Leonard (1914) *An Introduction to the Study of Language* (New York: Henry Holt)

A 1940 edition is available at https://openlibrary.org/books/OL24354840M/ An_introduction_to_the_study_of_language (accessed October 2015).

Bloomfield, Leonard (1933) *Language* (New York: Henry Holt)

Boas, Franz (1911) *Handbook of American Indian Languages* (Washington: Government Printing Office)

Available at https://archive.org/details/handbookamerica00fracgoog (accessed October 2015).

Bréal, Michel (1897) *Essay on Semantics (Essai de Sémantique)* (Paris: Hachette)

Available in the original French at https://archive.org/details/ essaidesmantiq00bruoft (accessed October 2015).

A translation by Nina Cust published as *Semantics: Studies in the Science of Meaning* (London: W Heinemann, 1900) is available at https://archive.org/details/ semanticsstudie00postgoog (accessed October 2015).

Broca, Paul (1861) 'Loss of speech, chronic softening and partial destruction of the anterior left lobe of the brain' ('Perte de la parole, ramollissement chronique et destruction partielle du lobe antérieur gauche du cerveau'), in *Bulletin de la Société Anthropologique*, vol. 2, pp. 235–8

Available in the original French at http://psychclassics.yorku.ca/Broca/perte.htm (accessed October 2015) where you can also click through to an English translation.

Brodmann, Korbinian (1909) *Comparative localization of the cerebral cortex (Vergleichende Lokalisationslehre der Grosshirnrinde)* (Leipzig: Johann Ambrosius Barth)

Available in the original German at http://digital.zbmed.de/zbmed/id/554966 (accessed October 2015).

Brown, Roger (1973) *A First Language: The Early Years* (Cambridge, MA: Harvard University Press)

Cheshire, Jenny (1982) 'Linguistic variation and social function', in Suzanne Romaine (ed.) *Sociolinguistic Variation in Speech Communities* (London: Edward Arnold)

Chomsky, Noam (1957) *Syntactic Structures* (The Hague: Mouton)

A second edition with an introduction by David Lightfoot is also available (Berlin: Mouton de Gruyter, 2002).

Chomsky, Noam (1959) 'A review of B F Skinner's *Verbal Behavior*', in *Language*, vol. 35, pp. 26–58, reprinted in Anthony Arnove (ed.) *The Essential Chomsky* (London: Bodley Head, 2008)

Also available at: www.chomsky.info/articles/1967----.htm (accessed October 2015), with an additional preface written by Chomsky in 1967.

Chomsky, Noam (1965) *Aspects of the Theory of Syntax* (Cambridge, MA: MIT Press)

Chomsky, Noam (1966) *Cartesian Linguistics: A Chapter in the History of Rationalist Thought* (New York: Harper & Row)

Chomsky, Noam and Maurice Halle (1968) *The Sound Pattern of English* (New York: Harper & Row)

Coates, Jennifer (2003) *Men Talk* (Oxford: Blackwell Publishing)

Condillac, Etienne Bonnot de (1746) *Essay on the Origin of Human Knowledge (Essai sur l'origine des connaissances humaines)* 2 vols. (Amsterdam: Pierre Mortier), translated and edited by Hans Aarsleff as *Essay on the Origin of Human Knowledge* (Cambridge: Cambridge University Press, 2001)

Crystal, David (2000) *Language Death* (Cambridge: Cambridge University Press)

Darwin, Charles (1859) *On the Origin of Species by Means of Natural Selection* (London: John Murray)
Available at http://darwin-online.org.uk (accessed October 2015).

Darwin, Charles (1871) *The Descent of Man, and Selection in Relation to Sex* (London: John Murray)
Available at http://darwin-online.org.uk (accessed October 2015).

Darwin, Charles (1872) *The Expression of the Emotions in Man and Animals* (London: John Murray)
Available at http://darwin-online.org.uk (accessed October 2015).

Darwin, Charles (1874) *The Descent of Man, and Selection in Relation to Sex*, 2nd edn (London: John Murray)
Available at http://darwin-online.org.uk (accessed October 2015).

Darwin, Charles (1877) 'A biographical sketch of an infant', in *Mind*, vol. 2, pp. 285–94
Available at http://darwin-online.org.uk (accessed October 2015).

Dax, Marc (1836) 'Lesions in the left hemisphere of the brain in relation to the loss of indications of thought' ('Lésions de la moitié gauche de l'encéphale coincident avec l'oublie des signes de la pensée'), in *Gazette Hebdomadaire de Médecine et de Chirurgie*, vol. 2, no. 17 (1865), pp. 259–60
Available in the original French at www2.biusante.parisdescartes.fr/livanc/index. las?dico=perio&chapitre=marc%20dax&p=1&do=page (accessed October 2015).

Descartes, René (1637) *Discourse on the Method of Rightly Conducting One's Reason and of Seeking Truth in the Sciences (Discours de la méthode pour bien conduire sa raison, et chercher la vérité dans les sciences)* (Leiden: Jan Maire), translated and edited by E Anscombe and P T Geach in *Descartes: Philosophical Writings* (London: Nelson, 1970)

Dionysius Thrax (c. 100 BCE) *The Art of Grammar (Tekhne grammatike),* translated by Thomas Davidson as *The Grammar of Dionysios Thrax* (St. Louis: Studley, 1874)
Available at https://archive.org/details/grammarofdionysi00dionuoft (accessed September 2015).
A more recent translation by Alan Kemp can be found in *Historiographia Linguistica*, vol. 13, no. 2–3 (1986), pp. 343–63.

Epicurus (c. 305 BCE) 'Letter to Herodotus', translated by George K Strodach in *Epicurus: The Art of Happiness* (New York: Penguin, 2012).

Exner, Sigmund (1894) *Outline of a physiological explanation of psychical phenomena (Entwurf zu einer physiologischen Erklärung der psychischen Erscheinungen)*, Vol. 1 (Leipzig and Vienna: Franz Deuticke)
Available in the original German at https://archive.org/details/ entwurfzueinerp00exnegoog (accessed October 2015).

Fairclough, Norman (1989) *Language and Power* (London: Longman)
A second edition of this work was published in 2001.

Fairclough, Norman (ed.) (1992) *Critical Language Awareness* (London: Longman), republished (Abingdon: Routledge, 2013).

'First Grammatical Treatise' (anonymous, 12th century), translated and edited by Einar Haugen as *First Grammatical Treatise: The Earliest Germanic Phonology* (New Jersey: Prentice Hall, 1950)

Available in the original Icelandic as part of an online collection of Old Norse texts at http://etext.old.no/gramm/ (accessed October 2015).

The original *Codex Wormianus* containing the treatise can be viewed at www.e-pages. dk/ku/621/, made available by the University of Copenhagen (accessed October 2015).

Fitch, Tecumseh (2010) *The Evolution of Language* (Cambridge: Cambridge University Press)

Fodor, Jerry (1975) *The Language of Thought* (Cambridge, MA: Harvard University Press)

Fowler, Joy (1986) 'The social stratification of *r* in New York City department stores, 24 years after Labov' (New York University: unpublished paper)

Frege, Gottlob (1892) 'On sense and reference' ('Über Sinn und Bedeutung'), in *Zeitschrift für Philosophie und philosophische Kritik*, issue 100, pp. 25–50

An English translation by Max Black is available at http://en.wikisource.org/wiki/On_Sense_and_Reference (accessed October 2015).

Gall, Franz Joseph and Johann Gaspar Spurzheim (1810) *The anatomy and physiology of the nervous system in general and the anatomy of the brain in particular (Anatomie et physiologie du système nerveux en général et anatomie du cerveau en particulier)*, Vol. 1 (Paris: F Schoell)

Available in the original French at http://gallica.bnf.fr/ark:/12148/bpt6k767165/f6.image (accessed October 2015).

Volume 2 (also Gall and Spurzheim) was published in 1812. Gall published Volume 3 in 1818 and Volume 4 in 1819.

Gauchat, Louis (1905) *Phonetic uniformity in the local speech of a Swiss commune (L'unité phonétique dans le patois d'une commune)* (Halle a.d. Saale: Max Niemeyer)

Available in the original French at www.archive.org/details/lunitphontiqued00gaucgoog (accessed September 2015).

Geoffrey of Monmouth (c. 1136) *The History of the Kings of Britain (Historia regum Britanniae)*

Both the original Latin and an English translation are available at http://books.google.co.uk (accessed September 2015).

A 1966 translation by Lewis Thorpe is published by Penguin Books.

Gessner Conrad (1555) *Mithridates, or On the differences between languages (Mithridates (sive) de differentiis linguarum)* (Zurich: Froschouer)

Available in the original Latin at http://books.google.co.uk/books/about/Mithridates_sive_de_differentiis_linguar.html?id=yTVUAAAAcAAJ&redir_esc=y (accessed September 2015).

Gilliéron, Jules and Edmont, Edmond (1902–1910), *Atlas linguistique de la France* (Paris: Honoré Champion)

Pages from the atlas can be viewed in Google Images and Wikimedia Commons (both accessed September 2015).

Greenberg, Joseph H (1963) 'Some universals of grammar with particular reference to the order of meaningful elements', in Joseph H Greenberg (ed.) (1963) *Universals of Language* (Cambridge, MA: MIT Press), pp. 58–90

Available at https://archive.org/details/universalsoflang00unse (accessed September 2015).

Greenberg, Joseph H (1986) 'On being a linguistic anthropologist', in *Annual Review of Anthropology*, vol. 15, pp. xii + 1–24
Available at www.jstor.org/stable/2155753 (accessed September 2015).

Grice, Paul (1989) *Studies in the Way of Words* (Cambridge, MA: Harvard University Press)
This edition includes the previously unpublished William James Lectures that Grice gave at Harvard in 1967.

Halliday, Michael A K (1975) *Learning How to Mean: Explorations in the Development of Language* (London: Edward Arnold)

Hauser, Marc, Noam Chomsky and W Tecumseh Fitch (2002) 'The faculty of language: what is it, who has it, and how did it evolve?', in *Science*, vol. 298, no. 5598, pp. 1569–79
Available at www.chomsky.info/articles/20021122.pdf (accessed September 2015).

Henry, George W (1941) *Sex Variants: A Study of Homosexual Patterns*, 2 vols (New York: Paul B Hoeber)

Hensel, Gottfried (1741) *Synopsis universae philologiae* (Nuremberg: Homann heirs)
Available at http://books.google.co.uk/books?id=IZJDAAAAcAAJ&printsec=frontcover&source=gbs_ge_summary_r&cad=0#v=onepage&q&f=false (accessed September 2015).

Herder, Johann Gottfried (1772) *Essay on the Origin of Language (Abhandlung über den Ursprung der Sprache)* (Berlin: Christian Voss), translated by Alexander Gode in John H Moran and Alexander Gode (eds) *On the Origin of Language* (Chicago: University of Chicago Press, 1966)
The original essay can be viewed at www.deutschestextarchiv.de/book/view/herder_abhandlung_1772?p=5 (accessed September 2015).

Herodotus (c. 450 BCE) *The Histories*, translated by Tom Holland (London: Penguin Classics, 2014)

Heschl, Richard L (1878) *On the anterior transverse temporal gyrus (Über die vordere quere Schläfenwindung des menschlichen Grosshirns)* (Vienna: Wilhelm Braumüller)
Available in the original German at http://ub-goobi-pr2.ub.uni-greifswald.de/viewer/image/PPN77082319X/5/ (accessed October 2015).

Hippocrates (400 BCE) 'On the Sacred Disease', translated by W H S Jones in *Hippocrates*, Vol. 2 (The Loeb Classical Library) (London: William Heinemann Ltd, 1923)
Available in the 1959 edition at https://archive.org/details/hippocrates02hippuoft (accessed October 2015).

Hjelmslev, Louis (1943) *On the foundation of a theory of language (Omkring sprogte-oriens grundlaeggelse)* (Copenhagen: B Lunos), translated by Francis Whitfield as *Prolegomena to a Theory of Language* (Madison, Wisconsin: University of Wisconsin Press, 1961)

Hockett, Charles F (1954) 'Two models of grammatical description', in Martin Joos (ed.) *Readings in Linguistics* (New York: American Council of Learned Societies, 1957), pp. 386–99
This paper was originally published in *Word*, vol. 10, pp. 210–31.
The second (1958) edition of Joos' book is available at https://archive.org/details/readingsinlingui00joos (accessed October 2015).

Hockett, Charles F (1960) 'The origin of speech', in *Scientific American*, vol. 203, pp. 88–111, reprinted in William Shi-Yi Wang (ed.) *Human Communication: Language and Its Psychobiological Bases* (*Scientific American*) (San Francisco: Freeman, 1982) pp. 4–12
Available at www.illc.uva.nl/LaCo/CLAS/clc13/papers/hockett60sciam.pdf (accessed September 2015).

Humboldt, Wilhelm von (1836) 'Introduction: on the diversity of human language construction and its influence on the mental development of the human species' ('Einleitung: über die Verschiedenheit des menschlichen Sprachbaues und ihren Einfluss auf die geistige Entwicklung des Menschengeschlechts'), translated from the German by Peter Heath in Michael Losonsky (ed.) *Humboldt: On Language* (Cambridge: Cambridge University Press, 1999)
This is the general introductory volume to *On the Kawi Language of the Island of Java (Über die Kawi-Sprache auf der Insel Java)* (Berlin: Royal Academy of Sciences, 1836) and is available in the original German at https://archive.org/stream/ berdieverschied00humbgoog#page/n9/mode/2up (accessed October 2015).

Hymes, Dell (1962) 'The ethnography of speaking', in T Gladwin and W C Sturtevant (eds) *Anthropology and Human Behavior* (Washington: Anthropological Society of Washington)
Available in two parts at: www.ohio.edu/people/thompsoc/Hymes.html and http://oak.cats.ohiou.edu/~thompsoc/Hymes2.html (both accessed September 2015).

Itard, Jean Marc Gaspard (1801) *On the Education of a Savage Man (De l'éducation d'un homme sauvage)* (Paris: Goujon fils), translated from the French by an unknown translator as *An Historical Account of the Discovery and Education of a Savage Man* (London: printed for Richard Phillips, 1802)
Available at https://archive.org/details/anhistoricalacc00itargoog (accessed October 2015).

Jackendoff, Ray (2002) *Foundations of Language: Brain, Meaning, Grammar, Evolution* (Oxford: Oxford University Press)

Jackson, John Hughlings (1874) 'On the nature of the duality of the brain', republished in *Brain*, vol. 1, issue 1–2 (1915), pp. 80–103

Jespersen, Otto (1922) *Language: Its Nature, Development and Origin* (London: George Allen & Unwin)
Available at www.archive.org/details/afa5370.0001.001.umich.edu (accessed September 2015).

Jespersen, Otto (1923) *Child Language: A book for parents (Börnesprog: En bog for forældre)* (Copenhagen: Gyldendal)

Jespersen, Otto (1925) *Mankind, Nation and Individual from a Linguistic Point of View* (Oslo: Harvard University Press)

Jones, Sir William (1786) 'The third anniversary lecture, on the Hindus, delivered 2nd of February, 1786', in *The Works of Sir William Jones*, Vol. 1 (London: G G and J Robinson and R H Evans, 1799)
Available at https://archive.org/details/worksofsirwillia01jone (accessed September 2015).

Joos, Martin (ed.) (1957) *Readings in Linguistics* (New York: American Council of Learned Societies)
The second (1958) edition is available at https://archive.org/details/ readingsinlingui00joos (accessed May 2015).

Katz, Jerrold and Jerry Fodor (1963) 'The structure of a semantic theory', in *Language*, vol. 39, no. 2, pp. 170–210

Available at www.jstor.org/stable/411200 (accessed October 2015).

Kloeke, Gesinus (1927) *The Dutch Expansion (De Hollandsche expansie)* (The Hague: Martinus Nijhoff)

A transcription of the original Dutch is available at www.dbnl.org/tekst/ kloe004holl01_01/ (accessed September 2015).

Kurath, Hans et al. (eds) (1939–43) *Linguistic Atlas of New England* (Providence: Brown University for the American Council of Learned Societies)

Kutas, Marta and Steven Hillyard (1980) 'Reading senseless sentences: brain potentials reflect semantic incongruity', in *Science*, vol. 207, no. 4427, pp. 203–5

La Mettrie, Julien Offray de (1748) *Man a Machine/Machine Man (L'Homme Machine)* (Leiden: Elie Luzac), translated by M W Calkins based on a version by Gertrude C Bussey in *Man a Machine* (Chicago: Open Court Publishing, 1912), pp. 83–150

Also available at https://archive.org/details/manmachine00lame (accessed September 2015).

A more recent English version is in Ann Thomson (trans./ed.) *La Mettrie: Machine Man and Other Writings* (Cambridge: Cambridge University Press, 1996), pp. 1–40.

Labov, William (1963) 'The social motivation of a sound change', in *Word*, vol. 19, pp. 273–309, reprinted in William Labov, *Sociolinguistic Patterns* (Philadelphia: University of Pennsylvania Press, 1972), pp. 1–42

Labov, William (1972a) 'The social stratification of (r) in New York City department stores', in William Labov, *Sociolinguistic Patterns* (Philadelphia: University of Pennsylvania Press), pp. 43–54

Labov, William (1972b) *Sociolinguistic Patterns* (Philadelphia: University of Pennsylvania Press)

Lakoff, George (1973) 'Hedges: a study in meaning criteria and the logic of fuzzy concepts', in *Journal of Philosophical Logic*, vol. 2, no. 4, pp. 458–508

Available at www.jstor.org/stable/30226076 (accessed October 2015).

Lakoff, Robin (1973) 'Language and Woman's Place', in *Language in Society*, vol. 2, no. 1, pp. 45–80

A pdf of Lakoff's original paper is available at http://web.stanford.edu/class/ linguist156/Lakoff_1973.pdf (accessed September 2015).

Lakoff, Robin (1975) *Language and Woman's Place* (New York: Harper & Row), reprinted in Robin Tolmach Lakoff, *Language and Woman's Place: Text and Commentaries* edited by Mary Bucholtz (New York: Oxford University Press, 2004)

This new edition of Lakoff's work contains not only this 2004 retrospective but also a wide selection of other related essays.

Lakoff, Robin Tolmach (2004) '*Language and woman's place* revisited', in Mary Bucholtz (ed.) *Language and Woman's Place: Text and Commentaries* (New York: Oxford University Press)

Lancelot, Claude and Antoine Arnauld (1660) *General and Rational Grammar (Grammaire générale et raisonnée)* (Paris: Pierre le Petit)

Available at www.academia.edu/9422035/1660_Grammaire_générale_et_ raisonnée_de_Port-Royal (accessed September 2015).

Legman, Gershon (1941) 'The language of homosexuality: an American glossary', in George W Henry et al., *Sex Variants: A Study of Homosexual Patterns*, Vol. 2 (New York: Paul B Hoeber)

Lenneberg, Eric (1967) *Biological Foundations of Language* (New York: John Wiley & Sons)

Levinson, Stephen C (1983) *Pragmatics* (Cambridge: Cambridge University Press)

Linguistic Institute Final Report (1964)
Available at http://fedora.dlib.indiana.edu/fedora/get/iudl:957732/OVERVIEW (accessed September 2015)

Linnaeus, Carl (1735) *Systema naturae* (Leiden: T Haak)
This first edition is available in the original Latin at http://biodiversitylibrary.org/page/728487 (accessed September 2015).

Linnaeus, Carl (1758) *Systema naturae*, 10th edn (Stockholm: L Salvius)
Available at www.biodiversitylibrary.org/item/10277#page/3/mode/1up (accessed October 2015).

Livia, Anna and Kira Hall (1997) *Queerly Phrased: Language, Gender and Sexuality* (Oxford: Oxford University Press)

Locke, John (1690) *An Essay Concerning Human Understanding* (London: Thomas Basset)

Lucretius (c. 49 BCE) *On the Nature of Things / On the Nature of the Universe (De rerum natura),* translated by R E Latham as *On the Nature of the Universe,* (Harmondsworth: Penguin, 1951)
Many other editions (both prose and verse translations) are available in hard copy and online.

Lutoslawski, Wincenty (1890) 'Principles of stylometry' ('Principes de stylométrie'), in *Revue des études grecques,* vol. 41, pp. 61–81

Lutoslawski, Wincenty (1897) *The Origin and Growth of Plato's Logic* (London: Longmans, Green & Co)
Available at https://archive.org/details/origingrowthofpl00lutoiala (accessed May 2015).

Lyons, John (1977) *Semantics,* Vol. 2 (Cambridge: Cambridge University Press)

Meillet, Antoine (1912) 'The Evolution of Grammatical Forms' ('L'évolution des formes grammaticales'), reprinted in Antoine Meillet, *Linguistique historique et linguistique générale* (Paris: E. Champion, 1921)
Available in the original French at http://ctlf.ens-lyon.fr/t_resul.asp?idtexte=2&nom=Meillet&prenom=Antoine (accessed September 2015).

Milroy, Lesley (1980) *Language and Social Networks* (Oxford: Blackwell)
A second edition of this text was published in 1987.

Müller, Friedrich Max (1861) *The Science of Language* (London: Longman, Green, Longman & Roberts), in F Max Müller, *Lectures on the Science of Language,* Vol. 1 (Cambridge: Cambridge University Press, 2013)
An 1885 edition is available at https://archive.org/details/lecturesonscien07mlgoog (accessed September 2015).

Müller, Friedrich Max (1864) *The Science of Language* (London: Longman, Green, Longman, Roberts & Green), in F Max Müller, *Lectures on the Science of Language,* Vol. 2 (Cambridge: Cambridge University Press, 2013)
An 1877 edition is available at https://archive.org/details/lecturesonscien02mluoft (accessed September 2015).

Nichols, Johanna (2012) 'Monogenesis or polygenesis: a single ancestral language for all humanity?', in Maggie Tallerman and Kathleen Gibson (eds) *The Oxford Handbook of Language Evolution* (Oxford: Oxford University Press), pp. 558–72

Osthoff, Hermann and Karl Brugmann (1878) 'Preface', in *Morphological Investigations in the Sphere of the Indo-European Languages (Morphologische Untersuchungen auf dem Gebiet der indogermanischen Sprachen)*, Vol. 1 (Leipzig: S Hirzel), pp. iii–xx
An English translation by Judy Haddon and Winfred Lehmann is available at www.utexas.edu/cola/centers/lrc/books/read14.html (accessed October 2015).
The Oxford Dictionary of English Grammar, revised edn, Sylvia Chalker and Edmund Weiner (eds) (Oxford: Oxford University Press, 1998)
Pāṇini (4th century BCE) *Eight Books (Ashtadhyayi)*
An English translation by Srisa Chandra Vasu (Allahabad: Indian Press, 1891) is available at www.wilbourhall.org/index.html#panini (accessed October 2015).
Partee, Barbara Hall (2005) 'Reflections of a formal semanticist as of Feb 2005'
Available online only at http://people.umass.edu/partee/docs/BHP_Essay_Feb05.pdf (accessed October 2015).
Pavlov, Ivan Petrovich (1928) *Lectures on Conditioned Reflexes: Twenty-five years of Objective Study of the Higher Nervous Activity (Behaviour) of Animals*, Vol. 1, translated by W Horsley Gantt (London: Martin Lawrence)
Penfield, Wilder and Lamar Roberts (1959) *Speech and Brain Mechanisms* (Princeton, NJ: Princeton University Press)
Piaget, Jean (1923) *The Language and Thought of the Child (La langage et la pensée chez l'enfant)* (Neuchatel: Delachaud & Niestlé)
Plato (c. 387–361 BCE) *Cratylus*, translated by C D C Reeve in John M Cooper (ed.) Plato, *Complete Works* (Indianapolis: Hackett, 1997)
Preyer, William (1881) *The Mind of the Child (Die Seele des Kindes)* (Leipzig: Thomas Grieben)
Available in the original German (2nd edn) at https://archive.org/details/dieseeledeskind03preygoog (accessed October 2015).
Also available in English (translated by H W Brown) at https://archive.org/details/mindofchildobser01preyuoft (Vol. 1) and https://archive.org/details/mindofchildobser02prey (Vol. 2) (both accessed October 2015).
Priscian (527) *Grammatical Foundations (Institutiones grammaticae)*
The original Latin text is available at http://kaali.linguist.jussieu.fr/CGL/text.jsp?id=T43 (accessed September 2015).
Robins, R H (1997) *A Short History of Linguistics*, 4th edn (London: Longman)
Rochefort, Charles de (1658) *Natural and moral history of the Antilles (Histoire naturelle et morale des îles Antilles de l'Amérique)* (Rotterdam: Arnould Leers)
The original French edition can be viewed at http://gallica.bnf.fr/ark:/12148/bpt6k74105c/f5.image (accessed September 2015).
The English translation, published in 1666 as *The History of the Caribby Islands*, is available at www.wdl.org/en/item/252/ (accessed September 2015).
Rosch, Eleanor (1971) 'On the internal structure of perceptual and semantic categories' (Psychology Dept., University of California, Berkeley: unpublished paper)
Rousseau, Jean-Jacques (1755) *Discourse on the Origins and Foundations of Inequality among Men (Discours sur l'origine et les fondements de l'inégalité parmi les hommes)* (Amsterdam: Marc Michel Rey), translated by Maurice Cranston as *A Discourse on Inequality* (London: Penguin, 1984)

Rousseau, Jean-Jacques (1762) *Émile, or Education (Émile ou de l'éducation)* (The Hague: Jean Néaulme)

Rousseau, Jean-Jacques (1781) *Essay on the Origin of Languages (Essai sur l'origine des langues)*, translated by John H Moran in John H Moran and Alexander Gode (eds) *On the Origin of Language* (Chicago: University of Chicago Press, 1966)

Ruhlen, Merritt and John Bengston (1994), 'Global etymologies', in Merritt Ruhlen, *On the Origin of Languages: Studies in Linguistic Taxonomy* (Stanford: Stanford University Press) pp. 277–336

Available as a pdf at http://merrittruhlen.com/files/Global.pdf (accessed September 2015).

Sanctius (Francisco Sánchez de las Brozas)(1562, 1587) *Minerva, or the Underlying Principles of the Latin Language (Minerva sive de causis linguae latinae)* (Salamanca: Renaut, 1587)

Available in the original Latin at http://iessapostol.juntaextremadura.net/latin/minerva/ (accessed October 2015).

Sapir, Edward (1921) *Language: An Introduction to the Study of Speech* (New York: Harcourt, Brace & Co)

Available at https://archive.org/details/languageanintrod00sapi (accessed October 2015).

Saussure, Ferdinand de (1916) *Course in General Linguistics (Cours de linguistique générale)* edited by Charles Bally and Albert Sechehaye (Paris: Payot), translated by Roy Harris as *Course in General Linguistics* (London: Duckworth, 1983)

Schleicher, August (1863) *Darwinism Tested by the Science of Language: An Open Letter to Dr Ernst Haeckel (Die Darwinsche Theorie und die Sprachwissenschaft – offenes Sendschreiben an Herrn Dr. Ernst Haeckel)* (Weimar: H Boehlau), translated by Alexander V W Bikkers as *Darwinism Tested by the Science of Language* (London: J C Hotten, 1869)

Available at https://archive.org/details/darwinismtestedb69schl (accessed September 2015).

Schleicher, August (1868) 'Fable in Proto-Indo-European' ('Fabel in indogermanischer Ursprache'), in *Contributions to comparative linguistics in the field of Aryan, Celtic and Slavic languages (Beiträge zur vergleichenden Sprachforschung auf dem Gebiete der arischen, celtischen und slawischen Sprachen)*, Vol. 5 (Berlin: Dümmler, 1868), pp. 206–8

Available at http://reader.digitale-sammlungen.de/de/fs1/object/display/bsb10588539_00216.html (accessed September 2015).

Schmeller, Johann (1821) *The Bavarian Dialects (Die Mundarten Bayerns)* (Munich: Karl Thienemann)

Available at https://archive.org/details/diemundartenbay00schmgoog (accessed September 2015).

Seuren, Pieter (1998) *Western Linguistics: An Historical Introduction* (Oxford: Blackwell)

Shattuck, Roger (1980) *The Forbidden Experiment: The Story of the Wild Boy of Avalon* (New York: Farrar Straus Giroux)

Skinner, Burrhus F (1957) *Verbal Behavior* (New York: Appleton)

Snow, Catherine (1972) 'Mothers' speech to children learning language', in *Child Development*, vol. 43, no. 2, pp. 549–65

Available at www.jstor.org/stable/1127555 (accessed October 2015).

Sperber, Dan and Deirdre Wilson (1995) *Relevance: Communication and Cognition*, 2nd edn (Oxford: Blackwell)

Stern, Clara and William Stern (1907) *The Language of Children (Die Kindersprache)* (Leipzig: Johann Ambrosius Barth)

Stern, Gustaf (1931) *Meaning and Change of Meaning: with Special Reference to the English Language* (Bloomington: Indiana University Press)
Available at https://archive.org/details/meaningchangeofm00ster (accessed October 2015).

Süssmilch, Johann Peter (1766) *Essay on the proof that the first language did not originate from man, but from the creator alone (Versuch eines Beweises, dass die erste Sprache ihren Ursprung nicht vom Menschen, sondern allein vom Schöpfer erhalten habe)* (Berlin: Buchladen der Realschule)
Available in the original German at https://archive.org/stream/ versucheinesbew00ssgoog#page/n6/mode/2up (accessed September 2015).

Svartvik, Jan (1968) *The Evans Statements: A Case for Forensic Linguistics* (Gothenburg Studies in English 20) (Gothenburg: University of Gothenburg)
Available in two parts at www.thetext.co.uk/Evans%20Statements%20 Part%201.pdf and www.thetext.co.uk/Evans%20Statements%20Part%202.pdf (both accessed October 2015).

Sweet, Henry (1877) *A Handbook of Phonetics* (Oxford: Clarendon Press)
Available at https://archive.org/details/handbookofphonet00swee (accessed October 2015).

Taine, Hippolyte (1876) 'The acquisition of language in children and the human species' ('De l'acquisition du langage chez les enfants et dans l'espèce humaine'), in *Revue Philosophique*, vol. 1, pp. 23–32, republished in English as 'Acquisition of language by children', in *Mind*, vol. 2 (1877), pp. 252–59

Thomas of Erfurt (c. 1310) *On the Modes of Signifying or Speculative Grammar (Tractatus de modis significandi seu grammatica speculativa)*, translated by G L Bursill-Hall as *Thomas of Erfurt: Grammatica Speculativa* (London: Longman, 1972)

Tiedemann, Dietrich (1787) *Observations on the Development of the Mental Faculties of Children (Beobachtungen über die Entwicklung der Seelenfähigkeiten bei Kindern)* (Altenburg: Oskar Bonde)
Available in the original German at https://archive.org/stream/ beobachtungenbe00tiedgoog#page/n2/mode/2up (accessed October 2015).
There is an English translation by Carl Murchison and Suzanne Langer in *The Pedagogical Seminary and Journal of Genetic Psychology*, vol. 34, issue 2 (1927), pp. 205–30.

Trier, Jost (1931) *German Vocabulary in the 'Sense District' of the Mind (Der deutsche Wortschatz im Sinnbezirk des Verstandes)* (Heidelberg: C Winter)

Trombetti, Alfredo (1905) *The Single Origin of Language (L'unità d'origine del linguaggio)* (Bologna: Luigi Beltrami)
Available in the original Italian at https://archive.org/details/ lunitdoriginede00tromgoog (accessed September 2015).

Trudgill, Peter (1974a) *Sociolinguistics* (Harmondsworth: Penguin), in *Sociolinguistics*, revised edn (Harmondsworth: Penguin, 1983)

Trudgill, Peter (1974b) *The Social Differentiation of English in Norwich* (Cambridge: Cambridge University Press)

Varro, Marcus Terentius (1st century BCE) *On the Latin Language (De lingua latina)*, translated by Roland G Kent as *Varro: On the Latin Language*, 2 Vols. (London: Heinemann, 1938)
Available at https://archive.org/details/onlatinlanguage01varruoft and https://archive.org/details/onlatinlanguage02varruoft (both accessed September 2015). This is a parallel edition with the Latin texts and also includes the remaining fragments.

Vesalius, Andreas (1543) *On the Fabric of the Human Body (De humani corporis fabrica)* (Basel: Ioannes Oporinus)
Available at http://archive.nlm.nih.gov/proj/ttp/flash/vesalius/vesalius.html (accessed October 2015). The illustrations of the brain can be found at the end.

Wallace, Alfred Russel (1895) 'The expressiveness of speech', in *Fortnightly Review*, vol. 58, pp. 528–43
Available at http://wallace-online.org/content/record?itemID=S518 (accessed September 2015).

Watson, John B (1913) 'Psychology as the behaviorist views it', in *Psychological Review*, vol. 20, pp. 158–77
Also available at http://psychclassics.yorku.ca/Watson/views.htm (accessed October 2015).

Wegener, Philipp (1897) 'On the dialects and local customs of the region of the River Ohre' ('Zur Kunde der Mundarten und des Volkstums im Gebiete der Ohre'), in *Geschichtsblätter für Stadt und Land Magdeburg*, vol. 32, pp. 326–64

Wells, Rulon S (1947) 'Immediate constituents', in Martin Joos (ed.) *Readings in Linguistics* (New York: American Council of Learned Societies, 1957), pp. 186–207
This paper was originally published in *Language*, vol. 23, no. 2, pp. 81–117 and is available at www.jstor.org/stable/410382 (accessed October 2015).
The second (1958) edition of Joos' book is available at https://archive.org/details/readingsinlingui00joos (accessed October 2015).

Wenker, Georg (1888–1923) *Language Atlas of the German Realm (Sprachatlas des Deutschen Reichs)* (Marburg)
Wenker's atlas first materialised as a collection of hand-drawn maps. More information about Wenker and his legacy can be found at http://regionalsprache.de/home.aspx (accessed September 2015).

Wernicke, Carl (1874) 'The Aphasia Symptom Complex: A Psychological Study on an Anatomical Basis' ('Der aphasische Symptomencomplex: Eine psychologische Studie auf anatomischer Basis') (Breslau: Max Cohn & Weigert), translated by Gertrude H Eggert in *Wernicke's Works on Aphasia: A Sourcebook and Review* (The Hague: Mouton, 1977)
Available in the original German at https://archive.org/details/deraphasischesy00werngoog (accessed October 2015).

Whitney, William Dwight (1867) *Language and the Study of Language* (New York: Charles Scribner)
The fourth edition is available at https://archive.org/stream/languagestudyofl00whituoft#page/n5/mode/2up (accessed September 2015).

Whorf, Benjamin Lee (1937) unpublished article 'Discussion of Hopi linguistics', in John B Carroll (ed.) *Language, Thought, and Reality: Selected Writings of Benjamin Lee Whorf* (Cambridge, MA: MIT Press, 1956) pp. 102–11

Available at https://archive.org/details/languagethoughtr00whor (accessed October 2015).

Whorf, Benjamin Lee (1938) 'Some verbal categories of Hopi', in John B Carroll (ed.) *Language, Thought, and Reality: Selected Writings of Benjamin Lee Whorf* (Cambridge, MA: MIT Press, 1956) pp. 112–24

Available at https://archive.org/details/languagethoughtr00whor (accessed October 2015).

Wilkins, John (1668) *An Essay Towards a Real Character* (London: Gellibrand & Martyn)

Available at http://books.google.co.uk/books/about/An_Essay_Towards_a_Real_Character_and_a.html?id=BCCtZjBtiEYC&redir_esc=y (accessed October 2015).

Wittgenstein, Ludwig (1921) 'Logical-philosophical treatise' ('Logisch-philosophische Abhandlung') in *Annalen der Naturphilosophie*, Vol. 14 (Leipzig: Reinhold Berger for Verlag Unesma GmbH), pp. 185–262

Wittgenstein, Ludwig (1922) *Tractatus Logico-Philosophicus* (originally 'Logisch-philosophische Abhandlung'), translated by Charles K Ogden (London: Kegan Paul)

Available at www.gutenberg.org/ebooks/5740 (accessed October 2015).

Wittgenstein, Ludwig (1953) *Philosophical Investigations* (*Philosophische Untersuchungen*), translated by Gertrude Anscombe (Oxford: Blackwell)

Wundt, Wilhelm (1900) *Language (Die Sprache)*, 2 vols (Leipzig: Engelmann)

Zadeh, Lofti (1965) 'Fuzzy sets', in *Information and Control*, vol. 8, issue 3, pp. 338–53

Available at www.sciencedirect.com/science/journal/00199958/8/3 (accessed October 2015).

Journals and societies
for the study of the history of linguistics

Societies

France
Société d'Histoire et d'Epistémologie des Sciences du Langage (founded 1978)
www.shesl.org/

Germany
Studienkreis Geschichte der Sprachwissenschaft (founded 1989)
www.elverdissen.de/~nodus/sgds.htm/

Great Britain
The Henry Sweet Society for the History of Linguistic Ideas (founded 1984)
www.henrysweet.org/

Italy
Società Italiana di Filosofia del Linguaggio (founded 1994)
http://web.dfc.unibo.it/sfl/

Spain
Sociedad Española de Historiografía Lingüística (SEHL) (founded 1995)
www.sehl.es/

United States
North American Association for the History of the Language Sciences (founded 1987)
http://naahols.org/

International Conference on the History of the Language Sciences (inaugurated 1978)
http://ichols-xiii.realvitur.pt/

Journals

Beiträge zur Geschichte der Sprachwissenschaft
The journal of the German Society for the History of Linguistics (Studienkreis Geschichte der Sprachwissenschaft).

Histoire Épistémologie Langage
The journal of the French Society for the History of Linguistics (Société d'Histoire et d'Épistémologie des Sciences du Langage).

Historiographia Linguistica
An international journal for the history of linguistics, edited by E F K Koerner and published three times a year (Amsterdam: John Benjamins).

Language & History
The journal of the Henry Sweet Society, due to be published three times a year from 2017.

Studies in the History of the Language Sciences
A companion series to *Historiographia Linguistica*, also published by John Benjamins.

Index

Figures and whole chapters are indicated in italics.